M. David Stone, author of *Getting the Most from WordStar and MailMerge,* has written and produced more than twenty high-level audio-visual pieces on subjects ranging from astronomy and general relativity to psychology and ape language experiments. He likes to think of himself as a translator, translating scientific material into "English." He has also contributed articles to several magazines such as *InfoWorld, PC Magazine,* and *Ahoy.*

i

To Linda

GETTING ON-LINE

A Guide to Accessing Computer Information Services

M. David Stone

A SPECTRUM BOOK

PRENTICE-HALL, INC.
Englewood Cliffs, New Jersey 07632

Library of Congress Cataloging in Publication Data

Stone, M. David.
    Getting on-line.

    "A Spectrum Book."
    Includes index.
    1. On-line data processing.   2. Information storage
and retrieval systems.   I. Title.
QA76.55.S86   1984   001.64   83-26870
ISBN 0-13-354416-8
ISBN 0-13-354408-7 (pbk.)

This book is available at a special discount when
ordered in bulk quantities. Contact Prentice-Hall, Inc.,
General Publishing Division, Special Sales, Englewood Cliffs, N.J. 07632.

A SPECTRUM BOOK

10 9 8 7 6 5 4 3 2 1

Printed in the United States of America

Editorial/production supervision by Cyndy Lyle Rymer
Manufacturing buyer: Joyce Levatino
Cover design by Hal Siegel

ISBN 0-13-354408-7 {PBK.}

ISBN 0-13-354416-8

Prentice-Hall International, Inc., *London*
Prentice-Hall of Australia Pty. Limited, *Sydney*
Prentice-Hall Canada Inc., *Toronto*
Prentice-Hall of India Private Limited, *New Delhi*
Prentice-Hall of Japan, Inc., *Tokyo*
Prentice-Hall of Southeast Asia Pte. Ltd., *Singapore*
Whitehall Books Limited, *Wellington, New Zealand*
Editora Prentice-Hall do Brasil Ltda., *Rio de Janeiro*

TRADEMARKS

The following are service marks, trademarks, or registered trademarks of their respective owners.

ADVANCED OFFICE CONCEPTS is a registered trademark. ALTOS is a registered trademark of Altos Computer Systems. SPIN is a registered trademark. PsycINFO is a registered trademark. AMERICA: HISTORY & LIFE is a registered trademark. Apple is a registered trademark of Apple Computer, Inc. Archives is a registered trademark of Archives Inc. Atari is a registered trademark of Atari, Inc. CBD OnLine is a registered trademark. POLLUTION ABSTRACTS is a registered trademark. REMARC is a registered trademark. CHEMICAL INDUSTRY NOTES is a registered trademark. CAS ONLINE is a registered trademark. CA SEARCH is a registered trademark. COLLEGE PRESS SERVICE is a registered trademark. CBM and PET are registered trademarks of Commodore Business Machines, Inc. Legislative Intelligence Week is a registered trademark. CompuPro is a registered trademark. CompuServe Information Service is a registered trademark of CompuServe Incorporated. ASI is a registered trademark. CIS/INDEX is a registered trademark. Connexions is a registered trademark. CYBERNET is a registered trademark of Control Data Corporation. PLATO is a registered trademark. DIALOG is a registered trademark of DIALOG Information Systems Services, Inc. ABI/INFORM is a registered trademark. DEC is a registered trademark of Digital Equipment Corporation. CP/M-80, CP/M, and CP/M-86/80 are registered trademarks of Digital Research, Inc. *Barron's National Business and Financial Weekly, The Wall Street Journal,* Dow Jones News Service, Dow Jones News, and Dow Jones News/Retrieval are registered trademarks of Dow Jones & Company, Inc. Principal International Businesses is a registered trademark. DUN'S MARKET IDENTIFIERS and DUN'S MILLION DOLLAR DIRECTORY are registered trademarks of Dun & Bradstreet, Inc. ENVIROLINE is a registered trademark. EXERPTA MEDICA is a registered trademark. Academic American Encyclopedia is a registered trademark of Grolier, Inc. Micromodem 100 is a registered trademark of Hayes Microcomputer

CONTENTS

7   SEARCH STRATEGY, 158

8   THE UTILITIES, 165
A Catalog

9   FREE SERVICES, 279
The Public Access Bulletin Boards

10   ON THE NEAR HORIZON, 284

APPENDIX, 294
Staying Current

PREFACE

There is a universe of information available, literally at your fingertips. All you have to know is where to look for it, and how. This book will help you find your way. It is a practical guide, suitable for everyone from novice to expert.

Knowing where to look is not a simple matter. There are hundreds of data bases available, each one specializing in a different kind of information. To add to the confusion, the number of data bases is growing. As of this writing, it is expected to double over the next 18 months.

Knowing how to look is not so simple either—not in terms of the mechanics of searching a data base, and not in terms of choosing the equipment you need for your purposes.

Fortunately, search strategies can be learned. Once learned, they can be improved. As for choosing the right equipment, a little planning can help avoid an expensive mistake. This is especially true in a marketplace where prices are falling and capabilities increasing on an almost daily basis.

The first six chapters tell you what you need to know before you get on-line.

Chapter 1, "Information Utilities," gives a general overview of the services available. Chapters 2 and 3 will introduce you to the kinds of equipment you need before you can use these services. Chapters 4 and 5 discuss software. Chapter 6 looks at some of the details of putting your system together.

These first six chapters include practical advice on how to choose the system that's right for you. They also include mini-reviews of specific hardware and software. The items reviewed were chosen to represent a range of what's available in each category. If you're a beginner, the reviews should give you a sense of what to look for in choosing a system. If you're an old hand at using data bases, these reviews should provide useful updates when you're shopping for new equipment or when you're looking for more sophisticated software to move up to.

If you're new to using information utilities, Chapter 7, "Search Strategies," should be particularly helpful. This chapter gives some tips on how to organize your search for information. Since the amount you pay for using a data base is usually based on how much time you spend on it rather than how much information you get from it, these tips will not only save you time, they will save you money.

The remainder of the book is mostly a catalog of information sources and an index to that catalog. Much of it can be read straight through, but you'll find that it's organized to act as a reference guide. You can use it to help decide which information services you may be interested in and as a starting point for organizing specific information searches. Chapter 8 covers the major information utilities. Chapter 9 covers computerized bulletin boards. Chapter 10 discusses graphics-oriented systems.

One last thing: Elsewhere in this book there is an acknowledgment section that lists a fair number of organizations that have helped in gathering the information for this book. There are two people I would like to single out here: Bill O'Brien and Danny Wexler. Both these individuals provided me with a great deal of help and information, often at odd hours, and always with generous amounts of their time. I probably would have been able to write this book without them, but it would not have been as good. Much thanks.

ACKNOWLEDGMENTS

The following companies have been more than generous in providing information and other help in putting this book together:

Dynamic Microprocessor Associates, Inc.
International Software Alliance
Binary Corporation
Transend Corporation
BIZCOMP Corporation
Hayes Microcomputer Products Inc.
Racal-Vadic
Radio Shack
BRS
Source Telecomputing Corporation

NewsNet
DELPHI (General Videotex Corporation)
Dow Jones News/Retrieval
CompuServe Information Service
DIALOG Information Services, Inc.
RCA MicroComputer Products
ONLINE, Inc.
Database Update
Cuadra Associates
Aslib

RCA MicroComputer Products
ONLINE, Inc.
Database Update
Cuadra Associates
Aslib

1

INFORMATION UTILITIES
A Look at What Is Available
and Where It Came From

The information utility is an idea whose time has come. At least that's what industry analysts have been saying lately. But what, exactly, is an information utility, and why has its time come?

The first question is easy. An information utility is just what it sounds like. It's an organization that will let you use its information, usually for a fee. If this sounds like a private pay-for-use library, you're right, but there are some important differences.

In the first place, this "library" is electronic, which means that it has an effectively unlimited supply of each item. An article is either there or it's not. It can't be out, it can't be misplaced, and just because somebody else is reading it at the moment doesn't mean that you can't read it too.

In the second place, this library is located wherever you want it to be. It can be in your home or office, on your desk or on your kitchen table—wherever is the most convenient for you.

And in the third place, an information utility is not a library in the first place. This makes it a rotten place to get a book (you wouldn't want to read one over a terminal anyway), but it also has its advantages. Many of the information utilities offer much wider services than you would expect if you think of them as just electronic libraries.

You can find communications services (electronic bulletin boards, electronic mail, electronic CB); you can find up-to-the-minute news directly from AP or UPI or from the latest update to an on-line electronic newspaper; you can find shopping services, often selling goods at a discount, and even a bartering service that arranges three-cornered deals for you. The point is that an information utility, unlike a library, is not in the business of providing books or magazines for you to read. It is in the business of providing *information*. All kinds of information.

The second question is a little harder to answer: Why is this an idea whose time has come?

The technically inclined will tell you that information utilities are the natural outgrowth of half a dozen different technologies coming of age. These include communications technologies (the information has to be delivered by phone lines, or cable, or broadcast television), space technology (much modern communication technology is dependent on satellites), and, of course, various computer technologies. There is the software technology, or computer-programming technology, that is used both to compile large masses of information (data bases) and to retrieve that information in useful ways; there is the technology of time-sharing that allows a single computer to interact with large numbers of terminals at the same time; and there is the continuing improvement in the technology of computer hardware so that a terminal, or small computer that can be used as a terminal, is now available for roughly the price of a television set.

Technology, of course, is not the whole story. It never is (despite what the technically inclined would have you think). The telephone was a terrific technical achievement, but that is not why there are telephones in virtually every house today. The phones are there because they fill a need. They help you communicate with the rest of the world.

The information utilities also fill a need—several needs in fact, depending on the service.

To begin with, from your point of view as a consumer (or potential consumer), there are three kinds of services available. They are described in industry jargon as transaction-based, communication-based, and information-based. We've touched on each of these already. Here's a closer look.

Transaction-Based Services

Transaction-based services are the bread-and-butter end of the information utilities. These include shopping services, bartering services, computerized classifieds, theater-ticket sales, plane reservations, and at-home banking. What they boil down to is shopping by computer.

These transaction-based services are probably not what you think of when you think of an information utility, but according to industry analysts, they are precisely the services that are likely to introduce most people to these systems. Ultimately, these are the services that will (probably) have the greatest effect on society and the greatest immediate impact on your life.

Consider doing your Christmas shopping from your living room instead of going through the hassle of fighting traffic, finding parking spaces, elbowing your way through crowds, and not finding what you were looking for in the first place. In fact, think about doing all your shopping from your living room. And remember, computerized shopping services (*today's* shopping services) are often less expensive than retail stores simply because they don't have the overhead—the rent, salespeople, or display models. In short, shopping by computer gives you all the advantages of discount stores but without the elbowing, the crowds, and the often rude sales staff.

Communication-Based Services

Communication-based services include electronic mail, computerized bulletin boards, and on-line conferences.

With electronic mail you can send a message to anyone else who uses the system. That message is earmarked for his or her "mailbox" and will be there to read the next time he or she signs on to the system. If you want to send the same message to more than one person, you can do that too. Electronic mail is faster than the post office but is nowhere near as cheap (in spite of spiraling postage costs).

Computerized bulletin boards function just like real bulletin boards. They let you enter a message that anyone can read if he or she feels like browsing through that particular bulletin board. More often than not, any given bulletin board is devoted to a single subject. Typically that subject is a hobby such as ham radio or photography. Often it is a particular computer; the Apple II perhaps, or the Commodore VIC-20. Sometimes it is a field of professional interest: law, medicine, or writing perhaps.

On-line conferences are no more than a written conversation between two or more people. Very often the conference amounts to a club or professional meeting, giving members the chance to share information and ideas. Sometimes the conference is a business meeting, discussing a possible sale or a proposed merger. Either way, the on-line conference serves much the same purpose as any other meeting. The major difference is that with on-line conferences, the meeting place is not a geographic location; it is a menu selection within a computer system.

On-line conferences can be open to all interested parties or restricted to a select few. They can be as formal or informal as the participants care to make them. At the most informal extreme, on-line "conferences" turn into CB emulation. This lets you get into a written conversation with anyone else who happens to be on the system. It functions very much like real CB or ham radio except that conversations are written rather than spoken, and the written version is more expensive.

Information-Based Services

Information-based services are the closest fit to the idea of an electronic library. They include everything from bibliographic research services that function as a sort of electronic card catalog to news services that give you the complete text of current wire-service news direct from UPI or AP. Also in this category are electronic newspapers, current stock-market quotes (usually with a few minutes' delay), and full text services that give you the complete text of whatever they cover. (Some possibilities are articles, court decisions, research papers, and encyclopedia entries.)

These information-based services are particularly helpful to anyone who needs to do research as part of his or her job. This includes lawyers (who research court decisions), writers (who do research for articles or books), doctors (who are trying to stay current or to be brought up to date on particular procedures or treatments), scientists (who generally conduct a thorough literature search before they do any scientific research of their own), financial advisors (who need background information on whatever it is they are giving advice about), and even business executives (who need information before they can make decisions).

These services can also be helpful to someone whose research needs are virtually non-existent. Just about everyone has had the frustrating experience of reading an article in a newspaper or magazine and then trying to find it again. There you are, recommending it to someone to read or in the middle of an argument and…where *did* you see that article on polar bears anyway? You could have sworn it said that eating polar-bear liver could give you Vitamin D poisoning. But if you can't find the article, there's not much you can do.

Of course, if you can't get by without the information, you could start searching through the back issues of all your newspapers and magazines.

Or you could go to the library and comb through *Reader's Guide to Periodical Literature,* the *New York Times Index,* and *Facts on File.*

Or you could walk over to your terminal, dial an information utility, and ask for all the articles on polar bears. When you find 3024 matches, you can try asking for articles with "polar bears" and "liver." When that comes up with 156 matches, you can try again, ask for all articles that contain the phrase "polar bears" and "liver" and "Vitamin D." When that brings you down to 16 matches, you can ask for the sources and see the list of the 16 articles. Eliminate articles in magazines that you don't read and you'll probably be left with a single bibliographic reference: the article you're looking for. (And if you don't find the article you wanted, you will probably find another reference with the same information—as long as you looked in an appropriate data base.)

Most of what you can do with these information-based services is identical to what you can do with their printed equivalent. Still, there are some important differences that give on-line services a real advantage.

The first difference is one of immediacy. With the electronic service, you can get the information as soon as it becomes available. You don't have to wait for printed material to be delivered anywhere. This may be important to you for business reasons, for instance, when dealing with stock-market prices or certain kinds of news stories.

The second difference is a matter of convenience. With the electronic information utility, you don't have to go out to buy a paper or wait for someone to bring it to you; you don't have to travel to the library; and you don't have to arrange your schedule to accommodate someone else's. Most of the information-based services are available for all but a few hours each day. They typically go off-line well after midnight and come back on-line before most people wake up.

The third and major difference is that with the electronic information utility, you can do these things more quickly, and often more cheaply.

This is a matter of simple cost accounting. If your time is worth $20 an hour, two hours of research cost you $40. If you cut the research time to 15 minutes by spending $20 on the information utility, that same research has cost you $25 ($20 to the information utility plus $5 of your time). Of course if your time is worth only $10 an hour, this same example would *increase* the cost of the research by $2.50. Still, the increased convenience may well be worth $2.50 to you. (And don't forget to figure in the travel time to and from the library.)

KINDS OF INFORMATION UTILITIES

So much for the kinds of *services* available. There are also variations in information utilities that deliver those services.

It's time for some definitions, but first a quick warning. This is a young field. The definitions for many words, and in some cases the spellings, are still up for grabs. I have tried to cover the most common variations, but you may well run across something here that's defined differently or spelled differently from the way you've seen it, or will see it, elsewhere. If so, don't let it throw you. It's just something you have to put up with in exchange for being a pioneer in the field. The payoff will come in one or two years, when everyone else is playing catch-up in an area you're already familiar with.

Basically there are four kinds of information utility, each one representing a different technology. They are teletext, videotex, computerized bulletin boards, and true on-line, interactive data bases.

Teletext

We'll start with an easy one, teletext. Teletext gets its name from the fact that it typically sends its information by way of television. It is, in effect, televised text—except that it can include graphics as well as text.

With teletext, information comes in "pages," with each page containing one screenful of information. Typically there are a few hundred pages available. They are sent "piggyback," right along with the regular television transmission. (The system crams the teletext information into the black bars that show up between normal television picture frames. You see those bars whenever your television picture rolls.)

Using teletext is simple. If you want to watch a television show, you use your television as usual. If you want to see the teletext pages, however, you need an adaptor (also known as a decoder, depending on who you're talking to).

Choosing among the teletext pages is a lot like choosing among TV channels except that you don't have to buy a *TV Guide* every week. The teletext pages include index pages, or table-of-contents pages, that tell you what's available on which page. The adaptor includes a keypad. You find the page number you want, punch it into the adaptor, and the page shows up on your television.

Teletext is a generic term that applies to several different specific systems. One of those systems is used by PBS, NBC, and CBS in their closed-caption system for the hearing-impaired.

Teletext systems have severe limitations. To begin with, like television itself, teletext is strictly one-way communication. You as the user cannot talk back to the system; you can only select pages. This limits the system's usefulness to information services—things like weather reports, news stories, or advertising. There is no way you can buy something over the system or use it for communications. Even within information-based services, moreover, many possibilities are ruled out with teletext because of its extremely limited ability to carry information.

Because the system is strictly one-way, the television station has no way of knowing which pages of information are being asked for at any given instant. To make sure that all the pages are available, the system has to keep broadcasting each of them, one after the other, and it has to keep doing that repeatedly.

A typical system will take about one second to transmit four pages. If the system is carrying 100 pages of information, then, it will take about 25 seconds to broadcast the entire sequence. You as the user choose the page you want and punch the number into your adaptor. Then you wait for it to show up on your screen. It may show up immediately, or it may take 25 seconds, or anywhere in between. (On the average, the wait will be about half the time it takes to broadcast the entire sequence, or about 12½ seconds.) However long it happens to take, though, even if it's the full 25 seconds, it's a tolerable wait.

Double the amount of information and you also double the waiting time. Double it twice, and the average waiting time goes to 50 seconds, with a maximum wait of one minute and 40 seconds. This is not a tolerable length of time, especially if the information is something you're anxious to see. ("What's the weather going to be, Mom? Can we go on the picnic?")

What this all adds up to is that there is a trade-off between how much information a teletext system can carry and how fast you as the user can expect to find the information you want.

This is the last you will see about teletext in this book. All the limitations of teletext systems stem from the fact that they are limited to one-way communication. This book is about getting on-line, and that means two-way communication between the system and you.

Which brings us to videotex.

Videotex (or Videotext)

Videotex is as tough to explain as teletext is easy.

Notice first that the word comes in two versions, videotex (without a final *t*) and videotext (with a final *t*). Although both versions are still used, it seems that videotex (to rhyme with Telex) is winning out. So videotex it is, in this book at least.

Unfortunately, the definition of videotex is at least as slippery as the spelling. Videotex is sometimes used to mean any system that puts information into a computer (as text or graphics or both), transmits that information by any means at all (phone lines, cable TV, or broadcast TV, or broadcast FM), and displays that information on a modified television set (in the form of pages). By this definition, teletext is a kind of videotex.

Another popular definition limits videotex to those systems that allow two-way communication. By this definition, teletext stands in sharp contrast to videotex.

In this more restricted definition, information is generally transmitted over the phone lines. In fact, it is the use of the phone lines, as opposed to one-way broadcast television, that allows the two-way transmission of information.

The mechanics of using this kind of videotex system (whatever your definition) are much the same as the mechanics of using a teletext system. You sit in front of your television with your adaptor, punch in the numbers of the pages you want (either from knowing them beforehand or as a choice from a menu), and the page shows up on your screen. The differences come from what goes on behind the scenes.

With this kind of system, you are connected directly to a computer, with your television-plus-adaptor functioning as a computer terminal. You ask the system directly for the information you want. The system responds by sending you the specific page of information you asked for. This means that the length of time you have to wait is not determined by how much information is in the system. And that, in turn, means you can have quick access to as many pages of information as the computer can hold.

How many pages? A bunch. Prestel, a British-based service, contains well over 250,000 pages.

How quickly you get the information varies from a couple of seconds on up. Waiting time is determined primarily by how many other people are using the system at the same time you are. Information utilities are constantly upgrading their facilities to provide faster response times.

There is a basic feedback loop involved. As any given utility adds more customers, its response time slows down. But then they can afford to invest in faster, more powerful, state-of-the-art computers and software, at which point the response time speeds up again. If the response time ever becomes intolerably long, the utility loses customers, which also speeds up the response time.

We are not through with trying to define videotex. To begin with, there are problems with both of the definitions we've looked at so far. Each defines videotex as a system that makes use of a modified television set. The problem is that videotex systems may have started out that way, but this is no longer necessarily true.

Prestel is the prime example of such a system. It was originally designed to be received by a television set equipped with an adaptor. Today there is software on the market that will let you use an Apple II to tie into Prestel, and there is a hardware/software combination that will let you use an IBM PC (or a "hardware compatible" clone). Still, no one argues that Prestel has stopped being a videotex service.

Complicating matters further is the fact that utilities like CompuServe Information Services call some of their services videotex but are intended to be used with virtually any computer or terminal.

Take your choice then. You can define videotex to include all computer-based, information systems.

Or you can define it to include only interactive systems.

Or only those systems that require special communications protocols.

Or only those systems where the information is transmitted in predetermined chunks, or pages (as opposed to the fully interactive data bases we will get to shortly).

Or you can define it to include only those systems that are capable of transmitting graphics as well as text.

Whichever definition you choose, be aware that other people are using the word differently. We will come back to this argument at the end of the book, but until we do, I am going to do my best to avoid the word altogether. It is useful, however, to make a differentiation between different kinds of information systems. I will, therefore, sometimes refer to a "Prestel-like" utility, meaning a system where information comes in pages, where the pages include graphics, and where the usual "terminal" is a television set with an adaptor.

Computerized Bulletin-Board Systems

We touched on computerized bulletin-board systems earlier, mentioning them as one kind of communication-based service. As the name implies, these computerized bulletin-board systems, or CBBSs, serve as an electronic bulletin board for exchanging messages. Some bulletin-board services are included within broad-scale information utilities such as THE SOURCE, but they deserve a separate listing here because most computerized bulletin-board systems function as small, independent information utilities.

CBBSs are so small and independent that it is hard to keep track of them. They are run by clubs, by computer stores, and even by individuals. Given the proper software (and such software exists for most popular computers), just about any computer can be set up as a bulletin-board system.

To use one of these CBBSs, you merely call up and log on to the system. (The exact procedure varies from one system to another.) Then you browse through the messages that others have left or leave messages of your own.

Most CBBSs specialize in some particular subject. You will find a sampling later in this book. I have made no attempt to list them, though, because these are small services and the listing changes at an appalling rate.

No one can give a definitive count of the number of CBBSs operating at any given instant. *The On-Line Computer Telephone Directory* lists over 600 bulletin boards, but Jim Cambron, who compiled the list, feels that 450 is a more accurate figure. Whatever the correct number, you will find a phone number in Chapter 9 that you can call for a current list. You will also find subscription information on *The On-Line Computer Telephone Directory,* which publishes its list four times a year.

Fully Interactive, Time-sharing Computer Systems

This last description—fully interactive, time-sharing computer systems—is a mouthful. Let's try breaking it into smaller pieces.

First, time-sharing is the technology that allows a large number of people to use the same computer at the same time. Notice that teletext has nothing to do with time-sharing because nobody is communicating with the computer. On the other hand, Prestel-like systems and fully interactive systems are practical *only* because of time-sharing. Without it, even the most powerful information-retrieval program imaginable would have limited usefulness. Only one person could use the computer at a time.

What really distinguishes this kind of system from a teletext system or a Prestel-like system, though, is the "fully interactive" part of the description.

The teletext system, being strictly one-way, is not at all interactive.

The Prestel-like system (with or without graphics) is interactive, but only to a limited degree. As a user, you're still confined to looking through tables-of-contents pages (menus) and making your choices from the lists provided to you. You do not have the option of bypassing the menus and going directly to some particular subject or subjects. In contrast, a fully interactive system gives you the ability to define your own subjects and lets the computer dig out the appropriate articles, or research data, or references.

A menu-based news service, for instance, might start by giving you a list of the day's headlines. You would then page through that list, one page at a time, until you saw something that interested you. At that point you could go to the story, read it, then come back to the headline menu. This is fine if you're just browsing through the day's news, but what if you're looking for a specific story—on the latest flight of the space shuttle perhaps? Why should you have to bother with reading page after page of menu? And what happens if you miss the headline of the story you're looking for?

With a fully interactive system, you would enter a command to find all stories dealing with the specific topic. Instead of looking through menus, you would enter "space shuttle," and the system would tell you how many stories fit your description. If the number is small enough to be manageable, you would ask for a list of those stories, then choose anything from the list that looked interesting. In effect, you create your own menu, tailored to your specific need of the moment.

The example we used earlier—polar-bear livers and Vitamin D poisoning—demonstrates the capabilities of a fully interactive system. We can take that example one step further. Suppose you're having trouble remembering just what the problem was with eating polar-bear liver. You know that it involved some kind of vitamin toxicity, but you can't remember what. In fact, you think it was Vitamin A poisoning. When you search for articles on polar-bear liver and Vitamin A poisoning, though, you don't find anything. At that point you can take a slightly different tack and try looking for articles on polar-bear liver and vitamin poisoning. Not only will the article show up (assuming it's listed), but your somewhat hazy recollection will be automatically corrected in the process.

DATA BASES

Another term we need to define at this early stage is *data base*.

A data base (two words), or database (one word), is any large collection of information in computer-readable form. Many data bases are strictly for private use within some particular organization. For purposes of this book, the only data bases we are interested in are those that are both available to interested segments of the general public and that can be reached by phone.

You will sometimes see the terms "data base" and "information utility" used interchangeably. Notice, though, that they are two very different things. A data base is a collection of information. Typically, an information utility offers more than one data base to choose from. Very often a data base will be available from more than one information utility.

Some people try to avoid this source of confusion by talking about data bases and data-base vendors. Unfortunately, that defines some systems out of existence, like computerized bulletin boards that do not charge a fee.

This brings us full circle to the question we started with at the beginning of this chapter: What's an information utility?

We started by defining an information utility as any organization that will let you use its information (or will let you use someone else's information), usually for a fee. This is as good a working definition as any, and the one we will stay with in this book. Still, be aware that the definition of information utility—like the definition of videotex—changes from one person to the next. Also be aware that many people use the terms "information utility" and "information service" interchangeably, so that THE SOURCE, for instance, would be called either an information utility or an information service.

In this book the terms will not be used interchangeably. Our working definition of a "utility" will be "an organization," while a "service" will be defined as "a kind of service" —meaning a bulletin-board service, or an electronic mail service, or a bibliographic reference service, or whatever.

Using these definitions, THE SOURCE is a large information utility that provides various kinds of information services, communications services, and transaction services. A computerized bulletin board, on the other hand, is a small information utility that provides only one kind of limited service.

That should be all the definitions we need for now. Here's a quick overview to help you put the pieces together.

Information utilities come in many variations, but the most interesting utilities for most of us are the large organizations that offer either a wide range of services or at least a wide range of data bases. Some of the better-known large utilities are THE SOURCE, CompuServe, DIALOG, Dow Jones News/Retrieval, and NewsNet.

Typically you can reach these large information utilities either by calling them directly or by calling through Telenet, Tymnet, or Uninet (three services that save you a long-distance phone charge). Then you log on, using your password and account number. Prices of these utilities range from a couple of dollars per hour to several hundred dollars per hour. Services range from electronic mail to full text data bases, from CB emulation to wire-service stories, from bulletin boards to patent searches.

Getting the information you want from a data base requires a knowledge of how the data base is structured. Basically there are two choices: command structure and menu structure.

- A command structure expects you to know the commands you need and to enter them with little or no prompting.
- A menu structure gives you menus that list your choices at each step along the way.

For those who are familiar with the particular data base, the command structure is faster and more powerful simply because you don't have to sit and wait while menus you don't need are written on the screen. For the new or occasional user, on the other hand, the menu structure is generally easier to understand and use. Some information utilities, including CompuServe and THE SOURCE, have introduced a dual structure. The user can either go into a command mode or rely on the menus to find his or her way around the system.

Notice, please, that the difference between menu structure and command structure refers to how you move around the utility or data base. It does not refer to how the information is presented to you. Any given utility can have a menu structure for moving around the utility but still contain one or more fully interactive data bases. Similarly, the utility can have a command structure but still present the information to you only through previously prepared menus or pages.

And that is just about all there is to say about information utilities in general. It's time to get down to the details.

2

HARDWARE PART I
Terminals

Before you can use any information utility, you need the proper equipment on your end of the phone line. "Proper equipment" in this case translates to a terminal and a modem.

Or a terminal with a built-in modem.

Or a computer that can act as a terminal, if it has the proper software.

Or any of a half dozen other combinations.

The truth is, when it comes to choosing equipment, there is an embarrassment of riches available. There are so many kinds of equipment to choose from—let alone specific equipment—that this is a good place to get lost and give up.

Of course if you already own a computer, part of your choice has been made, but there are still enough other choices to keep you busy.

Start with the basics:

- A terminal is a device with a keyboard (so you can type in commands) and a screen or printer (so you can read the information being sent to you).
- A modem, or modulator-demodulator, is a device for sending and receiving signals over the phone lines.

13

- Both terminals and modems come in all sorts of variations.
- Some terminals have built-in modems, some do not.
- Some are meant to be portable, some are not.
- Some include their own screen (or CRT), some do not. Some are meant to be used with a television. Still others are meant to be used with a printer.
- Some terminals look like portable typewriters, with the "typewriter" part being the printer.
- And some terminals are really computers being used as terminals.

Most of these differences don't matter all that much. The one that *does* matter is the difference between dumb terminals and smart terminals.

DUMB TERMINALS

A basic dumb terminal consists of a keyboard, a screen, and the associated electronics.

Because there is so little to them, dumb terminals are generally inexpensive. Precisely because there is so little to them, however, the capabilities of dumb terminals are severely limited. A dumb terminal will let you put information into the computer at the other end of the phone line, and it will let you get information out, but that's about it. Stripped-down models may have further limitations; they may, for instance, send and receive upper-case characters only.

The most important limitations of dumb terminals fall into three categories.

First, there are times when using a dumb terminal can be frustrating simply because you have to do everything manually. This means you have to know the phone number you want to call or else you have to look it up. Then you have to dial (or punch) the number in, and, finally, you have to carefully follow the log-on sequence of whatever system you're calling. This can be inconvenient if the number you're calling is busy, or if you can't get a good connection, or if you keep getting disconnected because you're not used to the procedure for logging on to the particular system. The first time you have to dial the same number four or five times in a row, you are going to start wishing there was a better way.

The second limitation of dumb terminals is that anything you want to send has to be typed manually, while you are on-line paying for the use of the phone and for the use of the utility. If you have to send a lot of information, and particularly if you are a rotten typist, this can be expensive.

The third limitation, and probably the most important one, is that if you are reading the incoming information off a screen, it is transient. As information comes in, it fills up the screen, scrolls up off the top, and is gone. Depending on the information you're getting (and paying for, remember), you might prefer to keep a copy.

If you think you'll need a record of your conversation with the computer, one possibility is to get a printing terminal.

A printing terminal is also a dumb terminal. Instead of consisting of a keyboard and screen, though, it consists of a keyboard and a printer (or electronic typewriter, which works out to the same thing).

With a printing terminal, anything you type at the keyboard is typed on the printer in front of you. Anything the computer sends back to you is also typed on the printer. When you're finished, you have a complete record, or hard copy, of the conversation.

Unfortunately, printers are much more expensive than cathode-ray tubes. As a result, a dumb printing terminal costs more than an equivalent CRT terminal. Also, being mechanical, a printing terminal will tend to break down more often.

Another problem with using a printing terminal is that you wind up with a record of the whole conversation: the parts you want, the parts you don't want, and even the parts you knew you didn't want while you were getting them or typing them in the first place.

The obvious answer to this problem is to stay with a screen-based terminal but to add a printer that you can turn on when you need it and off when you don't.

With this step, we have introduced our first electronically controlled option and have begun to give our terminal some smarts.

FIGURE 1. The TYMSHARE 110, a typical lightweight printing terminal.

SMART TERMINALS

Smart terminals are generally somewhat more expensive than dumb terminals simply because they contain more parts. In particular, they contain a local computer, or microprocessor, and at least some memory. (That's in addition to the keyboard and screen, of course.) This lets you do things like automatically dial phone numbers, automatically log on to various systems, or even capture incoming data and store it on disk or tape.

How smart is a smart terminal? It depends. In general, the more capabilities the terminal has (meaning the more electronic options available to you as a user), the smarter the terminal. Whether the particular terminal is considered "smart," or "very smart," or "brilliant," however, has nothing to do with any objective scale. It has everything to do with the manufacturer's marketing department and what it thinks will sell the equipment.

At the low end of the scale, a merely "smart" terminal may provide a few options to the user, little or no internal memory, and no capability at all for storing information on disk or tape.

At the high end of the scale, a brilliant terminal may be essentially indistinguishable from a fully equipped microcomputer system, with large amounts of internal memory and dual disk drives.

As you might expect, it works the other way too. If a terminal can be indistinguishable from a computer, then just about any computer can be used as a terminal as long as it has some way to connect to the phone system. We'll come back to computers later. Right now let's stay with terminals.

Scanset: A Not-So-Dumb Terminal

Scanset is an interesting example of a smart terminal. I say "interesting" because it is the first in a new generation of terminals that are aimed at people who don't generally use terminals, computers, or anything else with a keyboard.

The dead giveaway is size, particularly the size of the keyboard. The little calculator-style keys are arranged in the same way as a standard keyboard but they use only about two-thirds the width of a normal keyboard. This makes the terminal useless for touch typing and pretty much rules out the Scanset for anything that requires large amounts of typing, but that's obviously not what it was designed for.

The Scanset's "footprint," the measure of the amount of desk space it uses, is roughly a third the size of the footprint of a standard desk-top computer. This goes a long way toward shrinking a terminal down to a manageable size. In fact, it converts a terminal from something that will dominate its surroundings into something that can sit unobtrusively on a desk or table until needed. This has some obvious advantages.

Many executives wouldn't be caught dead with a full-sized terminal or fully equipped microcomputer system on their desk. Not only does it take up too much desk space, it looks too secretarial. The Scanset's small size, though, and its obviously useless keyboard, converts it from a secretarial tool into an executive toy—a gadget. The fact that you can also use it for something, like getting the latest stock prices, is merely a bonus.

The same size considerations apply at home. Where would you put a full-sized terminal if you had one? It certainly won't fit into the decor of most rooms. The Scanset, however, can sit comfortably on a table or desk next to a telephone and hardly be noticed.

Putting size considerations aside, Scanset has some useful, if minimal, smarts built in. Basically, it's one step up from a dumb terminal.

The Scanset frees you from the limitations and frustrations of doing everything manually. It does that in a straightforward way that is both easy to learn and easy to remember. It's even reasonably self-explanatory, which is a rare quality in anything having to do with computers.

The secret to the Scanset's ease of use is in the way it uses the six function keys at the top of the keyboard. These are unimaginatively labeled F1, F2, F3, and so forth, but with good reason: Their functions change depending on what you're doing. What makes life easy for you is that the bottom line on the screen provides descriptive labels for these keys. The labels thoughtfully change for you as the terminal switches from one mode to another.

When you turn on a Scanset, the first thing you see on the screen is a phone directory. This can hold up to 36 phone numbers. If you're turning it on for the first time, the phone directory is empty except for the numbers 1 through 36. At the bottom of the screen, above the function keys, are two labels. One says "DIAL." The other says "NEXT." If you choose the one that says "DIAL," Scanset will pick up the phone (using its built-in modem), and you will hear a dial tone through its built-in speaker. The directory, meanwhile, is replaced with a single word, "PHONE:" followed by a blinking cursor. The labels over the function keys are also changed. To make a call, you use the keyboard to punch in the phone number. To hang up, you hit the function key under the word "ABORT."

The entire process is designed to be simple and obvious, even for the first-time user. The rest of the Scanset functions, from entering numbers in the phone directory to automatically dialing a call, are just as well designed.

When you enter phone numbers in the directory, you are asked to enter a "LABEL," or name, as well as a phone number. Later, when you choose numbers to dial, you can look at the names instead of the phone numbers.

Once you have phone numbers in the directory, dialing becomes a simple matter of going to the first screen and picking a directory number between 1 and 36. Enter the number and Scanset dials it for you.

Thirty-six numbers make for a reasonably large phone directory. It is certainly more than you're likely to need for calling a few information utilities. If you have leftover room in the directory, though, it's not at all wasted. You can use Scanset as an automatic dialer. Enter your friends' phone numbers, your family's, your business associates', your home or office number, and you can let Scanset dial them for you too. Pick up your phone when you hear the ring over Scanset's speaker and tell Scanset to hang up.

You might, in fact, like to dial all your calls through Scanset. If a number is busy, you can keep redialing it automatically. (In fact, as I am writing this, I am using Scanset for just that purpose. The number I'm trying to reach has been busy all morning. If Scanset ever gets a ring instead of a busy signal, I'll stop writing and pick up my phone. Until then, I won't have to stop long enough to break my train of thought.)

Much more helpful than automatic dialing is Scanset's ability to automatically log on to a system.

Different systems require different log-on procedures. One might want you to begin by entering two carriage returns, wait for a response, then enter a "terminal identification code," wait for another response, enter a "network address," and so on. Another system might want you to wait for it to query you, after which you have to respond with an altogether different "terminal identifier," then wait for a response, enter a "User Identification," and so forth.

These log-on procedures are done purely by rote, like two spies making contact in a public place: Sign, countersign, counter-countersign. And like two spies making contact, the signs and countersigns have to be just so. If you type the wrong password, or you take too long, you'll often be thrown off the system and have to start again.

With Scanset, you don't have to worry about that. You can enter the entire log-on procedure for any particular system, then let Scanset take care of it automatically from then on.

Most log-on procedures, incidentally, take several steps of conversation between you and the host computer (the one you're talking to). Scanset allows for this. When you enter the procedure in Scanset's memory, you include a command to stop after each step and wait for the host computer to send its part of the conversation. Scanset sends its reply, then waits for the next prompt. One not-so-incidental advantage of all this is that the whole routine is speeded up because Scanset reacts faster, and "types" faster, than you do.

This automatic log-on capability is particularly helpful for utilities that can be reached in more than one way. Dow Jones News/Retrieval, for instance, can be reached through the Telenet, Tymnet, or Uninet systems. (We touched on these briefly in Chapter 1. They are three networks that, among other things, save you the cost of a long-distance call.)

Each of these systems has its own log-on procedure. (The procedures for Telenet and Tymnet are the two that I outlined earlier.) You may generally prefer to use one of these systems over the others, either out of habit or because it is closer, and therefore cheaper, to call. Still, you will at least occasionally be forced to use one of the other systems when your first choice has a computer down or when its phone is busy. In that case it is helpful to have both sets of phone numbers and both log-on procedures sitting in Scanset's memory. All you have to do then is choose between "Dow Jones— Tymnet," "Dow Jones—Telenet," and Dow Jones—Uninet" and let Scanset do its stuff.

A particularly nice aspect of the automatic log-on feature is that once you enter your password into Scanset's memory, no one else can get it out. It shows up on the screen with the rest of the log-on sequence but only as a series of dots. This is important since the password is what lets the utility know who is logging on to the system and who gets charged for the time. Once you've entered the password in Scanset's memory, moreover, you don't even have to remember what it was. And that means you don't have to keep scraps of paper hanging around where someone else might see your password and be able to use the utility at your expense. Keep in mind, though, that entering your password in Scanset's memory is *not* a good idea if you keep your Scanset in an office or some other easily accessible place. There is nothing to stop someone from logging on to a utility at your expense from your desk.

Scanset has one or two other features worth mentioning.

It has a "status screen" that lets you choose the basic settings to use. As with the rest of the Scanset features, this has been designed to be as simple as possible. Some of the choices border on the technical ("baud rate," "parity," "duplex," and a few other things we'll get to later). These choices do require some special knowledge before they can be used correctly, but they represent an absolute, irreducible minimum of special knowledge. The choices set at the factory will work for most information utilities.

In addition to the somewhat technical choices between communications settings, the status screen also lets you customize some Scanset features to taste. Among other things, you can choose the brightness of the screen, the volume of the speaker, and whether you want text to scroll off the screen or to start writing at the top of the screen each time it runs out of space.

One especially nice touch is that you can choose between 40 characters per line and 80 characters per line (that's the number of characters across the screen). Many information utilities assume that you have a 40-character screen width, which means that the information they send will fill only the left half of an 80-character screen. If you choose the 40-character option with Scanset, it doubles the width of the characters, making the text much easier to read.

Taken together, all of Scanset's smarts make the job of calling and logging on to an information utility much easier. They also eliminate a great deal of potential frustration. Once on-line, though, Scanset does little more than a dumb terminal.

If you want to send a message or post a message on a bulletin board, for example, you have to type it while you are on-line. Scanset does not have anything like enough memory to let you type it in beforehand, then send it from memory later. (Fortunately, Scanset's keyboard is adequate for medium-speed, two-finger typing.)

As for incoming information, Scanset by itself does just what a dumb terminal does. Text is written on the screen, then scrolls up into oblivion.

Notice, though, that I said "Scanset by itself." The terminal also has a built-in connector (or "port") for attaching a printer.

Scanset has exactly two on-line smart features. One is the ability to hang up the phone electronically. The other is the ability to turn the printer on and off electronically.

This brings us back to where we started the discussion of smart terminals. If you have a printer connected to Scanset, you can turn it on and off when needed. This means (in theory at least) that you will end up with a record of the information you want, available either to read later or to file away for your records. This is certainly better than having a printout of the entire conversation with the computer, and it is light years ahead of not having a printout at all, but there are two major problems with this kind of on-line editing.

First, you have to remember to turn the printer on and off, and second, you have to make your editing decisions on the go, with no opportunity to second-guess them later.

It would be more convenient to store incoming information in some way without printing it. Then you could edit it at your leisure after the conversation is over, when you're no longer on-line and paying for the time.

If you had that kind of memory capability, moreover, you could also type messages before you went on-line, then send them automatically.

You can get smart terminals with these capabilities. They come with different amounts of internal memory (for short-term storage of information), with or without external memory (for long-term storage), and with different capabilities for automatic dialing and automatic log-on.

But then, you can get computers with all these features as well. As I've already mentioned, smart terminals are essentially indistinguishable from equivalently equipped microcomputer systems. And virtually any microcomputer system can function as a terminal.

One last thing before we leave Scanset.

Three interesting "features" that come with Scanset are:

1. A free password for Dow Jones News/Retrieval and one free hour of time. (The usual one-time cost for the password is $50. The value of one hour's free time varies.)
2. A free registration on THE SOURCE and one free hour of on-line time. (Registration is normally $100.)
3. A six-month, free trial membership and one half hour of free time on COMP*U*STORE, a shopping service. (Membership is normally $25 for one year, $40 for two years.)

This brings up an important point to keep in mind if you don't own any equipment yet. Many information utilities have tie-ins with various products. These tie-ins will save you money in the form of a one-time registration fee, or membership fee. If you already know which utilities you want to use, you should take that into account in choosing your equipment—both hardware and software. If terminal A or computer A costs $160 more than terminal B but includes free registration on THE SOURCE (worth $100), then terminal A is really $40 cheaper than terminal B (*If* you're planning on getting a subscription to THE SOURCE anyway).

Now, briefly, on to the subject of computers as terminals.

COMPUTERS AS TERMINALS

Just about any computer can function as either a dumb terminal or a smart terminal as long as it has an RS-232 port (and very often even if it doesn't). This is a standard connector found on nearly all personal computers. If you don't know what an RS-232 port is, let it slip by for now; we'll come back to it later. Right now just take my word for it that this description covers virtually all personal computers.

Throughout the rest of this book the assumption will be that you are using a computer as a terminal—presumably a small personal or business computer. Different computers, though, have different capabilities and different configurations. They have different amounts of memory available (both internally and externally); they have different keyboard arrangements; they may or may not have programmable function keys (remember those log-on sequences); they may include an RS-232 port as standard or as an optional extra; they may not have an RS-232 port at all but have something that serves the same purpose. The list of variations goes on.

Having said all that, we will now proceed to ignore the differences for the time being. We'll get back to them in Chapter 6, where we will discuss specific features of some specific computers. First, though, we need to discuss modems and software.

All of which brings us, finally, to modems.

3

HARDWARE PART II
Modems

A computer or terminal by itself will not let you communicate with an information utility. Before you can do that, you need one other thing in the way of equipment: a modem.

A modem, once again, is the gadget that lets a computer transmit and receive information over phone lines. The word is short for *MOdulator-DEModulator,* which is a short description of what the device does. When sending information, a modem takes generated signals and *modulates* them, or converts them into a form that can be sent over the phone lines. When receiving information, it takes the modulated signals from the phone line and *demodulates* them, or converts them into a form that the computer can deal with.

As with terminals, modems are available in a number of variations. Fortunately, the modem is a simple beast so that the number of basic possibilities is relatively small (though there are additional options available to cloud the issue). The important variations fall into two categories. The first deals with technical choices, namely speed and signaling standards. The second deals with methods of connection, both to the computer and to the phone lines.

SPEED (BAUD RATE)

Speed of transmission is generally measured in something called baud rate, the most common rates being 300 baud and 1200 baud. These translate into transmission speeds of 30 characters per second and 120 characters per second. (Technical purists will argue that I cheated here, since baud rate is a measure of transmission speed, not a measure of how much information is moved. In practical terms, though, the conversion works, and I see no point in going into the technical definition.)

Until recently modems with a maximum transmission speed of 300 baud (30 characters per second) have been more or less *the* standard for the vast majority of users. First, they have been around for a long time. Second, they are more than adequate for most business needs and virtually all non-business needs. And third, they have been, until recently, much cheaper than 1200-baud modems. A standard joke about 1200-baud modems used to be, "They're available, but you might like to spend the money on something more useful. Like a car."

The difference in price between 300-baud modems and 1200-baud modems stems from the fact that signaling standards that work at low speeds simply do not work reliably, for technical reasons, at speeds much higher than 300 baud. 1200-baud modems therefore, must use different signaling standards and different, more expensive components. Even so, the price of 1200-baud modems has been coming down lately and will almost certainly continue to come down. The most inexpensive, stripped-down 1200-baud modems now cost only slightly more than the most expensive, option-laden 300-baud modems. This doesn't make them cheap, but it does bring them into the realm of the affordable.

For technical reasons, 1200 baud (120 characters per second) is pretty much the limit for reliable transmission of information over standard phone lines (so far at least). Modems exist that will operate at faster speeds but only on special, "conditioned" lines. The phone company, as you might expect, charges more for these special lines. As for the price of these high-speed modems, the old joke still applies. You'd probably prefer spending the money on a car.

You will occasionally see a reference to transmission speeds of less than 300 baud, 110 baud being the most common. These are generally older standards, established long ago and now limited to specialized equipment or networks. ("Long ago" in this context means any time before 1975.) The signaling standards in these older systems follow the same technical specifications that you will find in 300-baud modems. Some 300-baud modems can use these slower speeds as well. Others cannot. If you are concerned only with information utilities, these slower speeds are irrelevant.

1200-Baud Modems—Advantages and Disadvantages

Modems that work at 1200 baud (120 characters per second) are four times as fast as the "standard" 300-baud modems. This has obvious advantages if you are paying an information utility *and* the phone company some fixed amount per minute to receive a great deal of information that you can look through later at your leisure. The advantages are less compelling but still real if you are paying the utility an additional premium to use it at the faster rate.

If the work you are doing is highly interactive, the advantages of the higher speed are not so obvious. Most of your time will be spent entering information by hand, waiting for a response from the computer, and reading the response once it arrives. Relatively little time will be spent transmitting information. If the utility is billing you at a higher rate for the higher speed, this may wind up costing you more money for the same amount of information without even saving you much time.

Add to this the fact that 1200-baud modems are more expensive than 300-baud modems in the first place, and you may begin to wonder why anyone would want a 1200-baud modem at all.

The answer becomes obvious the first time you start paging through menus on an information utility. Thirty characters per second sounds fast enough, but not while you are sitting in front of your terminal watching the menus being written line by line on your screen. The problem is compounded by the very nature of a time-sharing system. Every so often the host computer (the utility) stops sending you information in the middle of a line while it does something for someone else.

Reading an electronic newspaper or magazine at 300 baud is even more annoying. Believe me, you can read faster than that. If 1200 baud is too fast, you can always save the article on disk or print it out and read it later.

In deciding whether you should get a 300-baud modem or a 1200-baud modem, there are several questions you have to ask yourself about the way you're likely to spend your time once you get on-line.

Is most of your on-line activity going to be highly interactive, in the form of CB simulation, or game-playing, or information searches? Do you plan to read through electronic newspapers while on-line? Do you plan to browse through bulletin boards and reply to them?

If your answer to any of these questions is yes, then using a 1200-baud modem is going to save you very little time, and will probably cost you more money. The limiting factor in these cases is not the speed of the modem; it is, variously, your reading speed, your typing speed, and your thinking speed. True, the actual transmission of data will be somewhat faster with the 1200-

baud modem, but you have to consider whether the marginal extra convenience of 1200 baud is worth the extra cost to you, both in initial costs and in later use. Your answer to that question is going to depend largely on how much you can afford to spend and how valuable your time is.

There are cases where a 1200-baud modem will save you time and money. You might, for example, be interested primarily in getting software for your computer from a Special-Interest Group bulletin board. (This is also known as downloading from an SIG.) In this kind of situation, where you are getting large amounts of information with little or no interaction between you and the information utility, a faster modem will save you significant amounts of time and money. Even if you plan to use your modem primarily for this sort of communication, though, you still have to consider whether it will save you enough money to cover the extra cost of the modem in the first place.

Finally, there is the question of compatibility. If your modem works at 1200 baud only and you want to use a bulletin board that works at 300 baud only, you won't be able to. The question is: Who do you expect to communicate with and what kind of modem do you need in order to communicate with them?

The last question brings us to the subject of modem compatibility, which brings us to signaling standards.

SIGNALING STANDARDS: BELL 103, BELL 113, BELL 202, BELL 212, RACAL-VADIC VA3400

Signaling standards are simply a set of agreed-upon technical specifications for modulating and demodulating the computer-generated information. And that's as technical as we are going to get.

Let's agree right at the outset that you don't need to bother with the technical details of modulation in order to use a modem any more than you need to bother with the technical details of audio modulation (AM) or frequency modulation (FM) in order to use an AM or FM radio. Still, you should be aware that just as there are different technical schemes used for radio transmission, there are also different technical schemes used for modems; and just as you can't use an AM radio to listen to FM signals, you can't use one kind of modem to communicate with a computer equipped with a different kind of modem.

Take the analogy one step further. When you buy a radio, you need to make sure that it's compatible with the station or stations you plan to listen to—i.e., do you need AM or FM?

When you buy a modem, you need to make sure that it's compatible with the information utility you plan to talk to. In this case, the standards go by the not-so-enchanting names of Bell 103, Bell 113, Bell 202, Bell 212, and Racal-Vadic VA3400.

You will notice that four of the five signaling standards contain the word "Bell" in their names, as in the late Bell Telephone Company. This is no accident. Each of these standards is named after a specific model of modem developed by and originally available from Bell Telephone. The fifth signaling standard, the Racal-Vadic VA3400, is named after a modem developed by a company named, unsurprisingly, Racal-Vadic.

The signaling standards used by any particular modem are easy enough to determine. Ads for the modem will usually say something like "Bell 103-compatible." So will the box the modem comes in.

You don't need to know much about the standards themselves, but before we look at the standards, there is some communications terminology that you will need to know.

Simplex versus Duplex

In general, transmission of information can be simplex or duplex. This is just another way of saying one-way or two-way.

A television transmission is a good example of simplex (one-way) transmissions.

Talking with someone over the phone is a good example of duplex (two-way) transmissions.

Half Duplex versus Full Duplex. Duplex transmission can be further divided into half duplex and full duplex.

Half duplex is two-way, but only one-way at a time. CB and ham radio provide a good example. There is communication going in both directions, but each side has to wait for the other to finish before it can begin sending.

Full duplex is two-way conversation, with both sides able to send at the same time. And we're back to the telephone for an example.

Full duplex, where both sides can send information simultaneously, is obviously more convenient than half duplex, where each side has to wait for the other to finish. There is a minor technical problem, though. Half-duplex systems are half duplex because they have to be that way. In the case of CB or ham radio, for example, the reason you can't listen at the same time that you're talking is that your receiver is tuned to the same frequency as your transmitter. If you try listening while talking, all you're going to hear is your own transmission.

Modems have the same basic problem. They communicate by way of audio frequencies, or audible tones. If two modems are communicating and both are using tones of the same pitch, they won't both be able to talk at the same time. In other words, they'll be limited to half-duplex communications. Fortunately, there's a way out of this problem—namely, have each modem transmit with one set of tones (transmission requires two separate tones) and listen for another set. The only catch is that you have to decide in advance which modem is transmitting which set of tones. (You can use this trick with radios also; you can get full duplex by transmitting on one frequency and listening on another.)

All this brings us to the idea of an originate mode and answer mode.

Originate Mode and Answer Mode

Most modems have a switch labeled "Originate—Answer." This determines which set of tones your modem is using to send information and which set it is listening to. If you are dealing exclusively with information utilities, you can simply set the switch in the originate mode and leave it there. In fact, you can save money by buying a modem that doesn't have this particular switch (or ability) in the first place. Before you do that, though, be absolutely sure that the originate mode is all you need. Should you ever exchange information or software with a friend, for instance, at least one of you has to be able to use the answer mode. (You and your friend simply agree beforehand which modem is going to be in which mode, then set the switches accordingly. By convention, the one who places the call is usually in the originate mode, but there is no real reason why you have to do it that way.)

Now back to the various modem standards.

Bell 103/Bell 113

The Bell 103 standard has been around the longest and is certainly the most widespread. In fact, if there is such a thing as *the* standard for modems, this is it.

Bell 103 is a full-duplex standard. You will usually see it referred to as having a maximum reliable speed of 300 baud, or 30 characters per second. Technically, this isn't so. The 103 standard is actually reliable over standard phone lines up to about 600 baud, or 60 characters per second. Still, as a practical matter, virtually all 103-compatible modems have a maximum speed of 300 baud. One or two manufacturers have models available with higher speeds, but there's no point in going out of your way to get one of these since there's hardly anyone you can talk to at the higher speed.

Some 103-compatible modems operate only at 300 baud; others allow for variable speed and can operate at some or all of the standard speeds between 0 baud and 300 baud.

The Bell 113 standard is identical to the Bell 103. The only difference is that where Bell 103 modems come with an originate-answer switch, Bell 113 modems come in originate-only models and answer-only models. The signaling standards are identical.

In any case, you will sometimes see modems referred to as "103-compatible"; you will sometimes see them referred to as "103/113-compatible"; and you will sometimes see them referred to as "100 series compatible." All of these references mean the same thing.

Bell 202

The Bell 202 standard is reliable up to 1200 baud, or 120 characters per second. This half-duplex standard is not very common. In fact, you need to be careful when buying a 1200-baud modem since many information utilities will not communicate with a Bell 202 modem. If you wind up with a Bell 202-compatible device, you may find yourself stuck with a modem you can't use.

Bell 212 or 212A

If you get a 1200-baud modem, you will almost certainly want it to be 212-compatible since this is the most common 1200-baud standard. Fortunately, most of the relatively inexpensive 1200-baud modems now coming on the market are 212-compatible.

The 212 standard is full duplex. As with Bell 103 modems, 212 modems have an answer mode and an orginate mode. In addition, many 212 modems have all sorts of extras, including lights on the front panel that tell you things like whether the modem is currently on the phone line or is in contact with another computer. When 212-compatible modems cost much more than they do now, these little extras added only a marginal additional cost of one or two hundred dollars. Now that prices are coming down, that additional cost no longer seems so minor. Some manufacturers are responding by offering plain-vanilla models that don't do anything fancy but work just fine and cost one or two hundred dollars less.

The official name for this standard is Bell 212A. Unless you are dealing with technical papers or technical purists, though, you will find that the "A" is usually dropped. Either way, "Bell 212" or "Bell 212A," it means the same thing.

Racal-Vadic VA3400

The Racal-Vadic VA3400 is also a full duplex, 1200-baud standard. This has been around longer than the Bell 212 standard but is not as widespread. While there are utilities that will communicate with a VA3400, there are few, if any, that require it. It is unlikely that you will find yourself needing this one unless, for instance, your home office uses it and you want to communicate with them as well as with information utilities.

Multiple Compatibility

As you may have already figured out, there are some good reasons for wanting the ability to communicate using more than one signaling standard. You might want to use a 1200-baud modem when you're sending or receiving a large amount of information but use a 300-baud modem when you're doing highly interactive work. Or you might want to use a 1200-baud modem to save time whenever possible but still be able to log on to a system that only operates at 300 baud.

One possibility, of course, is to buy one of each kind of modem that you need. But then you either have to go through the bother of disconnecting one and connecting the other each time you want to change or you have to buy a transfer switch, or T-switch, to switch back and forth between the two. (T-switches cost upward of $100.)

Fortunately, there's a simpler and cheaper way. You can get modems with multiple compatibilities, just as you can get a radio that receives both AM and FM. These multiple modems are literally that: two or three modems shoehorned into one box. They are much more convenient to use than separate modems. They are also less expensive, since they share the same box and some control circuitry.

The most common version of a multiple modem is the 103/212-compatible modem. This is the most common because it is the most useful for most people. Other combinations do exist, however, including triple modems, which are typically VA3400-compatible, 212-compatible, and 103-compatible. Being three modems in one, though, they are also expensive.

A Final Word on Choosing
Your Modem's Signaling Standards

Given all these possibilities for signaling standards, how do you know which one to choose? As far as information utilities are concerned, you can start by eliminating everything but the Bell 103 standard, as the most widespread to begin with, and the Bell 212 standard, as the most widespread 1200-baud standard. Be careful though. If you have some other telecommunications need in mind (communicating with the home office being the obvious example once again), check first and find out what standard the other system is using.

The next step is to decide between a 300-baud modem and a 1200-baud modem.

- If money is a concern, 300 baud is the obvious choice.
- If you want to be able to communicate with the largest number of information utilities (and other computer owners), then once again 300 baud is the obvious choice.
- If money is an important concern but time is important also, you should probably get a modem that is both 103-compatible and 212-compatible. You can use 1200 baud when it will save time and 300 baud when it will save money.
- Finally, if money is not a concern, you should still get the 103/212-compatible modem—even if you have no immediate use for the 300-baud capability. After all, the extra cost is no problem, and the extra capability may turn out to be useful someday.

What this advice adds up to is this: Get a 103-compatible modem. Then, if you can afford it, get the 212-compatibility also.

One other thing: If you already have a 103-compatible modem and you want to move up to a 212-compatible modem, you might consider modems that are 212-compatible only. Even so, consider the cost of a transfer switch and see if the cost of the modem plus the switch doesn't add up to the cost of a single 103/212-compatible device.

CONNECTING YOUR MODEM TO THE WORLD: DIRECT CONNECT VERSUS ACOUSTICAL CONNECT MODEMS

Once you've decided about signaling standards, you still have to decide how you want to connect the modem to the outside world, the "outside world" being the phone lines. You have exactly two choices. They are *direct connect* and *acoustical connect*.

Direct connect modems plug right into the phone line.

Acoustically connected (or acoustically coupled) modems communicate by way of a telephone handset, "talking" into the handset's microphone and listening over its speaker.

The Novation CAT-Acoustic

The Novation CAT is a typical example of a Bell 103-compatible, acoustically coupled modem. In function and description it is virtually identical to any number of similar devices. It has two switches, two status lights, one power cord, and one RS-232 connector so you can hook the modem up to your computer. (There's that term again, RS-232. Let it go by.)

The modem also has two rubber cups designed to hold a phone handset. At the bottom of one of the cups is a speaker so the modem can talk over the phone (into the telephone's microphone). At the bottom of the other cup is a microphone so the modem can listen (to the telephone speaker).

Once the modem is connected to your computer and plugged in, using it is simple.

One of the switches on the CAT is an on-off switch with two "on" positions. These are for answer mode and originate mode. To call an information utility, you turn the switch to "originate." The red light labeled "Power" lights up to tell you the modem is on and working.

The other switch gives you a choice between full-duplex mode (two-way conversation), half-duplex mode (two-way conversation but only one way at a time), and test mode (for checking out the modem if there seems to be a problem). Normally you leave it at full duplex and otherwise ignore it.

With the modem set to full duplex and in the originate mode, you pick up the phone and dial your chosen utility. When the computer on the other

FIGURE 2. The Novation CAT Acoustic, a typical 300 baud Bell 103-compatible acoustic modem. Photograph courtesy of Novation, Inc.

end picks up, you will hear a high-pitched tone after which you place the handset in the rubber cups. (There's a notation and an arrow on the modem to show you which side the cord goes on.)

After a short wait, the "Ready" light comes on. This tells you that the modems have established communication. You then go about your business at the keyboard and ignore the modem. (Unless something odd seems to be happening. If the host computer has stopped responding, for instance, you might glance over at the modem and see if the "Ready" light is still on.)

When you finish your session on-line, you sign off the system, take the handset out of the rubber cups, hang up the phone, and turn off the modem. That's pretty much all there is to say about it except for a short discussion about the switches.

Using the Full-Duplex/Half-Duplex Switch

You already know what the originate-answer switch does: It gives you the choice of being in the originate mode or the answer mode.

The settings on the second switch are "Full Duplex," "Half Duplex," and "Test."

The full-duplex setting assumes that the host computer will echo your transmissions back to you character by character. (It can do that only because both of you are operating at full duplex, meaning that communication can go both ways at the same time.) When you type a character on the keyboard, it is first sent to the host computer, then back to you before it shows up on your screen. This gives you an immediate confirmation that the character was received accurately by the utility's computer. If for some reason it was not received accurately, it will not show up on your screen accurately and you can either ignore it, or you can retype it, or otherwise correct the error.

The half-duplex setting is there in the rare event that you find yourself communicating with a computer that is not echoing your message. (This does not necessarily mean that you are not engaged in a full-duplex conversation. It is not possible to echo without full duplex, but it is possible to be in full-duplex mode without echoing. A minor source of confusion is that some systems make the distinction between duplex mode and echo mode while most do not. Ordinarily you will find "Full Duplex" to mean "Echo On" and "Half Duplex" to mean "Echo Off." This practice is so widespread that you may only get confused if you run into a system that does try to make the distinction.)

At any rate, if you leave the switch on the modem set at full duplex when the other system is not echoing, you won't see anything on the screen at all when you type information in. Set the switch at half duplex and the modem itself will echo the letter back to you. This way you will see your message on the screen and you will know that it is getting at least as far as the modem without problems.

If you happen to leave the switch set to half duplex when it should be at full duplex, you'll know it immediately. Every time you type a letter, you will see two letters on the screen: one echoed from the modem and one echoed from the utility's computer. If that happens, the solution is to check the modem and make sure the switch is set to full duplex.

It is also possible to wind up with three characters on the screen for each one typed, or to wind up with two characters even though the modem is set correctly. This is because some terminal-emulator programs also let you choose between full duplex and half duplex. If your software is set for half duplex, it will have the same effect as if your modem is set for half duplex; the software assumes no echo and puts the character on the screen. If your modem is also set for half duplex, it puts a second character on the screen. If the utility's computer is in fact echoing you, it puts a third character on the screen.

The third position on this switch is the "Test" setting. It's there to give you a way to test the modem and make sure it's working. Modems are such simple, reliable devices, though, that you should rarely, if ever, need to do that. Basically what the test setting does is let the modem listen to the same set of tones that it is sending. This lets you check out your modem and terminal by themselves, and can help you isolate any problems you are having.

Advantages and Disadvantages of Acoustically Coupled Modems

Acoustically coupled modems have one distinct advantage over direct connect modems. Because they are not connected directly to the phone system, they can be used virtually anywhere—in your home, your office, someone else's office, a hotel room, an airport—anywhere, in short, that you can find a phone with a standard handset. This makes them ideal for use with portable terminals. A journalist on assignment, or an executive keeping in touch with the home office, would definitely want his or her portable terminal hooked up to an acoustically coupled modem. So would a computer owner who takes his or her system back and forth between home and office or between city home and weekend retreat.

There are also some problems in using acoustically coupled modems.

The major one is that they cannot be used in a noisy environment. Random noises—people shouting, a radio in the background, a passing truck—can be picked up on the modem and generate garbage in the form of random characters on the screen. The rubber cups that the handset sits in can be made better or worse, but even the best can block out only so much noise. If you are printing the conversation as you go along, moreover, and you have a particularly noisy printer, you can even wind up generating garbage characters from the noise of the printer. That, to say the least, could be a serious obstacle to communications.

A second problem stems from the microphone found in the standard telephone handset. These microphones were designed to work with the human voice, not the computer voice. When you use them with an acoustical modem for any length of time, they tend to lose efficiency. Specifically, the carbon granules tend to pack together into clumps. You'll know that this is happening if you've been on-line for a while and then begin to have problems talking to the utility's computer.

The problem can be cured temporarily by taking the handset from the modem and shaking it vigorously or by rapping it against a hard surface once or twice. It can be cured permanently by replacing the standard handset microphone with a condenser microphone. These are sold in most computer stores. They cost roughly $10 to $20. To put one in your phone, you simply unscrew the mouthpiece from your handset, take out the standard microphone, and drop in the replacement.

Of course there's another way to cure this problem permanently: Don't get an acoustically coupled modem in the first place. Get a direct connect modem.

Direct Connect Modems

There are variations in even the most basic versions of direct connect modems.

Some, the Novation D-CAT for example, are connected between the telephone instrument (the part with the dial or buttons) and the telephone handset. (This will not work with an old-style phone where the handset cord is permanently connected. You need the kind with modular plugs. If you don't have one, your local phone company will be happy to install it for you, for a fee of course.)

The D-CAT eliminates the problem of random noise by electrically disconnecting the handset while the modem is sending and receiving data.

Other direct connect modems, including Radio Shack's Modem I and the Hayes Smartmodem 300, are connected to the phone system by plugging them directly into the wall socket. (Again, this won't work with an old-style phone. You need the newer kind, with the modular plugs.) These are connected in two different ways.

The Modem I is designed to go between the wall socket and the phone itself. The Modem I plugs into the wall. The phone plugs into the Modem I.

The Smartmodem is designed to be connected either by itself or in parallel with a phone, using a special "Y" connector that you have to purchase separately. (You can find these in most hardware stores. They are also called "T" connectors.)

Both the Smartmodem and the Modem I solve the noise problem the same way: by functioning as a stand-alone unit. When you're talking to the utility, the phone itself is hung up and the microphone is inactive.

What all direct connect modems have in common is that they are plugged directly into the phone system. If you listen over an extension phone, you can hear the modem's high-pitched whine, but the sound is never produced as sound. Instead, it is fed directly into the phone system as an electrical signal. Similarly, when the modem "listens" to the signal from another computer, it listens not to a sound, but to an electrical signal. Since it is not talking or listening by way of microphone and speaker in the first place, it cannot be fooled by local noise into generating garbage on the screen. You can, in short, make as much noise as you like around a direct connect modem and it will not interfere with communications. (Unless, of course, you pick up the extension, in which case the modem will hear whatever the microphone in the extension phone hears, and in which case you will definitely see garbage on the screen.)

The Radio Shack Modem I Direct Connect Modem

The Radio Shack Modem I is a basic, plain-vanilla, direct connect modem. In most ways it is equivalent to the Novation CAT acoustically coupled modem. The only important difference is in the method of connection.

The Modem I has five connectors, two switches, and two lights.

One connector is for the power cord.

Two connectors are used for plugging the Modem I into the phone system. One of these is a male connector at the end of a cord that plugs into the wall outlet. The other is a female connector where the cord from the phone plugs into the body of the modem.

The two remaining connectors are for connecting the modem to a computer. (These are both RS-232 connectors, in two variations.) One of these connectors is designed to be used specifically with the Radio Shack

Color Computer or with the Radio Shack TRS-80 Model I. The other is the "standard" RS-232 connector. It allows the Modem I to be used with any computer. (See Chapter 6 for more details.)

One of the switches on the modem determines which RS-232 port is being used.

The other switch, on the front of the modem, lets you choose between originate mode and answer mode. (Notice that there is no switch for choosing between full duplex and half duplex. The modem is full duplex only.)

The two lights are labeled "On" and "CD" (for "carrier detect").

Using the Modem I is even easier than using an acoustic modem. With the modem off, you dial the information utility. When the computer at the other end of the line answers the phone, you will hear its modem whining at you. At that point you flip the mode switch to originate and hang up the phone. The "On" light should come on immediately, quickly followed by the carrier detect light. After that you go about your business at the keyboard.

When you're finished, you log off the utility, wait for the carrier detect light to go off, and turn off the modem.

If you want to make a phone call, you can use the phone normally; just make sure the modem is off.

One last comment on direct connect modems in general. As with the Modem I, most direct connect modems plug directly into the wall jack. Because a poorly designed or malfunctioning device can wreak havoc on the phone lines, these modems must either be FCC-certified or, failing that, they must be connected through a device that will protect the phone lines.

Most modems are FCC-certified, and it will say so in the documentation and on the modem itself. If you somehow wind up with a non-certified modem, you can get the necessary connection device from your local phone company.

Finally, when you plug a modem into the phone lines, you are required to let your local phone company know about it. In particular, you have to give them some of your modem's specifications for their records. The manual that comes with the modem should include instructions along with a note that lists the information the phone company needs. These specifications are also on the modem itself, usually on the bottom of the unit.

Options

The modems we have looked at so far are simple, straightforward devices. Modems are available in both slightly stripped-down versions (originate only) and in more extravagant versions with additional features at extra cost.

A basic modem costs roughly $100 to $200 at list price. The Novation CAT, for instance, has a suggested retail price of $189. The Radio Shack Modem I has a suggested list price of $99.95.

For relatively little extra (about $100 more), you can get modems that will do things like dial the number for you, hang up electronically on command, and automatically answer the phone. These features are by no means essential but they are nice to have—particularly if you have software that takes full advantage of the modem's capabilities. There are any number of modems available with some or all of these extra features. We'll discuss a few of them later, after we've looked at the available software.

CONNECTING YOUR MODEM TO YOUR COMPUTER

There is, finally, one last basic variation on modems: how the modem is connected to the computer.

As you have certainly gathered by now, most modems can be connected to most computers through an RS-232 connector.

If you need the technical details—the nuts-and-bolts information on RS-232 standards and how to put a cable together—you will find them in Chapter 6 (Hardware, Part III—The Nitty-Gritty Details). For now we're going to stay with the very basic problem of determining whether the computer you have, or are planning to get, can be connected to a modem that has an RS-232 port in the first place.

The RS-232 Connection

The RS-232 port is an industry-wide "standard" that is found on most small computers. "Standard" goes in quotes here because manufacturers tend to modify that standard somewhat to suit their own needs. In practice, you have to check the manuals before you can hook up one piece of equipment to another even though both are using the same "standard" port.

The usual connector on the RS-232 port has room for 25 pins—and therefore 25 wires—that can be used to connect one piece of equipment to

FIGURE 3. An RS-232 connector. (Shown here on the back of a modem.) Note the 25 holes on the DB-25 connector.

another. All 25 wires are rarely if ever used, but they are there if needed. The connector also has a distinctive shape that makes it impossible for you to plug it in upside down (see photo). Some common uses for the RS-232 port are to connect a computer terminal to a computer, a printer to a computer, and a modem to a computer.

The connector usually found on the RS-232 port is called a DB-25 because of the 25 pins. This 25-pin connector, however, is not the only one that can be used. In fact, the RS-232 standard is based not on the connector, but on the technical standards established for the signals that are sent over the lines. These standards relate to which signals go on which lines and to the voltage levels used.

The following is a list of popular computers, all of which can be connected to a modem with an RS-232 port.

ALTOS
Atari 400, 800
Atari XL Series
Apple II, Apple II Plus, Apple IIe
Apple III
Commodore PET/CBM
Commodore VIC-20
Commodore 64
CompuPro
Cromemco
DEC Rainbow 100
IBM Personal Computer
KayPro II, 4, 10
NorthStar HORIZON
NorthStar Advantage
Osborne I, Osborne II
Osborne Executive
TRS-80 Model I
TRS-80 Model II, TRS-80 Model 12
TRS-80 Model III, TRS-80 Model 4
TRS-80 Color Computer
Texas Instruments TI-99/4A
Timex 1000, 1500, 2068
Vector Graphic—Vector 3, Vector 4

Some of the computers on this list come with RS-232 connectors as standard equipment, most often with the standard 25-pin connector. Others have RS-232 connectors as optional features. One or two do not have an RS-232 port, but do have another connector that serves the same function. You will find the particulars for each of these computers in Chapter 6.

Finally, you can add to this list any CP/M machine that is built around something called an S-100 bus structure. This is another widespread standard that is found in many small computers. If you don't know whether a particular computer has an S-100 bus, you can find out by asking.

In essence, the S-100 bus structure is a standard that has been established for both the slots that hold the computer boards and the electrical signals that go over each of the lines that the board connects to.

Any standard S-100 board, regardless of the manufacturer, will slip into any standard S-100 card cage and automatically make the right electrical connections work properly. If your computer uses a CP/M operating system, there's a good chance that it's built around the S-100 bus. (If you don't know what a CP/M operating system is, your computer doesn't use it.)

If your computer (or the computer you are thinking of getting) is not on this list and you are not sure whether it has an RS-232 port or the equivalent, you can ask your friendly neighborhood dealer, or read the manual that comes with the computer, or even call the manufacturer.

In any case, if your computer has an RS-232 port, be assured that you can connect it to any modem that also has an RS-232 port.

Modems for Computers Without an RS-232 Connector

So much for the vast majority of computers. What about computers that do not have an RS-232 port? And what about systems that have an RS-232 port but are already using it to tie the computer to a printer or some other piece of equipment?

There are two choices.

Even if your computer has only one RS-232 port, you can still connect it to two (or more) pieces of equipment by using a transfer switch, or T-switch. This will let you switch back and forth from the printer to the modem, depending on which one you want to use at any given moment.

With this kind of setup, however, you will not be able to print anything while you are on-line. If you want a hard copy of your conversation, you will have to save it to disk and print it later. This may or may not be a problem depending on whether you need to see a hard copy as you go along.

The second possibility is to get a modem specifically designed for your computer. There are modems available for the Apple II, for example, that plug into the Apple's game port. Similarly, there are modems designed specifically for Atari computers, the Commodore 64 or VIC-20, and others.

A common variation on this second possibility is the modem built on a computer board. These modems-on-a-board are designed to slip into a slot inside the computer. They are available for a number of machines, including the Apple II, the IBM PC, and any machine using the S-100 bus structure.

And that, finally, covers all the basic choices you have in choosing a modem.

CHOOSING YOUR MODEM

The first step in picking a modem is to decide on your budget. After that you can make your choices about the modem itself.

Decide first on the baud rate or rates you want and the signaling standards you need.

Next decide whether you want acoustical connect or direct connect. Acoustical connect is the preferred choice if you need the portability. In 300-baud modems, it also tends to be relatively inexpensive. (The most inexpensive 300-baud modems, though, are direct connect.) In 1200-baud modems, acoustic connect tends not to be available. Where it is available, it is more expensive than equivalent direct-connect modems and it typically uses the VA3400 standard. The 212 standard tends to be unreliable in an acoustically coupled modem.

Finally, decide whether you want an RS-232 modem, a modem that is specific to your system, or a modem that fits inside your computer.

Once you've made these choices, you can start looking at particular modems, and you can start considering the extra features you might like to have. In this chapter we have taken a look at two basic, plain-vanilla modems as examples of modems in general. In Chapter 6 you will find some additional reviews of specific modems including the Racal-Vadic VA212LC, the Bizcomp 1012, and the Hayes Smartmodem 1200. You will also find some notes on about 70 other modems. Taken together, these reviews and notes should give you a good idea of what's available.

Don't jump to Chapter 6 yet, though. Before reviewing specific modems, we need to take a look at some software because no matter what a modem is able to do, it can't do it by itself. It won't be able to do anything, in fact, unless you have software that can tell the modem to do it. (Some modems come with firmware—built-in programs permanently written on a computer chip—but that, for the moment, is beside the point.)

All of which brings us to the topic of software.

4

SOFTWARE PART I
A Look at Available Features

Once you have your computer plus a modem (and have them connected properly), you are almost ready to go on-line. The key word here is *almost.* Before you can actually do anything with the equipment, you need the appropriate computer program, or software, to do it with.

In this case, the appropriate program is known as a communications program, or a terminal-emulator program, or more simply, a terminal program.

Terminal programs come in two varieties. The simpler ones (read: cheaper ones) do little more than turn off most of the features of your computer so that it can act like a dumb terminal. This has the advantage of being inexpensive, but it has the same problem as getting a dumb terminal in the first place. You will quickly get frustrated because you cannot do more with your system.

The better (read: more expensive) terminal programs let you use your computer as a smart terminal. They also let you transfer files, meaning they will let you send files directly from disk or tape and will let you capture information and save it to disk or tape.

COMPUTERS AS DUMB TERMINALS

Atari's TeleLink I

Atari's TeleLink I is a good example of a rock-bottom, simple dumb terminal program.

TeleLink I comes in the form of a plug-in cartridge that works with the Atari 400 or 800 or any of the computers in the Atari XL series. The program itself is contained on a ROM chip, or Read Only Memory chip, inside the cartridge. (Translation: The TeleLink program is "written" into a memory chip that plugs into the computer.)

One clear advantage of a dumb terminal program is ease of use. The TeleLink I cartridge comes with a single folded-over page of printed instructions, equivalent to perhaps four or five typewritten pages. One measure of how simple the program is to use is that this single printed page contains all the information you need, even if you've never used a communications program before.

With TeleLink I, you do everything manually. To use the program, you plug in the cartridge and hit the reset button on the Atari. The program responds with the TeleLink sign-on message. To clear the screen and get ready for communications, you hit any key. Then you dial the phone. Once the modems have established a good connection, you go through the log-on procedure, then carry on your conversation with the host computer. When you're finished, you log off the system and hang up the phone.

TeleLink I gives you one or two simple conveniences. You can save information in the memory buffer, then send it to the printer if you have one. You can also choose between full duplex and half duplex. But that's about it.

TeleLink I, once again, is a basic dumb terminal program. There is little else that can be said about it. Similar programs are available for virtually any computer. They are easy to use, largely because they have so few features. But because they have so few features, they also have severe limitations.

The most important limitation of TeleLink I and similar programs is that you cannot use them to save anything to disk or tape, or to send anything that has already been saved on your disks or tape.

CP/M Computers

Next, a short digression about CP/M and about operating systems in general.

Even if you are relatively new to computers, you've probably seen or heard the term CP/M. The term is so widespread, in fact, that almost no one ever bothers to define it. Quite simply, the initials stand for "Control Program/Monitor." (You will sometimes see CP/M defined as "Control Program for Microcomputers." This definition sounds much more descriptive, but, unfortunately, it's wrong.)

CP/M is an example of what is known as an "operating system." It provides an "operating environment" for specific applications programs. In other words, CP/M (or any other operating system) takes care of the background chores in the computer system—things like telling the computer how to store files on the disks. It also provides various housekeeping utilities to help you with other chores, such as erasing files and renaming files. This means that someone who wants to write a computer program has a base to build on. Or, to put it another way, the programmer doesn't have to reinvent the wheel each time he or she writes a new program. What's more, a program written to work with a given operating system should work on any machine that is running that operating system, no matter who manufactured it. And that means that a program written on one CP/M machine should work on any CP/M machine.

CP/M has the well-deserved reputation of being the de facto standard in microcomputers. This is despite the fact that Atari, IBM, Apple, Radio Shack, and others have their own operating systems. Even taking these well-known exceptions into account, there are probably more CP/M computers on the market than any other kind (although IBM clones are catching up fast). There are also probably more programs written for CP/M than for any other single operating system (although MS-DOS, the operating system that the IBM PC uses, may close the gap there too). CP/M is so much the standard, in fact, that a small industry has grown up around hardware and software that provide CP/M capabilities for computers that are sold with other operating systems. Apple II and the IBM Personal Computer are the two obvious examples.

Computers that use the CP/M operating system can be lumped together and discussed as a group. Even so, specific computers have specific peculiarities. This is sometimes due to hardware differences and sometimes due to minor changes that computer manufacturers have made to their implementations of CP/M. These minor changes are usually billed as "features," or even as "improvements," but they function as hidden traps for off-the-shelf software that was written for standard CP/M.

It is important, therefore, that you realize that all discussions of CP/M software in this book are based on experience with that software on specific machines. In some cases the machine is an ALTOS, but in most cases it is a Vector Graphic Model 3 or 4. Where I am aware that a specific piece of software runs differently on other machines, I have said so. Do not make the mistake of assuming, however, that a piece of software that runs well on one CP/M machine will necessarily run well on another.

CP/M Computers as Dumb Terminals: DEC Rainbow

A very few computers, the DEC Rainbow 100 and Rainbow 100 +, for example, can act as dumb terminals all by themselves. With the Rainbow, the built-in option is called "Terminal Mode." Basically this is an extremely simple program that has been written into the Rainbow's PROM. (*Programmable* Read Only Memory this time.) In this case, the PROM, or memory chip, is permanently installed in the computer.

When you turn on the Rainbow, you're given a menu with several choices. One of these is "Terminal Mode." What this option does, essentially, is disconnect the keyboard and the screen from the rest of the computer. If you then connect a modem to the communications port, you have a perfectly adequate dumb terminal.

The operative word here is "adequate." The Rainbow's terminal-mode option is roughly equivalent to Atari's TeleLink I, except that the Rainbow will emulate DEC's VT102 terminal. As with TeleLink I, everything must be done manually. And as with TeleLink I, nothing can be saved to disk. The Rainbow will let you print information as you receive it, though. It also has an electronic toggle to turn the printer on and off.

The built-in communications option on the Rainbow is a relatively rare feature on microcomputers today. As communications become an increasingly important part of the microcomputer world, you can expect to see similar options on more systems.

COMPUTERS AS SMART TERMINALS

The only real problem with using the Atari, the Rainbow, or any other computer as a dumb terminal is that so much potential capability goes to waste.

The Rainbow 100 may have anywhere from 64K to 256K of internal memory. After you subtract the memory used by the operating system, you are still left with enough usable internal memory to hold anywhere from about 25 double-spaced typewritten pages on up to about 130 double-spaced pages (40K to 225K, if that means more to you). The Rainbow also has disk drives for external storage. These can store enough information on each disk to fill roughly 250 double-spaced typewritten pages. (That's 400K per disk after formating.)

When you use the Rainbow as a dumb terminal, all this memory, all this storage capability, might as well not be there. Incoming information is displayed on the screen, scrolls to the top, and disappears into oblivion.

Smart terminal programs make better use of the computer's potential. In addition to being able to send and receive information, a smart terminal program can, at the very minimum, also capture information and save it to disk. Most smart terminal programs are capable of more than that. Many are capable of much more.

SMART TERMINAL PROGRAMS: BASIC FEATURES

Before looking at specific programs, it will help to look at some of the features that a communications program can offer. A good place to begin is with some basic considerations, including the following:

Ease of Installation
System Commands
Menu-driven versus Command-driven Programs
Help Screens
Toggles
Information Capture and Memory Functions
Support of the X-On/X-Off Protocol
Control Over Parameters

Ease of Installation

Different computer systems work differently. In particular, they use different command codes to direct the movement of the cursor around the screen, or to clear the screen. This means that a computer program must be customized, or installed, to work on each specific system.

With programs (like TeleLink I), which are written for a specific computer, all the necessary customization is already provided. Programs that are written for CP/M, though, or for some other common operating system, are written to run on any number of different computers. As a result, these programs need to be installed for the particular system you want to use them on.

The simple phrase, "installing a program," covers a great deal of territory. It can mean anything from picking your computer from a list displayed on the screen to writing a program "patch" for your particular computer and assembling the program yourself. (Suffice it to say that if you don't know what that means, you won't know how to do it.)

Clearly, the easier it is to install a program, the better—especially if you don't know all that much about computers to begin with. The amount of difficulty you're willing to put up with is a personal decision, based on how much you already know and how much you are willing to learn as you go along. Still, a good rule of thumb is, "Easier is better." And assembling a program is something you shouldn't have to know about unless you want to get heavily into computers as computers rather than computers as tools for other purposes.

System Commands

System commands let you do useful things like check your disk directory, delete files from your disk, rename files, look at your files, and reset your system so you can change disks in mid-conversation.

Some programs won't let you do any of this without breaking the phone connection. This means that if you run out of disk space, you cannot change disks without hanging up first and then reestablishing the connection afterward.

Other programs do allow for system commands. Some let you leave the program, go to your operating system to do one or more chores, then go back into the program to pick up the conversation where you left off—all without breaking the phone connection. Still other programs let you do all these things without the bother of leaving the program and getting back into it. This accomplishes the same thing but more conveniently.

Obviously it is better to have access to system commands than not to have access to them. Being able to use them without leaving the program is icing on the cake.

Menu-Driven versus Command-Driven

As with any other program, communication programs can be menu-driven or command-driven. The same comment applies here that applies to data bases: The command format is faster and more powerful for those who are familiar with the program. The menu format is easier to use for those who are not familiar with the program.

Ideally, a program contains well-designed menus, but also gives you the ability to bypass those menus with simple, easy-to-enter commands. (WordStar does a good job of this as a word-processing program.) Some programs do this better than others. Some don't even make the attempt. Some can get along fine without it; a simple menu-driven program may have so few commands available that using the menu doesn't slow anything down.

Help Screens

There are two kinds of help screens. One kind functions as an extension of the user's manual, letting you find information about the various commands by asking the program instead of looking it up in the manual. This kind of help screen can be useful, but it generally doesn't tell you anything that you couldn't also find in the manual.

The second kind of help screen works differently. It reminds you of exactly which commands are available to you at any given instant. For example, if you are in interactive mode (interacting with a host system), your choice of commands may include turning the printer on or off, hanging up the phone electronically, and a few other things. This second kind of help screen will display these choices to you. This can be especially useful when you are first learning to use a program. It is even more helpful, though, if there is a way to turn the menu off so that once you are familiar with the program, you can get rid of it and have more of your screen free for incoming information.

Toggles

A toggle is a convenient, fast way to control what you are doing. It is a simple command that will alternately turn a feature on and off. A common toggle on communication programs controls the printer, typically with a ^P (Read: Control P). If the printer is on, ^P turns it off. If the printer is off, ^P turns it on.

Toggles are most convenient when they can be used directly from the interactive mode without first having to call up some menu or other. Even when toggles cannot be used in the interactive mode, they are still much more convenient than typing in a longer command.

Besides turning the printer on and off, toggles can be used to turn a help screen on and off or to turn the memory buffer on and off to start or stop capturing information.

Information Capture—Memory Functions

When you use a communications program (or any other program, for that matter), the first step is to load that program into your computer's memory. The memory that is left beyond what the program takes up is available for "working space." In a smart terminal program, this working space is generally known as a memory buffer; it is used as a place to store information that can later be saved to disk. (Dumb terminal programs ignore this working space.) The size of the memory buffer, which is to say the amount of information that can be captured at one time before saving it to disk, is limited. The exact size is a function of how much memory is in the computer in the first place and how much memory the program itself needs.

There are at least four capabilities that you must have in order to capture and save information conveniently.

- First, you need to be able to turn your memory buffer on and off at will. In other words, you need an easy way to tell your system when to start capturing information and when to stop. This lets you do a rough edit as you go, leaving out material that you know you don't want and saving valuable space in your buffer.

- Second, you need some way of knowing when the buffer is full or nearly full. A program that is capable of running out of memory without telling you about it is guaranteed to do just that at some point, no matter how careful you are in trying to prevent it from happening.
- Third, you need some way to save the information to disk once it has been captured in the memory buffer. This will let you save the information at any time, whether the buffer is full or not. Some programs can also be set to automatically save information to disk when the buffer is filled.
- Fourth, you should be able to clear the buffer without saving to disk if you decide that you don't want to keep the information after all.

Finally, in addition to the four capabilities that you must have, there is a fifth capability that you will probably also want, though it is by no means essential. This is the ability to tell the host computer to stop sending while you are saving a file or are otherwise engaged. Without this capability, you will lose any information that the host computer sends while you are saving the file.

X-On/X-Off Protocol

There is a standard method for telling the host computer when to wait and when to start up again. It is called the X-On/X-Off protocol. This is an important feature because your computer can do only one thing at a time. If you are busy with system commands, for example, or saving your captured information to disk, you cannot at the same time be capturing, or even looking at, information coming from the host computer.

The standard X-Off character, telling the other computer to stop, is a ^S (Control S). The standard X-On character, telling the other computer to start up again, is a ^Q (Control Q). Ideally, your communications program should automatically send the X-Off signal (Read: I'm busy. Hold up a second.) whenever you are doing something that will keep you from looking at incoming information. Similarly, it should automatically send the X-On signal (Read: I'm ready. Go on.) when you are ready to continue.

Even if your software does not support this protocol, you may be able to make use of it by manually sending a ^S and later a ^Q as appropriate. Whether you can do this or not depends on whether the program will let you send these particular control codes or whether it will interpret them as commands to itself. Some programs let you get around this problem with a "literal" command—meaning that the next character after the literal command is sent literally, without being interpreted by the program.

Control Over Parameters

A large number of parameters are involved in computer communications. Most of them have more or less standard settings and are permanently set in many communications programs. Still, you may have to deal with situations where the host computer expects a non-standard setting for some parameter or other. If so, it is important to have a program that will let you change the settings for that particular parameter.

The more parameters you have control over, the more flexibility you have in communications. But there is a trade-off here. The more parameters you have control over, the more difficult it is to learn how to use the program. And, of course, there is no point in paying for extra capabilities if you have no conceivable use for them. If all you expect to deal with are the large information utilities—THE SOURCE, Dow Jones, CompuServe, and the like—you don't need the extra flexibility. If you expect to communicate with some particular arcane utility (the computer in your home office comes to mind once again), you might need that extra flexibility. The trick is to first check out the systems you want to communicate with. Find out what parameter settings they need and then get a program that will let you set those parameters.

In any case, here is a list of the more common parameters that can be controlled by software. Some of these are self-explanatory. Others are not. Comments and explanations follow the list.

Duplex—Full or Half
Character Length, or Bits per Character
Stop Bits/Start Bits
Baud Rate
Parity

Duplex—Full or Half

This parameter choice is found on most communications programs, although not always under this name. It has exactly the same effect as the duplex switch on a modem. The difference is that if the modem is set to half duplex, the modem will echo the characters, while if the software is set to half duplex, the software will echo the characters. If you need to use half duplex, you should set *either* the software *or* the modem for it, not both. Otherwise both will echo the characters, and you will wind up with two characters on the screen ffoorr eeaacchh oonnee ttyyppeedd.

Character Length, or Bits per Character

Some programs give you a choice of the character length, or the number of bits per character, to use. The typical choices are seven or eight. This can mean one of two things, depending on the program.

"Bit" is short for "BInary digiT." This is the smallest unit of information that computers deal with. Inside a computer, a single bit is a high voltage or a low one, a switch that is on or off. To a 300-baud modem speaking over the phone lines, a single bit is one tone or the other. Whatever the physical reality, though, bits are represented as 1s and 0s.

Keyboard characters—letters, numbers, punctuation, and symbols—are represented by combinations of bits. These are simply an agreed-upon code, much as Morse code is an agreed-upon code. Part of the agreement is on how many bits are in each character. Obviously, if you allow only one bit per character, you have only two character codes available, 1 and 0. Two bits per character give you four codes: 00, 01, 10, and 11. Similarly, three bits per character give you eight codes, four bits give 16 codes, five bits give 32 codes, six bits give 64 codes, and seven bits give 128 codes.

One hundred twenty-eight codes happen to be enough for the number of characters on a keyboard. (There are 26 lower-case letters, plus 26 upper-case letters, plus 10 numbers, 0–9, plus about 30 punctuation marks and symbols, plus the 26 control characters, ^A through ^Z. Add in a few other things like the space key and you wind up with 128.) This means that you need only seven bits per character in order to represent everything you have to represent.

ASCII (American Standard Code for Information Interchange)

Computers generally deal with chunks of information, or bytes, that are eight bits long. The most widely accepted code for computer communications is ASCII, the American Standard Code for Information Interchange. This defines only seven bits per character. As a result, many computer systems work internally with seven bits per character. These systems essentially ignore the eighth bit by leaving it at zero, which has no effect whatsoever. Other computer systems use the eighth bit to define non-ASCII characters—typically reverse video or graphics characters.

That's all background for understanding the parameter choice of character length, or bits per character.

Once again, this parameter choice can mean one of two things, depending on the program. First, setting this at seven bits can mean that your system will actually be sending (and expecting to receive) seven bits per character. Similarly, setting the parameter at eight bits would mean that your system will be sending (and expecting to receive) eight bits per character. If this is what the parameter is doing, your setting for character length generally must agree with whatever the host computer is set for. For information utilities, this is almost always seven bits per character.

(At the risk of confusing the issue, I must add that these seven bits or eight bits per character are in addition to start bits, stop bits, and parity bits, which we will get to shortly. Also, to be technical about it, information utilities are usually set for seven bits per character *plus one parity bit* for a total of eight bits for each character, not including the start and stop bits. This "seven plus one" setting is exactly equivalent to a setting of eight character bits with no parity bit—all of which helps to increase the confusion around this issue.)

Other programs use the term "character length" differently. These programs are set to send and receive eight bits per character no matter what. If the host system is also sending eight bits per character or, equivalently, seven bits per character plus zero for the parity bit, this is not a problem. You can simply set your software for eight bits per character and not worry about it. If the host system is using the eighth bit, though, sometimes sending a 1 and sometimes a 0, you may get some strange effects on your screen or in your files. In that case you can set your system for seven bits, and it will automatically change the incoming eighth bit to zero no matter what the host computer sends.

Stop Bits/Start Bits (Asynchronous Communications)

Some programs include a parameter choice labeled "stop bits." The choice, if it is there, is between one stop bit or two.

All the programs we have discussed—in fact, all the *communications* we have discussed and will discuss in this book—are examples of asynchronous communication. The other choice, synchronous communication, would imply that the transmitting computer and the receiving computer are synchronized. This synchronization would mean that the receiving computer would know exactly when to expect a new character—when to expect it to start and when to expect it to stop. (Actually, the computers are synchronized only within blocks of characters, but there's no point in getting into the details.) While synchronous communication is possible in some situations, it is inconceivable in others. Whenever a person is involved in the communications, for example, individual characters will be typed with different lengths of time between them, and any attempt to keep the transmitter and receiver synchronized is doomed to failure.

Asynchronous communications programs—the only ones we are interested in—get around this problem by adding "start bits" and "stop bits" to each character that is sent. This added information tells the receiving computer where each character starts and where it stops.

Most systems running at 300 baud and above use one start bit and one stop bit. Slower systems generally use one start bit and two stop bits. Some programs let you choose which to use.

Parity

In addition to the bits that represent the characters themselves, and in addition to the start bits and stop bits, each character can also be sent with an additional bit called a parity bit. This parity bit does not have to be used, however. In fact, it usually is not used in microcomputer communications, which is why many programs do not include this as a parameter choice; these programs, in effect, are permanently set at Parity Off.

Other programs do include parity as a parameter choice. Typical settings are Parity Even, Parity Odd, and Parity Off. The parity bit, if it is used, is there to automatically check the accuracy of communications.

(If you are interested in the details, Parity Even means that the parity bit is always set so that the number of ones in the character plus the parity bit comes out to an even number. Parity Odd means that the parity bit is always set so that the number of ones in the character plus the parity bit comes out to an odd number. If the receiving system expects the parity to be even and it comes up with an odd number when adding the number of ones, it signals an error. Similarly, if it expects parity to be odd and it comes up with an even number, it will also signal an error. Parity Off means that the parity bit is not used.)

Under most conditions, you can leave this parameter set at Parity Off. If the host system requires a different setting, you simply set your system to match.

Baud Rate

Some communications programs let you choose the baud rate to use. This means that if you have a modem that can work at 300 baud and 1200 baud, you can choose the speed at which you want to communicate. Without this capability, you are stuck with the speed the computer is set at.

There is a rather large "if" that goes with this feature. A program with this choice on its parameter menu will work if, and *only* if, your computer has its baud rate under software control.

In general, the older your system, the less likely it is to have this capability. The baud rate in most older systems is completely under hardware control, meaning that the baud rate is controlled by a switch inside the machine. Some computers in this category are the Apple II, the TRS-80 Models I and II, and the Commodore PET/CBM.

Newer computers often have their baud rates under software control. Some examples are the Rainbow 100, the Vector 4, the Apple III, the TRS-80 Models III and 4, and the IBM PC.

At least one computer, the Vector 3, falls somewhere between these two categories. This computer allows for limited software control over its baud rate but requires an implementation of that capability different from that used by other computers. This means that programs that will control baud rates on other computers will not necessarily be able to control the Vector 3's baud rate.

The moral here is simple. If you want the ability to control your baud rate, make sure that the program you're looking at will work on your computer.

SMART TERMINAL PROGRAMS: ADDITIONAL CAPABILITIES

We have covered most of the basic features available on communications programs but we have by no means exhausted the possibilities. Here is a list of some of the more common additional capabilities to be had. As with the list of parameters, some of these are self-explanatory, others are not. Comments and explanations follow the list.

Automatic Dialing
Automatic Log On
Parameter Files
Send and Receive Files Directly from or Directly to Disk
Protocol File Transfer (Downloading and Uploading)
Ignore or Filter Out Incoming Characters
Translate Incoming or Outgoing Characters from One Coding System to Another
Emulate Specific Terminals

Automatic Dialing

Automatic dialing is pretty much what it sounds like. This feature will let you enter a phone number either from the keyboard or from a disk file; then it will automatically dial the number for you (assuming that your modem is capable of dialing, or that you have a separate automatic dialer).

Many programs with an auto-dial feature also have some way to let you store numbers. This means that you can store the number under a label—a name, initials, or whatever—then dial it by simply entering the label. You might, for example, list the number of Dow Jones Information Services as DJ. When you tell the program to dial DJ, it looks up the number, tells the modem to pick up the phone and dial, then lets the modem establish communications.

Automatic Log On

Automatic log on is also pretty much what it sounds like: a feature that will automatically log you on to a system.

This works differently in different programs, but there are a few general comments that are worth passing along, if only because they are often overlooked in user manuals.

The first step in automatic log on is to use your text editor or word processor to create a file with all the information you need to send.

For example:

The log-on procedure with CompuServe starts when you send a ^C.
CompuServe prompts you with "User ID:"

You answer with your identification number, which will be something like "77777,7777."

CompuServe prompts you with "Password:"

You answer with your password, which may be "MAIL.CHECK."

If you typed in everything correctly, you will be logged on to the system.

Your part of the log-on procedure, then, reads:

```
^C[Return]
77777,7777 [Return]
MAIL.CHECK [Return]
```

And this is what your sign-on file should look like. Two comments on this. First, each line should start in the first column of your screen and end with a carriage return. Second, in most programs the ^C has to be a Control C. I typed it in here by using a "^" sign, which is a capital six on my keyboard, and then using a capital C. This is not a Control C and will not generally be sent as one, although some programs will do the conversion for you.

Once you have created your log-on file, the exact procedure for using it varies, depending on the particular communications program. Some programs will let you send files one line at a time. This allows you to send the first line of your log-on file, wait for the response, send the second line, wait for the response, and so on. This reduces the log-on procedure to hitting a single key two or three times.

Other programs won't send files one line at a time but will send individual lines on command. This means that you write a slightly different log-on file that tells the program to stop after each line, then wait for a command before sending the next line. This works out to essentially the same procedure when it comes down to logging on to the system; it is only the log-on file that looks different.

Still other programs will let you tell the program what response to wait for before sending the message. This reduces the log-on procedure to telling the program which file to use.

Whatever the mechanics of the automatic log on, it is a convenient way to save time and typing. And just as the auto-dial feature saves you from having to memorize or look up phone numbers each time you call a utility, the auto-log-on feature saves you from having to memorize or look up the different log-on sequences and passwords.

Parameter Files

Most programs that let you change communications parameters also let you store the changes in some way. Some let you create several copies of the program, each of which will come up with different parameter settings. Others let you create separate parameter files that you can use to automatically load different parameters into the program. If you are going to be communicating with several information utilities, each of which requires different parameters, this feature becomes important. Without it, you will have to change parameters nearly every time you go into the program.

Send and Receive Files
Directly from or Directly to Disk

Most smart terminal programs will also let you send files directly from your disks or save them directly to your disks. These features are reasonably self-explanatory but there is one possible source of confusion; it stems from the distinction between text files (ASCII files) and command files (programs).

Any program that can send and receive files can send and receive text files. It can do that, moreover, with any host system that it can communicate with in the first place. This is not a capability that you're likely to use very much with an information utility. It can be useful, though. With this feature a writer can send an article or a book to an editor. Similarly, a salesman or an executive on a business trip can send a written report to the office.

Just because a program can send and receive text files, though, it does not necessarily mean that it can send and receive command files.

All of which brings us to the subject of protocol file transfer.

Protocol File Transfer (Downloading and Uploading)

Receiving a command file, or program, is known as downloading that program. Sending a program is known as uploading. Either way, the process is a bit trickier than dealing with an ASCII file.

With ASCII files—that is, files stored in ASCII code—there is no need for special protocols. With command files, though, meaning files that are stored in binary format, you can run into a problem.

First, binary files have various control codes built into them that tend to confuse the transfer process.

Second, telephone lines are noisy. This means that you will at least occasionally have a noise-generated mistake in the transmission. These mistakes are usually tolerable in an ASCII file, where you can see the mistake and correct it easily enough. They are not tolerable in a command file, where it is nearly impossible to see a mistake until it shows up as a mysterious bug in the program.

Transferring binary files, then, requires well-defined protocols that let the receiving system check the incoming information for accuracy. These protocols also give the receiving system the ability to let the transmitting system know that there has been an error and that a block of information must be retransmitted.

What all this adds up to is that ASCII files can be sent by protocol file transfer but they don't need to be. Binary files, on the other hand, *must* be sent by protocol file transfer.

If you are interested in downloading programs from an information utility, there is one other thing that you should be aware of: Different programs use different sets of protocols. It doesn't help to have a program capable of protocol file transfer unless the computer on the other end of the line uses the same program, or at least the same protocols. And that means that if you're interested in downloading programs from a particular information utility, you have to get a communications program that has the same protocols as that utility.

Ignore or Filter Out Incoming Characters

Occasionally an information utility will send a control code that affects your system in strange ways. The more sophisticated the program you are using and the more features it has, the more likely this is to happen. Under such conditions it is useful to be able to tell your program to filter out, or ignore, the incoming character that is producing the strange effects. In general, programs that are likely to need this feature have it; the rest do not.

Translate Incoming or Outgoing Characters

ASCII is the most widely accepted code for computer communication in this country, but it is not the only one. IBM, for instance, has its own code, EBCDIC (Extended Binary Coded Decimal Interchange Code). (This is *not* used in the IBM PC. The PC uses ASCII.) If you are using ASCII and need to communicate with a computer that uses one of these other codes (EBCDIC at your home office, for instance), it will be necessary to have one computer or the other translating incoming and outgoing characters from one code to the other. Some programs will let you do this.

Emulate Specific Terminals

All communications programs are terminal emulators in the sense that they let your computer act as a terminal. In general, though, they limit you to entering and correcting text on a one-line-at-a-time basis. This is sufficient for entering menu choices or simple command lines but it is severely limiting when dealing with longer entries. In entering a bulletin-board message while on-line, for example, making changes becomes a chore because of the one-line-at-a-time limitation.

Some host computers are programmed so they can control certain specific terminals on a full-screen basis rather than on a one-line-at-a-time basis. This means that the host computer can move your cursor around the entire screen as necessary *if* you have the proper terminal. In some cases the programming includes graphics capabilities as well.

Some communications programs can emulate one or more of these specific terminals, thus providing you with all the capabilities of the terminal that is being emulated. Keep in mind, though, that this makes a difference only if you are signed on to a system that is programmed to take advantage of these capabilities.

We still have not covered every possible feature to be found in every available communications program. Many programs will let you set up your own bulletin-board system, for example, or they may have additional features that relate to transferring files. Even so, we have covered the most common features available and certainly the most important ones that relate to using information utilities. If you have managed to digest everything up to this point, you have a pretty good idea of what a communications program can do. You should also have some idea of the features that you want and need.

All of which means that you should be ready to look at some specific programs.

5

SOFTWARE PART II
A Look at Some Real Programs

This chapter consists of short reviews of representative terminal programs. Keep in mind that comments on each of these programs are based on a particular version of that program. More recent revisions may or may not be available by the time you read this book. If they are available, they may or may not have added new features, successfully cured old bugs, or, for that matter, inadvertently added new bugs.

In any case, the following "mini reviews" should be read less as reviews of specific programs than as a guide to the features that are available in a range of programs at a range of prices. Use these comments as a starting point, by all means, but don't treat them as the last word on the subject.

In general, the software is listed in order of increasing capabilities.

SOFTCOM for CP/M

Name: SOFTCOM Data Communications Utility
Revision: 1.2

Company: The Software Store
706 Chippewa Square
Marquette, MI 49855
Phone: (906) 228-7622

Available for: CP/M operating system only. For virtually all computers based on Z-80, 8080, or 8085.

Special requirements: 32K bytes memory minimum.

Format: Comes on 8-inch, single-sided, single-density disk. Also available on 5-inch disk in the following formats: Superbrain, Micropolis/Vector Graphic, NorthStar, Osborne I, Televideo, Apple CP/M, Otrona, Multi-Tech, Sanyo, KayPro II, Heath/Zenith, MITS Hardsector, Morrow, Eagle II, Archives, Xerox 820, ALTOS. Check for current availability of other formats.

Price: $150 (for single CPU license).

SOFTCOM is as easy to use as any program I have ever seen. More than that, it is easy to install on most systems, and it comes with a straightforward, well-written and, above all, useful User's Manual. This last feat is unusual enough to deserve special mention. The User's Manual tells me what I want to know pretty much in the order I want to know it. What's more, it tells me all this in readable English.

The only problem with the manual is that it has occasional chunks of technical information that often use terms without first defining them. Ideally, these chunks should have been put in the back in a technical appendix, out of the way. Please note that my complaint is not that the manual is bad, because it isn't. Even the technical parts are well written for those who have the background to understand them. If you don't have the background, you will still find the manual extremely helpful if you have the courage to ignore the more technical sections.

The program itself, I'm happy to say, is easy to use.

SOFTCOM comes as a single-disk file, SOFTCOMU. The "U" stands for "uninstalled." The first time you go into the program (by booting up the disk and typing SOFTCOMU), the program comes up with a screen that tells you what it does, tells you that you must install it first, and tells you to press the carriage return to go ahead with the installation.

Pressing the carriage return provides you with the SOFTCOM parameter menu. The User's Manual tells you that most of the menu choices can be ignored for the moment but that there are four numbers you must enter before you can use the program. They are the numbers for your modem status port, your modem data port, your transmit buffer empty, and receive buffer full.

This is the point where you might get lost if you are not familiar with computers. The Software Store, however, has thoughtfully listed the appropriate numbers for more than 100 different systems. If yours is not on this list, you should still be able to get the numbers from your computer manuals, even if you don't know what they mean. (Whether you will actually be able to do that, of course, is a function of how well your computer manuals are written.) If you have problems in finding the numbers, you can call the dealer who sold you the computer, or call the manufacturer. (The SOFTCOM manual also lists three other methods for determining the numbers yourself. These are technical in nature, though. I suspect that anyone who understands what the manual is talking about will already know how to do it without being told.)

Once you get the numbers, simply enter them into the parameter menu, after which SOFTCOM is ready to use.

This installation procedure, which The Software Store has clearly done its best to make as simple as possible, is the most difficult part of using SOFTCOM. I have described it in some detail because it demonstrates the care that went into the writing of this program—and its documentation. The work has paid off. SOFTCOM is easy to learn as well as easy to use.

To use SOFTCOM with an information utility, you boot up your disk and enter the program. The first thing you see is the main menu. To get past the menu and into the interactive mode—that is, to get ready to talk to the host computer—you hit the carriage return. Then you dial the phone (manually). Once the modems have established communication, you struggle through the log-on procedure (manually again) and go about your business with the utility.

SOFTCOM gives you several useful on-line capabilities.

First, you can exit to CP/M from the main menu, perform system commands, and quickly get back into SOFTCOM without disturbing anything.

The menu also gives you two useful toggles, one to turn the printer on or off, the other to turn the memory buffer on or off to start or stop capturing the conversation.

You can exit the interactive mode, go to the main menu, and save captured information to disk whenever you like. If you haven't saved it by the time your memory buffer is running out of room (down to about 4K bytes, or a little over three typewritten, double-spaced pages), SOFTCOM tells you about it in no uncertain terms by flashing a message on the screen while still in interactive mode.

If you want to save the information at that point, you hit the "command" key (usually the "ESCAPE" key, but you can define it otherwise). This takes you back to the main menu, where you choose option 4, "Empty Memory Buffer to Disk." SOFTCOM asks you for a file name to use, checks to make sure that no file with that name exists yet, then writes the information to disk. When it's finished, you can go back to interactive mode and continue the conversation.

If you decide you don't need the information you've captured up to that point, you can clear it from memory simply by exiting to CP/M. SOFTCOM will remind you that you have information in the memory buffer and will ask you if you want to save it to disk. You answer no, exit to CP/M, then go right back into the program. The buffer will be emptied; everything else remains undisturbed.

Finally, SOFTCOM is also capable of computer-to-computer file transfer, which lets you receive files and save them directly to disk or send files directly from disk. In direct-file transfer, SOFTCOM can use X-On/X-Off protocol, meaning that the computer that is receiving can automatically tell the other computer to wait when the memory buffer is full. This lets the receiving computer save the information to disk without losing anything. The program is also capable of protocol file transfer, using its own error-checking protocols.

SOFTCOM's parameter menu contains several items in addition to those you need to enter when installing the program. These include full duplex and half duplex, seven bits or eight bits per character, and several other choices that relate to file-transfer functions. For the most part, these parameters can be left the way they are set when you buy the program.

A final convenience worth mentioning is that SOFTCOM lets you create different SOFTCOM files with different parameters. This means you can create a customized file for each utility you use.

There is one important convenience that SOFTCOM lacks: It does not support X-On/X-Off protocol in interactive mode. This means that whenever you leave the interactive mode to turn the printer or memory buffer on or off or to save a file, you lose any information that is coming in unless you remember to manually send a command to the host system to stop and wait. Usually the command is ^S (Control S) to stop and ^Q (Control Q) to start up again. Even without this feature, though, SOFTCOM is a useful and easy-to-use smart terminal program. If you're using a CP/M operating system, it is well worth looking at.

T.H.E. SMART TERMINAL for Atari

Name: T.H.E. SMART TERMINAL

Revision: 3.5

Company: Binary Corporation
3237 Woodward Ave.
Berkley, MI 48072
Phone: (313) 548-0533

Available for: Atari 400, 800, 1200, and XL series computers.

Special Requirements:
16K RAM for cassette version.
24K RAM for disk version.
Cassette recorder or one disk drive.

Format: Cassette or disk.

Price: $49.95. Disk or tape. (The tape also contains the disk version of the program, meaning you can move up to a disk without having to buy another program.)

T.H.E. SMART TERMINAL does for the Atari what SOFTCOM does for CP/M. Like SOFTCOM, T.H.E. SMART TERMINAL is simple to use. Also like SOFTCOM, the program comes with a straightforward, well-written manual that will get you up and running quickly and almost certainly without problems. It tells you exactly what you need to know, leading you through the process step by step. It even reminds you to make a backup copy of the disk before you do anything else.

Because this program is designed to work with a specific computer, there is normally no installation required. One exception: If you're using the Atari 800 with the 80-column card sold by the Bit-3 Company, you need to install the program for it. You'll find detailed instructions for installation in Appendix B of the manual.

Boot up the disk with T.H.E. SMART TERMINAL on it and you'll find yourself at the program's main menu. Putting the Atari in dumb terminal mode is as simple as reading the menu and choosing "T" for "Terminal." As shipped, the program is set to work with most utilities, so you can simply call NewsNet or THE SOURCE at that point and carry on a conversation.

If you need to change any of the settings, you can choose "C," for "Configuration Menu." This will let you adjust several parameters, including the baud rate and duplex setting. The configuration menu also has an option for saving the configuration on disk. You can, in fact, save as many different configurations as you need.

Another menu choice is "R," for "Receive Data." This captures the conversation in the computer memory. One nice touch with T.H.E. SMART TERMINAL is that you can divide the memory into as many as ten buffer areas and save different information to each one. This can be useful for the selective erasure of information. You may, for example, have just received something that you know you'll want to keep. If you take a moment, you can tell the system to close that buffer and open another. If the next batch of information turns out to be useless for your purposes, you can erase it to clear valuable memory space and still leave the first batch of information untouched.

Other choices on the main menu let you erase specified buffers, send information from a buffer to the printer or disk, read information into a buffer from disk, or send information from the buffer.

The menu also gives you the choice of sending or receiving data "with verify," meaning that you can use a file-transfer protocol. The particular protocol used, the XMODEM protocol, is in public domain and is widespread. It is found on most CP/M bulletin boards and is often called the CPMUG, or CP/M User's Group protocol. It is also found on most Atari AMIS Systems. (AMIS systems, for "Atari Message and Information Service," are Atari-based bulletin boards.)

My only negative reaction to the program is that many of the things you'll want to do require two steps. To send a disk file, for example, you have to read the file into a memory buffer, then send it from the buffer. This is a roundabout method, but it works. The drawback is that you cannot send a file that is longer than can fit into the memory. You have to break long files into shorter segments, then send them piecemeal.

Still, T.H.E. SMART TERMINAL is a useful program. It turns your Atari into a smart terminal, as advertised. It will certainly take care of most casual communications needs.

Transend for Apple

Name: Transend (Levels 1, 2, and 3)

Revision: 3.0

Company: Transend Corporation
           2190 Paragon Drive
           San Jose, CA 95131
           Phone: (408) 946-7400

Available for: Apple II, Apple IIe

Requirements:
>Minimum 48K RAM. One disk drive (Transend 3 requires two drives).
>Apple DOS 3.3

Format: Disk.

Price:
>Transend 1: $89.
>Transend 2: $149.
>Transend 3: $275.

I am not a big fan of copy-protected programs—to put it mildly.

Disks can be destroyed. Not often if you're careful, but it does happen. Spill some coffee on a disk or get some graphite on one, or even some dust, and you may be in trouble. A file can even be ruined by a random electrical surge courtesy of your local power company. Or if you use the disk enough, you can wear it out.

The inability to create backup disks may be tolerable for games or other non-essential programs. It is not tolerable when dealing with something like a communications program that you need *now*, when you need it—not days or weeks later when you finally receive a replacement disk.

On top of the inconvenience, I also find it objectionable to pay a replacement charge for something I've already bought once. (What you're usually paying for when you buy a program, don't forget, is the right to use that program.) And, not so incidentally, what happens if the company goes out of business or stops supporting the particular program?

So much for the tirade. Unfortunately, copy-protected disks are the norm when dealing with programs written for the Apple (or the IBM PC, for that matter, although I'm told that the copy-protection schemes for the PC tend to be easier to get around). In the real world, if you have an Apple, you have to live with what you can get.

Having said all that, I also have to say that Transend Corporation, to its credit, has come up with a more or less reasonable compromise between copy protection on the one hand and the need for backups on the other. The program comes not with one disk, but two: a master copy and a backup copy. The idea is to use one disk on a daily basis and to store the other in a safe place. If you do something disastrous to the first disk, you can send it to Transend for a replacement copy. (The current charge for a replacement disk is $25 after the 90-day warranty period.) In the meantime, you have the backup copy to tide you over. (But you had better not manage to ruin that one too.)

As for the program itself...

Transend is available in three levels: Transend 1, 2, or 3. This means that you can buy just as much or just as little communications ability as you need. As your needs increase, you can move from one level to the next for just the cost of the upgrade. Even better, when you move to a higher level, the commands for the "lower level" capabilities remain the same, which means that instead of having to learn an entirely new set of commands, you need to learn only the commands for the new capabilities.

Transend 1 turns your Apple into an intelligent terminal. It will let you communicate with just about any information utility, and it will let you send or receive text files.

Transend 2 adds verified file transfer, meaning file transfer with error-checking protocols. (The protocol is proprietary. The same protocol is used on Transend PC for the IBM PC.)

Transend 3, finally, adds electronic mail capabilities; you can automatically transmit files to as many as 128 other Apples. (Once you give the system its orders about who to send the messages to, and when to send the messages, it will go about its business while you go about yours. The other computers must also be running Transend.)

All three levels of Transend are completely menu-driven, meaning that you can find your way around the program simply by making choices from the menus as they come up. As I've pointed out elsewhere, this is helpful for the new or occasional user but it can be annoying and time-consuming once you know what you're doing. Fortunately, you can make most of your choices off-line, where at least they won't cost you anything.

Each time you make a choice, the program highlights the menu items you've chosen and asks you to confirm it. This is another feature that can become annoying once you're familiar with the program. You have the option of turning this off, though.

The number of parameters you can define with Transend is too long to list here, but that fact alone is worth mentioning. The point is, you can change just about any parameter you might need to change. (This includes baud rate if the serial card in your Apple allows for software control of baud rate. Transend can handle 1200 baud, if your equipment can.)

One other nice feature is Transend's update policy. Updates are free during the 90-day warranty period and $20 after that. This is more than reasonable and deserves praise.

Finally, with a machine as popular as the Apple, where a small industry has grown up around supplying add-ons to the system, it is a difficult task indeed to write a terminal program that will work with all possible combinations of equipment. Transend makes the effort. The manual lists 15 printer interfaces, five modem interfaces (serial cards or communication cards), five specific modems (including two from Transend Corporation), and three 80-column video cards that the program will work with. In addition, it will work with any RS-232 modem and, once again according to the manual, Transend Corporation "regularly adds interfaces to the above list."

This doesn't guarantee that Transend will work with your particular combination of equipment of course. But it does increase the odds.

In any case, before you choose this or any other program for the Apple, be sure to double-check that it will work with your system.

ASCII EXPRESS, P-TERM, Z-TERM for Apple II

NOTE: Southwestern Data Systems sells three communications programs that are nearly identical except for the operating systems under which they run. These are grouped together as "The Professional" series. ASCII Express "The Professional" runs under Apple DOS and is the version that is reviewed here. P-Term "The Professional" and Z-Term "The Professional" are similar to ASCII Express in capabilities. P-Term runs on the Apple under UCSD Pascal. Z-Term runs on the Apple under the Microsoft implementation of CP/M. As of this writing, ASCII Express is the most recently revised of the series and is, therefore, one generation ahead of the others. The major difference, I am told, is that ASCII Express is compatible with a larger number of Apple boards. Otherwise the three programs are substantially the same.

Name: ASCII Express "The Professional."

Revision: 4.20.

Company: Southwestern Data Systems
         P.O. Box 582
         Santee, CA 92071
         Phone: (619) 562-3221

Available for: Apple II, Apple II Plus, Apple IIe, Apple III (using Apple II emulation mode), Apple-compatible computers.

Special requirements (for ASCII Express):
Minimum 48K RAM.
Apple DOS 3.3 or "a close variation."
Will not work with PRODOS.

Format (for ASCII Express): Apple DOS 3.3

Price: $129.95

ASCII Express "The Professional," or "AE Pro" as it is also known, is one of the more sophisticated communications programs available for the Apple and Apple-compatible machines. In addition to providing basic smart terminal functions, meaning the ability to capture information and save it to disk, the program offers such niceties as auto-dial, auto-log-on, protocol file transfer, terminal emulation, unattended operation, and on-line help when asked for. It even has its own text editor.

One measure of the sophistication of this program is that there are 40 different commands available from the command prompt. This is enough to have forced the program's authors to break the main command menu into two parts. It's also enough that a new user is in danger of feeling overwhelmed—particularly if this is his or her first communications program.

Much to their credit, the program authors (Bill Blue and Mark Robbins) have taken this possibility into account. Both the software and the instruction manual are designed to ease the new user into the program.

The instruction manual in particular deserves praise. At more than 300 pages, it can look intimidating. Open it, however, and the first thing you'll notice are the tabs that divide it into more manageable sections. One of these sections is labeled "Introduction." It is one of the most intelligently designed introductions to a program that I have seen.

The manual contains a very quick (one page) overview of the program and a few preliminaries ("How to Use This Manual"). Then it gets down to business. It starts with such basics as reminding you to save your sales receipt for proof-of-purchase, after which it quickly and clearly walks you through everything you need to know to get the program up and running.

The first step, not so incidentally, is to make a copy of the program. This brings up an important point: AE Pro is *not* copy-protected. You can make backup copies; you can put the program on a hard disk if you have one; you can even run the program from a disk emulator. All this makes the program that much more useful for serious communications.

The next step is a kind of preliminary installation. Before AE Pro can run on your system, you have to enter a minimal amount of information. First, the program needs to know whether you can display lower case. Second, it needs to know the modem or serial card that you're using and which slot that card is in. Third, it needs to know the "console device" or display device and which slot that card is in.

When you boot up the (copied) disk for the first time, you find yourself in the installation program. The program prompts you for each piece of information that it needs. You can choose from a list of possibilities for both the communications device and the display device. The prompts are reasonably self-explanatory. The introduction in the manual explains them in more detail if you need it.

The AE Pro literature says that this program supports all Apple-compatible modems, serial interfaces, and display devices. The menu choices in the program list about 25 modems and serial cards. The display devices are listed by type and are explained more fully in the manual. One nice touch is that for most display devices you can simply choose "Auto" and let AE Pro identify the device.

For most systems, this takes care of the minimal installation of AE Pro. If you have a printer or certain external modems, there is a little more to do, but the manual clearly identifies these situations and gives you the information you need.

Once you've made it through the installation procedure, the manual takes you through a familiarization run to help you get started. It shows you how to call up the command menus and explains how to use them. (The menus are there as reminders only. Once you know the commands, you can ignore the menus.) The manual walks you through one or two sample sessions on-line. First it shows you how to dial a number, how to establish contact with another system, and how to hang up. Next it shows you how to capture information in the memory buffer, turn the buffer on and off, clear the buffer, and a few other simple things. The real value of this walk-through is that it introduces you to the most important commands and lets you ignore the rest for the time being.

There are one or two minor mistakes in the introduction. The manual's version of Menu 1 is missing a command that shows up on-screen, and the manual's version of Menu 2 lists the commands in the wrong order. Also, the manual says that when AE Pro detects a carrier, it will clear your screen and display the prompt **AE: Term—>**. The version I used in working on an Apple III did not clear the screen. This kind of mistake is not all that important, though; it doesn't affect the way you use the program and is not likely to be confusing.

One last point about the manual: It is designed around levels of understanding of both the program and of telecommunications in general. In addition to the Tutorial Section, there is a section on Basic Operation, a section on Advanced Operation, and a section on Advanced Programming and Utilities. This sort of division makes the learning process nearly painless. Start with the simplest capabilities of the program, learn how to use them and be comfortable with them, then move up to higher levels only when you're ready for it.

When you are ready to move up, there's plenty to move up to:

• The program will let you turn the printer on or off at any time.

• It will let you turn the memory buffer on or off at any time. It will also let you clear the buffer, save it to disk, or load a disk file into the buffer.

• It will let you—in a kind of instant replay of your conversation—review the information that's in the buffer.

• It will let you save files that are too long to fit in your memory buffer.

• It will let you send and receive files directly to and from disk, with or without full error-checking protocols. (AE Pro uses the Christensen protocol. This is yet another name for the XMODEM, MODEM7, or CPMUG protocol. This is a widespread, public domain protocol, which makes AE Pro compatible with a large number of other programs.)

• It will let you filter out control codes that are being sent by the host computer and are inadvertently interfering with communications.

• It will let you perform various operating-system functions from within the program, including "Catalog" (for a list of disk files) and "Delete."

• It will automatically dial and log on to a system. You can even set it up to dial a utility, log on, ask for some specific information, save that information to disk, log off, and hang up the phone.

As long as the above list is, it represents only some of the capabilities of AE Pro. One of the more impressive features of this program is the degree of flexibility designed into it. There is little that you could ask for in a communications program that you can't get out of ASCII Express if you know how to coax the program into working for you.

The terminal-emulation capabilities of the program provide a good example of AE Pro's flexibility. As mentioned elsewhere, some host computers are programmed to talk to specific terminals on a full-screen basis. Depending on the system, this may give you full-screen text editing or limited graphics capabilities. As shipped, AE Pro includes conversion tables to make your Apple emulate about a dozen different terminals, including a Hazeltine 1500 or 1510, an IBM 3101, an ADM-3A, and a DEC VT52. This is already more than most terminal programs will do for you, but AE Pro goes even further. It will let you custom-design your own terminal-emulation table. The manual shows you how.

The choices provided by the installation program are similarly flexible. Nearly every default value in the program can be changed. The list of choices alone runs over three pages in the table of contents.

One last feature that should be mentioned: the built-in text editor. I'm not impressed with it as a text processor. It is essentially line-oriented, which means that you are (mostly) restricted to doing things one line a time. I am impressed that it is there at all, however. It lets you manipulate the information in your memory buffer without having to leave the program.

For example: with most communications programs, if you're on-line and want to send someone a portion of a file, you have two choices. You can either send the whole file or you can leave the communications program, call up your word processor, go into the file, delete what you don't want to send, go back to the communications program, and—finally—send the file. With AE Pro you have a third choice. Load the file into your memory buffer, use AE Pro's text editor to delete what you don't want, then send the information from the buffer. This is not only easier, it's faster and cheaper as well.

The text editor also has a few other useful functions, including the ability to redefine the line width or change case. This can be useful when communicating with a computer that expects a specific line width or can deal only with upper case, for example. One nice touch on the editor is that many of the commands are user-definable. As shipped, most of the cursor control commands are set to match WordStar commands. If you use another word processor, though, it's nice to know that you can change AE Pro's text editor to match the commands that you're used to.

All these features (and more) put ASCII Express high on any list of full-featured communications programs. If you're running Apple DOS 3.3, don't skip AE Pro when you're looking for a communications program. And don't forget Z-Term if you're running CP/M on your Apple, or P-Term if you're running Pascal.

ASCOM for CP/M, CP/M-86 and MS-DOS (Including IBM PC)

Name: ASCOM Asynchronous Communications Control Program.

Revision: 2.2.

Company: Dynamic Microprocessor Associates
545 Fifth Ave.
New York, NY 10017
Phone: (212) 687-7115

Distributors:
WESTICO
25 Van Zant St.
Norwalk, CT 06855
Phone: (203) 853-6880

LIFEBOAT
1651 Third Ave.
New York, NY 10028
Phone: (212) 860-0300

Available for: CP/M, CP/M-86 and MS-DOS (IBM PC).

Format: CP/M version comes on 8-inch, single-sided, single-density disk. The program is also available in other formats for virtually any CP/M, CP/M-86, or MS-DOS system.

Price: $175.

ASCOM is not a program for neophyte computer users. This is not a negative comment about the program. After all, a Porsche 911 T is not a car for novice drivers, and a space shuttle is not a vehicle for novice pilots. In all three cases there is a great deal of potential available if you know how to use it. In all three cases, though, if you don't know what you're doing, you can quickly find yourself in trouble.

DMA bills ASCOM as an "Asynchronous Communications Control Program." This will tell you that "ASCOM" is short for "ASynchronous Communications," but unless you already know what the term means, that's about all it will tell you. (In case you've forgotten by now, it means having varying lengths of time between each character, and it means putting start bits and stop bits around each character.)

As you might suppose, any program that starts out by expecting you to know what "asynchronous communications" means is going to expect you to know more as well. It is at least going to expect you to be willing to learn along the way, and it is not going to go overly much out of its way to teach you.

All this is largely true, and DMA makes no apologies for it. It is a direct outgrowth of an explicit design philosophy. As originally conceived, the program was meant for people who already knew what they were doing when it came to communications, and it was meant, in particular, for those who wanted some fairly sophisticated abilities in a communications program.

DMA's design philosophy is beginning to change. The current version of ASCOM contains menus and help screens. These make the program a little easier to learn than it used to be. The next revision, currently under development, should be still easier, with newly designed menus and help screens.

The effect of the original design philosophy shows, however, in the current User's Manual as well as in the program. The manual is well written in the sense of being clear if you have the background to understand it. It is also well written in the sense of having few or no outright mistakes in it. (At least I didn't find any). But it tends to give less information than you might want if you are new to computers or new to communications programs.

Even if you're already well versed in communications, you're going to have to struggle with the manual a bit before you can get the most out of the program. The commands are listed alphabetically. If you go through the entire manual, trying out each command in turn, you will repeatedly run into instances where something won't work properly until you understand how to use another command that doesn't show up until ten pages later.

All this makes the User's Manual a rotten tutorial but an excellent reference guide after you're at least vaguely familiar with the program.

The program itself is much like the User's Manual: difficult to use until you have gained an idea of how it's organized, after which it becomes remarkably easy and straightforward to use.

It is possible to do everything in the program through the menus. They help when you're first learning the program, but they are also clumsy and not particularly self-explanatory. Once you're familiar with the program, you can ignore the menus and enter the commands directly.

ASCOM also contains help screens, but as with the menus, they are clumsy to use. Like the User's Guide, they function better as reminders than as introductions to the program's capabilities.

What makes ASCOM worth the work is that once you learn how to use the program, you will find that it is extremely flexible. It is rich in commands and will do just about everything for you but whistle a tune and tickle you under the chin.

The easiest way to use ASCOM is to write a batch file, or parameter file, for each information utility you deal with on a regular basis. These files can not only contain the commands to set ASCOM for the proper parameters, they can also contain phone numbers to dial, automatic log-on instructions, instructions to open a file to capture the information, instructions to automatically save the information to disk when the memory buffer is full, and more. Once you have the batch file written, you have only to enter the file name and everything else is done automatically.

If this isn't enough for you, ASCOM has a few additional conveniences. Not the least of these is that the program has its own system commands. These let you perform your housekeeping chores without having to leave the program. And there's more.

- ASCOM can control your baud rate if your system has its baud rate under software control.

- It can send and receive text files.

- It can download and upload program files.

- It can filter out control codes that are sent by the host computer and are interfering with communications.

- It can be set to translate incoming or outgoing characters from one code to another.

- It includes a choice of protocols for downloading or uploading. One of these (on both the CP/M and MS-DOS versions) is the CP/M User's Group protocol. This, as I've mentioned elsewhere, is commonly found on CP/M and other bulletin boards.

- One very nice touch, finally, is that you can run another program from within ASCOM. This means, for instance, that you can go into your word processor, create a batch file for immediate use, and go right back into ASCOM without going out of the program and into your operating system. This is a minor savings in time and effort, but it is still an extra step you don't have to take.

One warning: Normally when you order ASCOM, you specify the computer you're using, and the program is patched for that computer before being sent to you. If you somehow wind up with a program that hasn't been patched for your system, you will have to write an assembly language patch yourself. The User's Manual gives three examples. It also tells you, "This [assembly language] file should be assembled and then used to overlay the interface area in the ASCOM.COM file." If that sentence doesn't make sense to you, the examples aren't going to help very much either. Moral: Unless you want to write your own assembly language patch, make sure that you're getting the pre-patched version for your system. This usually won't be a problem, but it doesn't hurt to double-check.

If you are new to computers, you probably don't want—and don't need— anything as sophisticated as ASCOM. On the other hand, if you plan to get heavily into computer communications and you want to make sure that you won't be limited by your communications software, ASCOM is one program you should definitely look at.

ASCOM on the IBM PC

All the comments on the CP/M version of this program apply to the IBM version as well. In fact, there are only two differences worth noting. First, where the CP/M version uses a ^A (Control A) or the like, the IBM version makes use of the function keys on the machine, and second, the IBM version outlines the working area of the screen—for no particular reason that I can see. In conversational mode this outline comes nearly flush to the leftmost column of text. Some people find this attractive, others find it distracting. It's little things like this that make it important to play with a program before you commit yourself to buying it.

CHOOSING A COMMUNICATIONS PROGRAM

The programs we have looked at, from the extremely simple but limited Telelink I in Chapter 4 to the complex but powerful ASCOM, cover a wide range of capabilities. Somewhere within that range there is a program suitable for your needs

Before you start looking at specific programs, you need to consider three areas:

- First, how much do you know about computers and what degree of complexity are you willing to deal with? If you are new to computers, and don't want to invest a great deal of time in learning how to use a communications program, you obviously do not want a program like ASCOM, which may overwhelm you by its flexibility and richness of commands. On the other hand, if you already know something about computers and are willing to invest the time, then ASCOM—or something like it—may be exactly the right program for you.
- Second, what hardware do you have or are you planning to get? There is no point in demanding automatic dialing from your software if your modem isn't capable of dialing the phone. And if you do want automatic dialing, make sure that the automatic dialing on the software will work with the particular modem that you want.
- Third, consider the capabilities you need now and those you might want in the future. If you are new to computers, you might be considering a simple-to-use, dumb terminal program like TeleLink I. But if you already know that you are going to need the ability to save incoming information to disk, there is no point

in buying a dumb terminal program—no matter how little you know about computers and no matter how much you want to keep it that way.

Another thing to keep in mind: If you want the capability of downloading programs from some particular utility or utilities, you must find out the protocols you'll need and make sure that the program you buy can use those protocols. One more or less standard protocol that we've already touched on is the CP/M User's Group, or CPMUG protocol. This is used by most CP/M bulletin boards and by many other bulletin boards as well. It is also known as the XMODEM protocol, the MODEM7 protocol, and occasionally as the Ward Christensen protocol after the public benefactor who wrote it.

This particular protocol is in public domain. It is available on programs that you can get through CP/M User's Groups for roughly the price of the disk they come on. Also, because the CPMUG protocol is so widespread, much commerical software (including ASCOM and T.H.E. SMART TERMINAL) includes this as one of the options for transferring programs. If you are interested in downloading programs from a User's Group bulletin board, you will want a program that has this capability—particularly if you are running a CP/M system.

Any of the features we have looked at may or may not be important to you. In addition, there are other possibilities. You may be considering setting up your own bulletin board, for example, in which case you will want a piece of software that will automatically answer the phone and generally provide bulletin-board functions.

The best approach to choosing software is to make a list of the capabilities you want and then look for a program that closely matches the list. It is unlikely that you'll find an exact match, but at least you'll be able to make your compromises by decision rather than by ignorance.

A LIST OF TERMINAL PROGRAMS

Finally, here is a list of terminal programs along with some comments on each one. There are two disclaimers you should keep in mind about this list.

First, it is by no means exhaustive and is not meant to be. It is, rather, representative. I have made an effort to cover a wide range of computers and to include at least one program for each computer. For more popular systems, like the Apple II, I have generally included several programs.

Second, and more important, the inclusion of a program on this list does not constitute a recommendation. Given the range of equipment involved and the sheer number of programs, it is impossible to become thoroughly familiar with all of them. Where I have used a program enough to be familiar with it, and where I do feel comfortable recommending it, I have said so. Otherwise you should treat the list as a convenient starting point and no more.

One other thing. Many of the programs listed here are available in different versions for different computers, or even for different operating systems. Rather than try to group them by system, I've listed them alphabetically, then cross-referenced them to the computers covered in Chapter 6. For a list of the programs for any given computer, look at the software notes for that computer in Chapter 6.

ASCII Express, "The Professional"

Southwestern Data Systems
P.O. Box 582
Santee, CA 92071
Phone: (619) 562-3221

This is a sophisticated smart terminal program for the Apple II running Apple DOS. Features include auto-dial, auto-log on, the ability to capture information and save it to disk, and the ability to transfer files to and from disk. CPMUG is included as a protocol for file transfer. For more details on ASCII Express and other programs in "The Professional" series, see the review earlier in this chapter.

Apple Access III

Apple Computer, Inc.
20525 Mariani Ave.
Cupertino, CA 95014
Phone: (408) 996-1010

Operating System: Apple SOS.

This is Apple Computer's terminal program for the Apple III running Apple SOS.

ASCOM

Dynamic Microprocessor Associates
545 Fifth Ave.
New York, NY 10017
Phone: (212) 687-7115

ASCOM is a smart terminal program that works with most CP/M machines (including the Apple when running CP/M). It is also available in a CP/M-86 version and an MS-DOS version for the IBM PC and other machines. Features include auto-dial, auto-log on, the ability to capture information and save it to disk, and the ability to transfer files to and from disk. File transfer makes use of a choice of protocols, including CPMUG protocol. For further details, see the review of ASCOM earlier in this chapter.

Chameleon

Atari Incorporated
1265 Borregas Ave.
Sunnyvale, CA 94086
Phone: (408) 745-2000

This is a smart terminal program that works with any of the Atari computers. Features include the ability to send and receive files and the ability to emulate several terminals. For more details, see comments under Atari 400 in Chapter 6.

CONECT

Vector Graphic, Inc.
500 North Ventu Park Road
Thousand Oaks, CA 91320
Phone: (805) 499-5831

CONECT is a smart terminal program for Vector Graphic computers only. Features include auto-dial, auto-log on, the ability to capture information and save it to disk, and the ability to transfer files to and from disk.

CROSSTALK

MicroStuf, Inc.
Box 33337
Decatur, GA 30033
Phone: (404) 952-0267

CROSSTALK is a smart terminal program available for most CP/M systems (including the Apple when running CP/M). A version is also available for the IBM PC. Features include auto-dial, auto-log on, the ability to capture information and save it to disk, and the ability to transfer files to and from disk.

Data-Trans

ABT Microcomputer Software
55 Wheeler St.
Cambridge, MA 02138
Phone: (617) 492-7100

For the Apple II. Features include auto-dial, auto-log on, and the ability to communicate at 300 baud or 1200 baud.

DataLink II

Link Systems
1640 19th St.
Santa Monica, CA 90404
Phone: (213) 453-8921

DataLink II is a smart terminal program for the Apple II running Pascal. Features include auto-dial, auto-log on, the ability to capture information and save it to disk, and the ability to transfer files to and from disk. Choice of protocols in file transfer does not include CPMUG protocol.

DataLink III, for the Apple III, and a version of DataLink for the IBM PC are currently under development. (They should be available by the time you read this.) These will have all the capabilities of DataLink II, plus some added features.

Dow Jones Software

Dow Jones Market Analyzer
Dow Jones Market Manager
Dow Jones Market Microscope

Dow Jones & Company, Inc.
P.O. Box 300
Princeton, NJ 08540
Phone: (800) 257-5114
        (609) 452-1551 (in New Jersey)

Dow Jones has three communications programs. They come in versions for the Apple II running Apple DOS and for the IBM PC running MS-DOS. Each program is a straightforward smart terminal program that will work with any on-line service, but each also has additional capabilities for working with information downloaded from Dow Jones. All three let you manipulate financial information received from Dow Jones News/Retrieval. You can create reports, or even graphs, to analyze the data. Each of these programs is meant for a slightly different kind of financial analysis. Check with Dow Jones or your dealer to see which one best fits your needs.

All three of these programs come with a subscription to Dow Jones News/Retrieval. All three are capable of auto-dial and auto-log on, but only with Dow Jones.

EasyComm 64

Commodore Business Machines
487 Devon Park Road
Wayne, PA 19807
Phone: (215) 431-9100

EasyComm 64 is a smart terminal program for the Commdore 64. Features include auto-dial, the ability to capture information and save it to disk, and the ability to transfer files to and from disk.

Hayes Terminal Program

Hayes Microcomputer Products, Inc.
5835 Peachtree Corners East
Norcross, GA 30092
Phone: (404) 449-8791

The Hayes Terminal Program is specifically for the Apple II using a Hayes modem. The program comes in two versions: one for the Hayes Micromodem II and one for the Hayes Smartmodem. Either version can be used with Apple DOS, Pascal, or CP/M. Features include auto-dial, the ability to capture information and save it to disk, and the ability to transfer files to and from disk. File transfer does not include CPMUG protocol as a choice.

INTELLITERM

MicroCorp
913 Walnut St.
Philadelphia, PA 19107
Phone: (215) 627-7997

INTELLITERM is available in a version for the IBM PC and other MS-DOS systems, and in versions for the TRS-80 Model I and Model III running TRSDOS or LDOS. According to Radio Shack, it should be able to run on the Model 4 as well. Features in all versions include auto-dial, auto-log on, and automatic loading of parameters.

The MS-DOS version has additional capabilities as well. It comes in two levels, basic and advanced. Both allow protocol file transfer with XMODEM protocol. Both also have several other, more sophisticated capabilities. These include some unique features that help to ensure the proper transmission of ASCII files even when not using protocol file transfer. One interesting feature is the ability to simultaneously transfer files in both directions with full protocol file transfer. The advanced level of INTELLITERM adds sophisticated bulletin-board capabilities. If you start with the basic level, you can upgrade to the advanced level at any time.

InterLync

Starside Engineering
P.O. Box 18306
Rochester, NY 14618

InterLync is a smart terminal program for the IBM PC using MS-DOS. Features include the ability to capture information and save it to disk and the ability to transfer files to and from disk. CPMUG (XMODEM) protocol is used for file transfer.

Lync

International Software Alliance (Distributor)
1835 Mission Ridge Road
Santa Barbara, CA 93103
Phone: (805) 966-3077

Lync is a smart terminal program that will run on most CP/M machines. Other versions are available for the IBM PC, the Victor 9000, the TRS-80 Models I and III, and the TRS-80 Model II/12.

Features in the terminal mode include the ability to capture information and save it to disk. In addition to the terminal mode, Lync has a file-transfer capability with full error-checking protocols and a remote mode for operating the system from another location. CPMUG protocol is not included as a choice in file transfer but "will probably be added to the next revision." As of this writing, the MS-DOS versions of Lync are machine-specific for the IBM PC and Victor 9000 only. A generic MS-DOS version is under development. The version for the TRS-80 Models I and III operates under TRSDOS. According to Radio Shack, it should also work on the Model 4. The version for the TRS-80 Model II runs under Pickles and Trout CP/M or Lifeboat CP/M.

The Apple II CP/M version of Lync includes a simplified installation menu for use with the Hayes Micromodem II.

Micro Link II

Digital Marketing Corp.
2363 Boulevard Circle
Walnut Creek, CA 94595
Phone: (415) 947-1000

Micro Link II is a smart terminal program for various computers that run CP/M, MS-DOS, or CP/M-86. Unlike many programs, Micro Link II comes only in specific versions for specific machines rather than in generic versions that need to be installed. This means that you can use the program only if there's a version available for your machine. It also means that you don't have to worry about installing the program once you get it. Versions of Micro Link II are available for the Apple II running CP/M, the IBM PC, and various other specific systems.

Features include auto-dial, auto-log on, the ability to capture information and save it to disk, and the ability to transfer files to and from disk. CPMUG protocol is included as a choice in transferring files.

MICRO/Terminal

MICROCOM, Inc.
1400A Providence Highway
Norwood, MA 02062
Phone: (617) 762-9310

A smart terminal program for the Apple III running Apple SOS. Features include auto-dial, auto-log on, the ability to capture information and save it to disk, and the ability to transfer files to and from disk. MICRO/Terminal used to be available for the Apple II and IBM PC as well. Microcom has withdrawn those versions from the market, however, in favor of Microcom's ERA 2 Communications Package (listed under modems). Microcom still offers support for the Apple II and IBM PC versions of MICRO/Terminal.

Move-it

Woolf Software Systems
6754 Eton Ave.
Canoga Park, CA 91303
Phone: (213) 703-8112

Move-it is a smart terminal program that comes in versions for CP/M, CP/M-86, and MS-DOS systems. Features include auto-dial, the ability to capture information and save it to disk, and the ability to transfer files to and from disk.

MTERM

Micro-Systems Software, Inc.
4301-18 Oak Circle
Boca Raton, FL 33431
Phone: (800) 327-8724
       (305) 983-3390

MTERM is available for the Apple II running Apple DOS, the IBM PC running MS-DOS, the Zenith Z-100, and TRS-80 Models I, III, and 4. Features of MTERM include auto-dial, auto-log on, the ability to capture information and save it to disk, and protocol file transfer with another system running MTERM.

MTERM for TRS-80 Models I and III comes on a bootable disk with Micro-Systems' TDOS. The version for TRS-80 Model 4 runs on Micro-Systems' DOSPLUS IV or Radio Shack's TRSDOS. As of this writing, a version for the TRS-80 Model II/12 is under development. Check with Micro-Systems for current availability.

Omniterm

Lindberg Systems
49 Beechmont St.
Worcester, MA 01609
Phone: (617) 852-0233

Also available from:
Microperipheral Corp.
2565 152nd Ave., N.E.
Redmond, WA 98052
Phone: (206) 881-7544

Omniterm is available for the TRS-80 Models I and III running TRSDOS. (According to Radio Shack, this means that it should work on the Model 4 also.) Features include the ability to capture information and save it to disk and the ability to transfer files directly to or from disk.

P.I.T.S.—Pascal Interactive Terminal Software

Software Sorcery, Inc.
7927 Jones Branch Drive, Suite 400
McLean, VA 22102
Phone: (703) 471-0572

P.I.T.S. is for the Apple II. As the name implies, it runs under Pascal. Features include auto-dial and the ability to capture information and save it to disk. P.I.T.S. will also let you print information as it comes in, but if your printer can't keep up, you will lose characters. The program works at 300 baud only. It comes with the source code. (Software Sorcery also publishes a bulletin-board program for the Apple.)

P-Term "The Professional"

Southwestern Data Systems
P.O. Box 582-1
Santee, CA 92071
Phone: (619) 562-3221

A sophisticated smart terminal program for the Apple II running Pascal. P-Term is very much like ASCII Express except that it is written to run under UCSD Pascal rather than Apple DOS. For details on "The Professional" series, see the review of ASCII Express, P-Term, and Z-Term earlier in this chapter.

PC-Talk

The Headlands Press, Inc.
P.O. Box 862
Tiburon, CA 94920

PC-Talk, as the name suggests, is a smart terminal program for the IBM PC. It runs under MS-DOS. This program is interesting if for no other reason than that the early versions are essentially free. The program author encourages people to make copies of the program and hand them out, asking only for a $25 donation from anyone who feels the program is worth it. The first version of this program, I am told, had bugs, but the second version works just fine.

Features include auto-dial, the ability to capture information and save it to disk, and the ability to transfer files to and from disk.

PC/InterComm

Mark of the Unicorn
222 3rd St.
Cambridge, MA 02142
Phone: (617) 576-2760

A smart terminal program for the IBM PC running MS-DOS. Features include the ability to capture information and save it to disk and the ability to transfer files to and from disk. InterComm will make your IBM PC emulate a DEC VT100 terminal. This will let the host system do a number of things, including drawing graphs on your screen. Whether you can make use of this feature or not depends on the computer you're talking to.

Sci-Mate

Institute for Scientific Information
3501 Market St.
Philadelphia, PA 19104
Phone: (215) 386-0100

Sci-Mate is available for most CP/M systems, including the Apple II running CP/M. It is also available for the IBM PC running CP/M-86. Features include auto-dial, auto-log on, and the ability to capture information and save it to disk. The most interesting feature, though, is that it provides menu-driven searching on five large bibliographic information-retrieval systems: Dialog, BRS, National Library of Medicine (NLM), ORBIT Search Service, and Institute for Scientific Information (ISI). These five utilities each have a different command structure. If you use more than one of them, and particularly if you don't use them too often, it's easy to get the different commands confused. Sci-Mate lets you use a single set of commands for all five systems. You tell Sci-Mate the system you're dealing with and it will generate the appropriate commands for that system. You only have to learn Sci-Mate's menu-driven commands. If you're on a system that Sci-Mate doesn't know how to talk to, you can turn the "translation" capability off and deal with the system directly.

This program is named Sci-Mate because it's aimed primarily at scientists who want to conduct their own literature searches. (Searching through "the literature" is a routine step before starting any scientific research.) The program will work just as well for anyone else who uses these five information utilities.

Smartcom II

Hayes Microcomputer Products, Inc.
5835 Peachtree Corners East
Norcross, GA 30092
Phone: (404) 449-8791

Smartcom II is another program that comes only in specific versions for specific machines rather than in generic versions that need to be installed. As of this writing, it is available only for the IBM PC. Versions for the DEC Rainbow, the Xerox 820, and the Kaypro II are under development.

Features include auto-dial, auto-log on, the ability to capture information and save it to disk, and the ability to transfer files to and from disk. CPMUG protocol is not included as a choice in transferring files.

SOFTCOM

The Software Store
706 Chippewa Square
Marquette, MI 49855
Phone: (906) 228-7622

SOFTCOM is a smart terminal program for CP/M. Features include the ability to capture information and save it to disk and the ability to transfer files to and from disk. CPMUG protocol is not included as a choice in protocol file transfer. For more details, see the review on SOFTCOM earlier in this chapter.

Softerm

Softronics
6626 Prince Edward
Memphis, TN 38119
Phone: (901) 683-6805

Softerm is a smart terminal program for the Apple II. Features include auto-dial, the ability to capture information and save it to disk, and the ability to transfer files to and from disk. Protocol file transfer includes XMODEM protocol as an option. Softerm can emulate 20 different terminals. Although Softerm runs under Apple DOS, it can read and write Pascal and CP/M files.

ST80-III

Small Business Systems Group
6 Carlisle Road
Westford, MA 01886
Phone: (617) 692-3800

For the TRS-80 Models I, III, and 4, and for the TRS-80 Models II and 12. Features include auto-dial, auto-log on, and the ability to capture information and save it to disk.

The version for the Model I and III works under NEWDOS 80, LDOS, and TRSDOS. It will also work on the Model 4 using the Model III operating system, but it will not work on the Model 4 using the Model 4 operating system (TRSDOS 6.0).

There are two versions for the Model II/12. One runs under TRSDOS 2.0. The other runs under Lifeboat CP/M version 2.2. The CP/M version will not run under Pickles and Trout CP/M or Radio Shack CP/M+.

T.H.E. SMART TERMINAL

Binary Corp.
3237 Woodward Ave.
Berkley, MI 48072
Phone: (313) 548-0533

T.H.E. SMART TERMINAL is for all Atari Computers running Atari OS, Atari DOS, Atari XL OS, or Atari XL DOS. Features include the ability to capture information and save it to disk and the ability to load information from disk into the memory buffer, then send it from the memory buffer. Files longer than the available memory cannot be transferred unless you can break them into smaller parts. CPMUG (XMODEM) protocol is used for file transfer. For more details, see the review on T.H.E. SMART TERMINAL earlier in this chapter.

TeleLink I

Atari Incorporated
1265 Borregas Ave.
Sunnyvale, CA 94086
Phone: (408) 745-2000

TeleLink I is a cartridge-based dumb terminal program for Atari computers. It will run under Atari OS, Atari DOS, Atari XL OS, or Atari XL DOS. Like any dumb terminal program, it has little in the way of features. For further details, see the discussion of TeleLink I in Chapter 4.

TeleLink II

Atari Incorporated
1265 Borregas Ave.
Sunnyvale, CA 94086
Phone: (408) 745-2000

TeleLink II is also a cartridge-based program for Atari computers. Like TeleLink I, it is basically a dumb terminal program with one or two minor refinements. It will run under Atari OS, Atari DOS, Atari XL OS, or Atari XL DOS. For more details, see software notes for the Atari 400 in Chapter 6.

TELPAC

U.S. Robotics
1123 West Washington
Chicago, IL 60607
Phone: (312) 733-0497

TELPAC is a smart terminal program from U.S. Robotics, a leading modem manufacturer. TELPAC is available for the IBM PC running MS-DOS, the TRS-80 Model II and 12 running TRSDOS, the TRS-80 Model III running TRSDOS, and for CP/M systems, including the Apple II using CP/M. Features include auto-dial (with U.S. Robotics' modems), auto-log on, the ability to capture information and save it to disk, and the ability to transfer files to and from disk.

Terminal Emulator II

Texas Instruments Incorporated
P.O. Box 10508
Lubbock, TX 79408
Phone: (806) 741-2000

Terminal Emulator II is Texas Instruments' terminal program for the TI-99/4A. For details, see software notes for the TI-99/4A in Chapter 6.

Transend (Levels 1, 2, and 3)

Transend Corp.
2190 Paragon Drive
San Jose, CA 95131
Phoe: (408) 946-7400

Transend is a smart terminal program for the Apple II running Apple DOS. Features include auto-dial, the ability to capture information and save it to disk, and the ability to transfer files to and from disk. Transend 1 does not include protocol file-transfer capabilities; Transend 2 and 3 do. CPMUG protocol is not a choice for file transfer. For more details, see the review of Transend earlier in this chapter.

Transend/PC

Transend/PC is also from Transend Corporation. As the name implies, it is meant for the IBM PC. This is not simply a rewritten version of the Apple II program, though. About the only things the two versions share are the name and some general features. These include auto-dial, the ability to capture information and save it to disk, and the ability to transfer files to and from disk. CPMUG (XMODEM) protocol can be used for file transfer.

TSMART

> Microperipheral Corp.
> 2565 152nd Ave., N.E.
> Redmond, WA 98052
> Phone: (206) 881-7544

TSMART is a smart terminal program for the Atari 400 or 800. Features include auto-dial, the ability to capture information and save it to disk, and the ability to transfer files directly to or from disk. TSMART works only with Microperipheral's Microconnection.

Uniterm/80

> Apparat, Inc.
> 4401 South Tamarac Pkwy.
> Denver, CO 80237
> Phone: (303) 741-1778

Uniterm is a smart terminal program for the TRS-80 Model I and III running TRSDOS or NEWDOS 80. According to Radio Shack, it should also work on the Model 4. Features include the ability to capture information and save it to disk. Files cannot be transferred directly to or from disk. Instead, they must be put into the memory buffer first, then sent to the modem or disk as appropriate.

VICTERM and VICTERM 40

> Commodore Business Machines
> 487 Devon Park Road
> Wayne, PA 19807
> Phone: (215) 687-9750

VICTERM is a basic dumb terminal program for the VIC 20 or Commodore 64. The program is available separately or as part of the package when you buy the VICMODEM.

VICTERM 40 is a smart terminal program for the VIC only. In addition to giving the VIC smart terminal capabilities, it reformats the screen to 40 characters per line.

For more information, see the software notes on the VIC 20 in Chapter 6.

Videotex

Radio Shack
1800 Tandy Center
Forth Worth, TX 76102
Phone: (817) 390-2000

Videotex is a dumb terminal program available for the TRS-80 Color Computer, the TRS-80 Models I, III, and 4, and the TRS-80 Models II and 12. The Color Computer version comes as a plug-in cartridge. The version for the Models I, III, and 4 comes on tape but can be converted to disk. The Model II/12 version comes on disk. All work in essentially the same way—as a dumb terminal with few features. For more information on this, see the software notes on the Color Computer in Chapter 6.

Videotex Plus

Radio Shack
One Tandy Center
Fort Worth, TX 76102
Phone: (817) 390-2000

As the name implies, Videotex Plus is a slightly smarter version of the Videotex program. It is currently under development and should be available for TRS-80 Models I, III, and 4 shortly.

Z-TERM "The Professional"

Southwestern Data Systems
P.O. Box 582-1
Santee, CA 92071
Phone: (619) 562-3221

A sophisticated smart terminal program for the Apple II running CP/M. Z-Term is very much like ASCII Express except that it is written to run under Microsoft CP/M rather than Apple DOS. For details on Southwestern Data Systems' "Professional" series, see the review of ASCII Express, P-Term, and Z-Term earlier in this chapter.

HARDWARE PART III
The Nitty-Gritty

This chapter is divided into three sections—modems, terminals, and computers, and a discussion of how to connect them to each other. But not in that order.

The first section continues the discussion of the RS-232 standard; it gives details on connecting computers to modems in general.

The second section contains reviews and notes on specific terminals and computers. These include Scanset; Zenith ZT-1; the RCA Videotex Data Terminal and All-Purpose Terminals; Apple II, II Plus, and IIe; Apple III; TRS-80 PT-210 Printing Terminal; TRS-80 Models I, II, III, 4, and 12; TRS-80 Color Computer; Commodore PET/CBM; VIC-20 and Commodore 64; Timex 1000, 1500, and 2068; IBM PC; Atari 400, 800, and the new Atari XL series; the Osborne I, Osborne II, and Executive; the KayPro II, 4, and 10; the Texas Instruments TI-99/4A, Vector 3 (as an example of an S-100 bus, CP/M machine); and Digital Equipment Corporation's Rainbow 100. The section gives information on hardware peculiarities, compatible modems, and compatible software.

The third section contains reviews and notes on specific modems. These include the Racal-Vadic 212LC, the Bizcomp 1012, and the Hayes Smartmodem 1200. The section also includes a list of about 70 additional modems. If you don't already own a modem, this is the one section you won't want to skip, although you may want to bypass some of the technical details at the end of each review.

SECTION I: PUTTING IT ALL TOGETHER, OR RS-232 REVISITED

Ideally, you shouldn't have to read this section.

In Chapter 3 we breezed through a discussion of the RS-232 standard, mostly by listing some computers that can be connected to a modem with an RS-232 port.

In the best of all possible worlds, that should be enough; the only thing you should have to know is that if there is an RS-232 port on your computer and an RS-232 port on your modem, all you have to do is to plug in a cable with appropriate connectors on each end and forget about it.

Unfortunately, it's not always that simple.

If you buy your equipment at list price through a retail store, it should be that simple. The main reason for paying list price is precisely so that the dealer will take care of the technical details.

On the other hand, if the dealer doesn't quite know what he or she is doing, or if you saved money by buying your equipment through discount mail order, you may find yourself with a modem, a computer, and a cable and not know how to put them together. If that's your situation, keep reading. Otherwise skip to Section II.

There are only two points you need to remember from Chapter 3.

First, the RS-232 standard refers not to a particular kind of connector but to the technical standards established for the signals that are sent over the lines. Second, the most common connector used with the RS-232 standard contains 25 pins and is known as a DB-25.

The RS-232 standard defines the voltage that goes over the wires. We can ignore that. For our purposes it is much more important to know that the standard also defines which wire is used for which signal. This part of the standard is what determines how to connect any given computer to any given modem.

If you look head-on at a DB-25 connector, you will see that each of the pins (on a male connector) or each of the holes (on a female connector) has a number next to it—1 to 25. If you look at a 25-wire cable, you will find that each of the 25 wires is clearly marked with a different color or stripe so that you will know which wire to attach at which number on each side of the cable.

FIGURE 4. A DB–25 connector. Notice that each of the holes on the connector is numbered.

Each of these 25 lines (meaning pins, holes, or wires) has an assigned function (except for one, which in the official version of the standard is not used at all). I am not going to list those functions here, however, because there are only three lines that are really important for connecting computers to modems. These are lines two, three, and seven.

Data Communications Equipment and Data Terminal Equipment

Most computers can be connected to most modems by using just three lines. The exact method of connection depends on how the computer and modem are wired. Most often it depends on how the computer is wired since virtually all RS-232 modems are wired in the same way.

The choices in wiring are exactly two. Equipment can be wired as data communications equipment (DCE) or as data terminal equipment (DTE).

Data communications equipment (DCE) expects to send information on line two and receive information on line three.

Data terminal equipment (DTE) expects to send information on line three and receive it on line two.

This works out nicely if a terminal wired as data *terminal* equipment is connected to a modem that is wired as data *communications* equipment. All you need is a straight through connection; you connect line two on the terminal to line two on the modem and line three on the terminal to line three on the modem. (Ignore the other lines for the moment.) Data will be sent from the modem on line two and will be received at the terminal at line two. Similarly, it will be sent from the terminal on line three and arrive at the modem on line three.

This simple, straightforward method of cabling, as you might suppose, is precisely the point of having two standard kinds of wiring in the first place.

The confusion starts when you are dealing with a computer instead of a terminal.

Modems are unarguably data communications equipment (DCE) and are always wired that way.

Terminals are unarguably data terminal equipment (DTE) and are always wired that way.

Computers, though, are flexible. They can be used as terminals or they can have terminals connected to them. Even when a computer is not being used as a terminal, moreover, it can still be connected to a modem so that remote terminals can reach it. One result of this flexibility is that there is no clear choice between wiring a computer as data communications equipment (DCE) or as data terminal equipment (DTE). And that, of course, means that some computers are wired one way and some are wired the other way.

Computers that are wired as data terminal equipment are connected to a modem with a straight-through cable, just as a terminal is connected.

For computers that are wired as data communications equipment (DCE), though, a straight-through cable will not work. Both the computer and the modem will be sending data on line two and both will be "listening" for data on line 3.

The solution, when connecting a modem to a computer wired as data communications equipment, is to cross lines 2 and 3—that is, the wire that starts at pin 2 on each end of the cable ends up at pin 3 at the connector on the other end. This means that data will be sent from the modem at pin two but will be received at the computer at pin three, where the computer is listening for it. Similarly, data will be sent from the computer at pin 2 and arrive at the modem at pin three, where the modem is listening for it.

Putting the Cable Together (If You Have To)

The mechanics of putting a cable together are pretty simple. First you have to have a cable with a DB-25 connector at each end. I mention this because you might otherwise make the mistake of ordering a modem by mail order with the assumption that a cable will come along with it. It usually won't unless you order the cable also.

You should be aware too that you can buy cables and connectors separately. In addition, you can buy cables that have 25 wires in them or cables with fewer wires. The latter are usually somewhat cheaper.

DB-25 connectors come in two forms. In one version the pins are part of the connector and the wires are soldered to the pins. In the other version the pins are actually attached to the wires and the connector itself has holes that the pins fit through. In either case, at the base of the connector there is a kind of clamp that serves to hold the cable in place and hide the individual wires. If you open up that base, you can see which version of the connector you have.

Depending on the version, you can either solder and unsolder wires to the pins or you can use a special tool called a pin extractor to push pins out of the various holes or put them in. This, of course, is what lets you cross wires in the cable. If you are buying the version with the pins attached to the wires, you should be aware that you can buy cables that already have the pins attached or you can buy the pins separately and attach them yourself. Unless you really enjoy fooling around with this sort of thing, I suggest that at the very least you make sure that the cable you buy already has the pins attached to the wires.

Once you have the cable (with the bases of the connectors open, the pins attached to the wires, if necessary, and with your pin extractor or your soldering gun at the ready), all you need to do is to find out whether the computer is wired as DCE or DTE. This information should be somewhere in your computer documentation. If you can't find it, you can always call your dealer or the company. Another possibility is to arbitrarily assume that the computer is wired in one way or the other. If the cabling doesn't work based on your first assumption, you can go back and wire it the other way.

If the computer is wired as DCE (Data Communications Equipment), you cross lines two and three.

If the computer is wired as DTE (Data Terminal Equipment), you connect lines two and three straight through.

The only other line you need to connect (usually) is seven, which is connected straight through in either case. (This is the signal ground.)

These three lines—two, three, and seven—are the only ones you need to connect in nearly all cases. They are sufficient to let the computer support most functions of most modems.

Depending on how your system is set up, you may also want to connect line one straight through. This is the protective ground. It electrically connects the chassis of computer and modem and ensures that all the equipment is at the same ground potential. This is usually considered a good idea, but not always. If your modem and computer are plugged into different lines, you may have slightly different electrical potentials on each line. If so, connecting the protective ground can cause problems. Also be aware that some manufacturers don't make use of line one, in which case connecting the line would be pointless.

Another line you might want to connect, if you have an auto-answer modem, is line twenty. This line tells the modem when the computer is on so that the modem knows when it's okay to answer the phone. (If you don't want to bother with line twenty, there are usually ways to fool the modem into thinking that the computer is always on. Typically, auto-answer modems have a switch that you can set to either make use of line twenty or to bypass it.)

If you read through your computer manual and your modem manual, you will usually find that most of the other lines are not used. If you want to match up whatever lines are used, go right ahead. *But be careful.* If you connect pins where they do not belong (which may mean a straight through connection in some cases), it is possible to send a voltage from computer to modem (or modem to computer) that will damage a circuit.

Moral: Do not, under any conditions, use the cable to connect a pin on the computer to a pin on the modem unless you are absolutely sure that it will do no damage.

Lines that you don't need can be clipped off or simply not be inserted in the connector, but be careful here too. Loose wires must be cut cleanly so they won't accidentally make electrical contact where they shouldn't. Any loose pins should be wrapped in electrician's tape for the same reason.

Once you have your cable wired, you only have to plug it into the computer and modem, then test the system to see if it works. If it doesn't, the most likely problem is with the cable. You may have the wrong information about how the computer's DB-25 is wired, DCE or DTE. Go back and rewire it the other way before looking for problems in the computer or modem.

Cables that cross lines two and three, incidentally, are known as "null modem cables." There is no standard null modem cable though; there are different versions for different computers. Each of these does something different with the other lines.

If Your Computer's RS-232 Port Does Not Have a DB-25

Up to this point the entire discussion of cabling has assumed that your computer has a DB-25 connector on its RS-232 port. This is a reasonable assumption since the DB-25 is far and away the most common connector used. Reasonable or not, however, the assumption doesn't help much if the computer you're dealing with is using something else for a connector. In that case you will have to get a cable with the appropriate connector on the computer end. You will also have to study your computer manual to determine which lines are being used for which signals.

There are four, or possibly five, lines you are interested in. They are:

TXD, or transmit data, which should be connected to line 2 of the modem;
RXD, or receive data, which should be connected to line 3 of the modem;
Signal ground, which should be connected to line 7 of the modem;
Protective ground, which can be connected to line 1 of the modem (but which, once again, can cause a problem in some cases).
Finally, if you have an auto-answer modem, you might want to connect the DTR, or data terminal ready line. This can be connected to line 20 of the modem.

You should also take a look at Section II of this chapter. It contains useful notes for connecting modems to several specific computers.

SECTION II: COMPUTERS AND TERMINALS: SHORT REVIEWS AND HELPFUL HINTS

This section covers several specific computers and terminals, including most popular small computers and some representative CP/M systems.

The section can be used in one of two ways, depending on whether you already own a system or have yet to buy one.

If you do not as yet own a computer or terminal, you might like to browse through the section, skipping over the more technical notes. Keep in mind that various computers and terminals can be grouped into categories. The equipment reviewed here was chosen to be representative of those categories. If you're looking for a system that will act as a terminal, you should find these reviews useful, at the very least, in helping you to decide the category of equipment you should be looking at.

If you already have one of the machines covered here (or a similar, hardware-compatible system), there is no point in reading the whole section. Just take a look at the notes on your computer or terminal for information about setting it up. In addition to notes about cabling and about the kind of connectors you need, you will find notes about compatible modems and software. Where appropriate, you will find a list of modems or software designed for the particular computer. You can then check these lists against the notes on modems at the end of this chapter and against the notes on software at the end of Chapter 5.

The section covers the following specific computers and terminals. They are listed here in alphabetical order within category.

TERMINALS

RCA Videotex Data Terminal
RCA All-Purpose Terminals (APT)
Scanset
TRS-80 PT-210
Zenith ZT-1

INEXPENSIVE COMPUTERS

Atari 400
Commodore VIC-20
Commodore 64
TRS-80 Color Computer
Texas Instruments TI-99/4A
Timex 1000, 1500, 2068

POPULAR SMALL COMPUTERS

Atari 800
Atari 600XL, 800XL, 1400XL, 1450XLD

Apple II, II Plus, IIe (Most comments on the Apple II also apply to the various Apple-compatible machines, including the Franklin ACE, the BASIS 108, and the ORANGE + TWO.)

Apple III

Commodore PET/CBM

IBM Personal Computer (Most comments on the IBM PC also apply to various IBM PC-compatible machines, including the Eagle, the COMPAQ, the Hyperion, and the Columbia.)

KayPro II, 4, 10

Osborne I, II

Osborne Executive

TRS-80 Model I

TRS-80 Model II, Model 12

TRS-80 Model III, Model 4

CP/M COMPUTERS

Vector Graphic Vector 3 (Comments on the Vector 3 also apply to most other S-100 bus, Z-80 systems.)

DUAL PROCESSOR COMPUTERS

DEC Rainbow 100

Prices and specifications are subject to whims of the manufacturers and may have changed by the time you read this.

Here are two notes that apply to many of the systems covered here.

RS-232 Ports and Serial Ports

RS-232 ports are serial ports. This has to do with the way they transmit data: serially or one bit at a time.

Since all RS-232 ports are serial ports, and since the vast majority of serial ports on computers are RS-232 ports, you will often see the two terms used synonymously. This is not correct, however, and it can get you in trouble. Connecting an RS-232 serial port to another kind of serial port that uses different voltages can, and most probably will, result in wisps of smoke rising from your valuable equipment. Moral: Do not assume that a connector labeled "Serial Port" is, in fact, an RS-232 port unless the computer documentation (or the modem documentation, for that matter) says it is.

Serial Ports and Parallel Ports

Many systems come equipped with parallel ports as well as, or instead of, serial ports. The difference is that in a parallel port the eight data bits for each character travel in parallel—eight bits at a time along eight different wires— instead of traveling serially—one bit at a time—along one wire.

The most common kind of parallel port is called a Centronics (or Centronics-compatible) parallel interface. Like the RS-232 connector, this is a common standard for connecting computer equipment. Printers typically come with either an RS-232 connector or a Centronics parallel connector. Where the notes in this section mention a Centronics-compatible printer port, be aware that to use it, you need either a printer with a Centronics-compatible interface or a separate device to convert the signals from your computer so that it will work with the interface your printer uses.

TERMINALS: DUMB AND NOT SO DUMB

If you are expressly interested in communicating with an information utility, and if you have no interest in or desire for a computer at all, you might consider getting a terminal. There are more terminals available than we can conveniently list here, much less take a close look at. The following represents a fair sampling of relatively inexpensive terminals.

Scanset

Manufacturer: The French Matra Corp.
Sold in North America exclusively by:
    TYMSHARE
    Equipment Product Marketing
    20705 Valley Green Drive
    Cupertino, CA 95014
    Phone: (408) 446-6510

Availability: Direct from TYMSHARE or through distributors. (Call TYMSHARE for your closest distributor.)

Support: TYMSHARE offers two basic maintenance programs: a "Fixed-Price Repair" and an "Extended Limited Warranty." The first choice amounts to a standing charge for repair regardless of the problem. This is currently $95 for the 410 and 415. It will be slightly higher for the 415 HS and the XL models. The second choice amounts to a one-year renewable service contract. This is currently $85 per year for the 410 and 415. The contract is also available with an exchange option. If you choose this option, TYMSHARE will ship you a replacement Scanset immediately upon notification of a problem. Otherwise you have to wait for your Scanset to be fixed and returned.

Price: Standard Models (without built-in phone handset):
    $495...Model 410 (without modem or automatic dialer)
    $695...Model 415 (with modem and automatic dialer)
    $1295...Model 415HS (with 300/1200-baud modem and automatic dialer)
    XL Models (with built-in phone handset):
    $1895...(XL equivalent to Model 415)

FIGURE 5. The Scanset with a printer (the 3M Whisper Writer 1000).

The XL is also available without a modem but only on a special-order basis. A 300/1200-baud version should be available by the time this book is published, but as of this writing, the price has not yet been decided.

Features: Includes monitor screen.

Available with or without built-in modem. (Both a 300-baud, 103-compatible modem and a 300/1200-baud, 103/212-compatible modem are available. Both modems are full or half duplex, originate only.)

Automatic dialing. (This feature will work only with the built-in modem. Remembers up to 36 phone numbers. Can use either pulse dialing or tone dialing.)

Automatic log on with password protection. (Once you've entered the password, it cannot be read by others.) Scanset can store up to 16 different log on sequences. Four of these can be stored along with the appropriate telephone numbers so that a single command will take you through dialing and log on.

Screen width: Can change from 80-character width to 40-character width at any time.

Small size: Keyboard and screen are in one small package that fits on desk or table with room to spare.

Can attach printer (see note on page 95).

Can turn printer on and off at any time while on-line.

Comes with passwords to and free registration for Dow Jones News/Retrieval and THE SOURCE. Also a six-month trial membership to COMP*U*STORE shopping service.

Drawbacks: Keyboard is too small for typing.

Cannot capture incoming information except as hard copy on optional printer.

Comments: Because of its small size, Scanset is ideal for an executive desk or anyplace else where space is at a premium. Precisely because of its small size, however, Scanset's keyboard is useless for typing. If your interaction with an information utility is going to be limited to choosing a number from a menu or giving short commands such as "GO PAGE X," Scanset is more than adequate. If you are planning to do anything that involves typing, such as leaving messages on a bulletin board or sending electronic mail, look elsewhere.

For a closer look at Scanset, see Chapter 2.

Notes for Connecting to Printer: Scanset comes with a 9-pin RS-449 connector. This supplies the appropriate signals for a printer equipped with an RS-232 port. The User's Manual includes an appendix that shows how to configure cables for several popular printers, including the Epson MX 80. Cables are also available from TYMSHARE.

Notes for Connecting to Modem: Scanset Models 415, 415 HS, and XL each contain a built-in modem.

Model 410 comes without a modem but with a cable that ends in a standard male DB-25, RS-232 connector. This can be plugged into any standard RS-232 modem wired as DCE.

Zenith ZT-1

Manufacturer: Zenith Data Systems
1000 Milwaukee Ave.
Glenview, IL 60025
Phone: (312) 391-8860

Availability: Local Heath and Zenith dealers.

Support: Equipment repaired at Zenith Data Systems Authorized Service Stations, including HeathKit Electronic Centers. Terminal can also be returned to factory for repair.

Price: ZT-1 is $549. Related models range in price from $399 to $579, depending on whether they come with or without a monitor, built-in modem, or RS-232 port. In addition, if you want to put it together yourself, Heath sells three versions of the terminal as kits.

Features: ZT-1 comes with built-in 300-baud, 103-compatible modem. (Modem is full or half duplex, with originate, answer, and auto-answer capabilities.)

Automatic dialing. Remembers up to 26 numbers of 21 digits each. (Pulse only.)

Automatic log on with password protection.

The ZT-1 comes in three basic versions: ZT-1, ZT-1A, ZT-11. (There is also a ZT-10 but this is just a ZT-11 without a modem.)

The ZT-1 is customized for CompuServe so that you can enter the entire log on sequence. For any other utility, you can enter everything up to, but not including, the password.

FIGURE 6. Zenith ZT-1.

The ZT-1A is customized for THE SOURCE so that you can enter the entire log on sequence for THE SOURCE. Once again, though, when dealing with any other utility, you can enter everything up to, but not including, the password.

Finally, the ZT-11 will let you enter the entire log on sequence, including the password, for each number in the directory. The lack of customization makes for marginally more work in entering the log on sequences in the first place, but this extra work is more than made up for by the increased ease of use when logging on to various systems. If you are looking at the Zenith ZT series terminal, the ZT-11 is definitely the version to look at. (The ZT-11 also has an RS-232 port. The ZT-1 does not.)

Screen width: 80 characters.

The ZT-1 comes with a full-size keyboard and a separate monitor.

Can attach printer (see note below).

Can turn printer on and off at any time while on-line. Can also print a screen at a time rather than printing continuously as the information comes in.

Comes with passwords to, free registration for, and one free hour on Dow Jones News/Retrieval, THE SOURCE, and CompuServe. Also comes with a six-month trial membership to COMP*U*STORE.

Comments: The ZT-1 is comparable in most respects to the Scanset. A comparison of features—automatic dialing, automatic log on, and especially the reliance on carefully designed, self-explanatory menus—reveals more similarities than differences.

This is not to say that there are no differences, though.

The most important of these, and the major advantage of the ZT-1 over the Scanset, is the full-sized keyboard on the ZT-1. As a touch-typist, I can vouch for its comfortable feel. The ZT-1 is well-suited for typing messages on bulletin boards or for sending electronic mail. In fact, when not being used as a terminal, the ZT-1 can be used as an electronic typewriter if you have it attached to a printer. There is one important change from a standard keyboard that you may find bothersome though.

On a standard keyboard the shift lock is released by hitting the shift key. On this keyboard the shift lock is released by hitting the shift lock key itself. If you are a touch-typist, or even a fast two-finger typist, this takes some getting used to.

There are a few nice touches on the ZT-1. There is, for example, a clock display in the upper right-hand corner. When you're on-line, time really is money. This built-in clock can help you keep track of just how much you're spending. (If you would rather not be reminded, you can turn it off. The ZTX-10 and ZTX-11 do not have the clock.)

In addition to automatic dialing in originate mode, the ZT-1's modem also allows manual originate, manual answer, and auto-answer. These additional capabilities aren't needed in dealing with an information utility, but you might want them for other purposes.

Not all the differences between Scanset and ZT-1 are in Zenith's favor. To begin with, the screen on the Zenith is significantly more difficult to read. (If you don't like the screen, you can buy the terminal without a monitor, then buy a separate monitor.)

Another disadvantage on the Zenith is that the dialer is pulse only. This means that you cannot call a remote data base by Sprint or MCI, both of which require tone dialing.

One last and much more important disadvantage of the ZT-1 is that it is not quite as easy to use as the Scanset. Despite the obvious (and largely successful) effort to include a series of well-designed, self-explanatory menus, the ZT-1 stumbles in one or two places. In particular, the prompts for auto-log on leave much room for confusion. The User's Manual doesn't help matters either. The instructions and examples for entering log-on sequences manage to be both skimpy and convoluted. They are confusing enough so that I finally gave up trying to make this feature work on my own and wound up calling the company for help. It turned out that the procedure is simple—once you know what it is. The confusion apparently stems from the differences between the various versions of the terminal. In any case, it would be nice if Zenith would rewrite this section of the manual. (Zenith tells me that this is "in the works.")

Notes for Connecting to Printer: The ZT-1 comes equipped with a Centronics-compatible parallel printer port on the rear of the keyboard unit.

Notes for Connecting to Modem: The ZT-1 comes with a built-in 300-baud, 103-compatible modem and no way to attach anything else. The ZT-10 and the ZT-11, however, both come with RS-232 ports. These can handle up to 9600 baud, which means that they are also suitable for direct connection to a computer.

The ZT-10 comes without a built-in modem. The ZT-11 comes with one. Either model can be connected to an external modem through the terminal's RS-232 port. If the modem is capable of dialing, you can use the auto-dial feature on the terminal to dial through the modem. (And if you get a modem that can use tone dialing as well as pulse dialing, you can use the modem to call through Sprint or MCI.) The RS-232 port on the ZT-10/ZT-11 is wired as DTE. A straight through connection of lines 2, 3, and 7 will support most functions of most modems.

RCA Videotex Data Terminal

Manufacturer: RCA MicroComputer Products
New Holland Ave.
Lancaster, PA 17604
Phone: (800) 233-0094
(717) 393-0446 (in Pennsylvania)

Availability: Computer and electronics retail stores or RCA distributors.

Support: Currently must be shipped to RCA for repair. Third-party maintenance may be available by the time you read this.

Price: $399 (Model VP 3501. This model includes a built-in 300-baud modem, a calculator keypad, and an RF-modulator to allow use of a TV for the monitor screen. Stripped-down models are available for less.)

Features: Can be used with either a separate monitor or with a TV.

Is available with or without a built-in 300-baud, 103-compatible modem. (Modem is full or half duplex, originate only.)

Calculator-style keypad simplifies entry of numbers.

Cassette recorder interface is available for use with an audio cassette recorder. This gives you the ability to record incoming information on tape, then read it later at your leisure.

Screen width: Choice of 24 lines of 40 characters each or 12 lines of 20 characters each.

Size: Unit is small enough to fit into a briefcase with room to spare (16.5" by 7" by 2").

Can attach printer (see note below).

There is no provision for turning a printer on and off while on-line.

Comes with passwords to, free registration for, and one free hour on Dow Jones News/Retrieval and CompuServe.

Drawbacks: Membrane keys make touch-typing difficult.

Does not include automatic dialing or automatic log on capabilities.

Comments: The RCA Videotex Data Terminal is an interesting departure from most terminals. To begin with, it is "briefcase portable," meaning that it is small enough to fit into a briefcase, light enough to carry easily, and rugged enough to survive the trip. In addition, the VP 3501 can use any television set as a monitor screen. There is even an acoustic coupler available as an option for those times when you can't use the built-in direct connect modem. All this makes the VP 3501 a worthwhile candidate for a traveling companion. It is certainly suitable for sending and receiving electronic mail to and from the office. There are limits to how much text you will want to read from a television screen, though, even at the setting of 20 characters per line.

FIGURE 7. RCA Videotex Data Terminal. Photograph courtesy of RCA MicroComputer Products.

A second difference between the RCA Videotex terminal and most other terminals is that it is not limited to transmission of text. The local computer chip (the one inside the terminal) can control colors and sounds to create graphics and music. This makes the VP 3501 suitable for use with Prestel-like systems as well. (Assuming that the particular system uses appropriate commands for this particular terminal. The term "Prestel-*like*" is carefully chosen here. This terminal does *not* use the same protocols as Prestel and will *not* work on the Prestel system. There are some in-house graphics-oriented systems that use the RCA terminal, though.)

The VP 3501 has a membrane keyboard. You can look at this as either a feature or a drawback.

As a feature, the keyboard is part of what makes the VP 3501 a rugged piece of equipment, better able to withstand travel and "hostile environments." (Read: It's peanut-butter-and-jelly proof. Also coffee spill-proof.)

As a drawback, this same keyboard will slow you down if you are a touch-typist. I hasten to add, however, that it is much easier to type on than other membrane keyboards I have seen.

Notes for Connecting to Printer: The VP 3501 provides minimal printer capabilities. A connector on the back of the unit can be used with any printer equipped with an RS-232 interface. There are limitations though.

Normally a printer connection includes other lines for "handshaking" between the printer and the terminal. If the printer can't keep up with the incoming information, it uses these other lines to send a signal, telling the terminal to wait. The VP 3501 does not have any handshaking capabilities. This means that unless your printer either has a buffer or can manage an honest 30 characters per second, you will lose information.

Notes for Connecting to Modem: The VP 3501 contains its own 300-baud, 103-compatible modem.

RCA All-Purpose Terminals

Manufacturer: RCA MicroComputer Products
New Holland Ave.
Lancaster, PA 17604
Phone: (800) 233-0094
(717) 393-0446 (in Pennsylvania)

Availability: Computer and electronics retail stores or RCA distributors.

Support: Must be shipped to RCA for repair.

Price: APT-VP-4801 (full keystroke keyboard)
      With 12-inch monitor. $598
      Without monitor. $399
  APT-VP-3801 (membrane keyboard)
      With 12-inch monitor. $598
      Without monitor. $399
  Monitor (VP-3012D). $229

Features: Can be used with either a separate monitor or with a TV.

Automatic dialing can remember up to 26 phone numbers (pulse dialing or tone dialing).

Automatic log on with password protection can store the appropriate log on sequence for each of the 26 phone numbers in the directory.

Comes with built-in 300-baud, 103-compatible modem. Functions include originate, answer, and auto-answer, at full or half duplex.

Calculator-style keypad simplifies entry of numbers.

Screen width: Menu choice of 80 characters per line or 40 characters per line. (Can change while on-line.)

Size: Keyboard unit is small enough to fit into a briefcase with room to spare. Monitor is optional.

Can attach printer (see note below).

Printer can be turned on and off at any time while on-line.

Comes with passwords to and free registration for Dow Jones News/Retrieval and CompuServe.

Comments: The RCA APT models are the newest addition to the RCA line. Like Scanset and the Zenith ZT-1, the features on these terminals are menu-driven. These features include automatic dialing and automatic log on. As an additional convenience, you can also store the specific communications requirements (including full duplex or half, seven bits or eight bits per character) along with each phone number.

All this makes the APT models directly competitive with the Scanset and Zenith terminals. At the same time, though, the design of the keyboard unit retains the briefcase portability of the RCA VP 3501.

100

FIGURE 8. RCA All-Purpose Terminal, shown here with full-stroke keyboard. Photograph courtesy of RCA MicroComputer Products.

Unlike the 3501, the APT model comes in two versions, offering you a choice between a membrane keyboard for ruggedness or a full keystroke keyboard for faster typing.

The APT model includes a Centronics-compatible printer port. It can also operate at up to 9600 baud for use with a high-speed modem (or direct connection to a computer, for that matter).

The major difference between the APT models and the 3501 is that the APT models have no color capabilities. On the other hand, the monitor available with the APT is much better than a TV screen for reading text.

All this makes the APT models more suitable than the VP 3501 for any application that is concerned only with transmission of text. If you're interested in using the graphics or sound capabilities of the VP 3501, of course, the APT model is automatically ruled out.

Notes for Connecting to Printer: The APT model comes equipped with a Centronics-compatible parallel printer port.

Notes for Connecting to Modem: The APT model also includes an RS-232 port using a standard DB-25 connector. You can use this to connect the terminal to an RS-232, 1200-baud modem. The DB-25 is wired DTE, which means that you only need a straight through connection to the modem. (As noted earlier, you can also use the RS-232 port to connect the terminal directly to a computer for speeds up to 9600 baud.)

TRS-80 PT-210 Printing Terminal (Portable Data Terminal)

Manufacturer: Radio Shack
One Tandy Center
Fort Worth, Texas 76102
Phone: (817) 390-3011

Availability: Radio Shack retail stores and Radio Shack computer centers.

Support: Equipment is repaired through any local Radio Shack store.

Price: $995.

Features: The TRS-80 Portable Data Terminal consists of a keyboard, a thermal printer, a built-in modem, and the associated electronics. It is typical of terminals built around a thermal printer.

The built-in acoustic modem is 103-compatible, originate only. It can be set to 110 baud or 300 baud.

The TRS-80 PT-210 is about the size of a small portable typewriter.

Drawbacks: Cannot read incoming information except as hard copy on a printer. This uses a lot of paper. Because this is a thermal printer, moreover, it requires a special kind of paper. If you run out, you can't make do with something else. All this is true of any printing terminal that is built around a thermal printer.

COMPUTERS THAT CAN BE USED AS TERMINALS

There are a number of popular small computers around, any one of which you may already have or may be considering getting. Any of these systems can also be used as a terminal. Some come with appropriate ports as standard, some do not. Some come with disk drives as standard, some do not. Some come with 64K or more of internal memory as standard, some do not. But, once again, any of these computers can function as terminals: either dumb terminals or smart terminals. And all of them have software available to let them function either way.

I've divided the systems into two groups labeled "Inexpensive Computers" and "Popular Small Computers." This division is somewhat arbitrary since there is an overlap in the two groups. In general, though, what distinguishes the "inexpensive" computers from their more expensive relatives and accounts for their low price is their stripped-down condition. The package typically includes a keyboard, a minimal amount of internal memory, and a central processing unit, or CPU (the actual computer inside the box). Video screens, external memory, additional internal memory, and other options all need to be added. Most of these computers also cut costs on the keyboard, which means that they are not really suitable for any application that includes a great deal of typing. (The VIC-20 and the TRS-80 Color Computer are possible exceptions to this rule.)

A close look at the TRS-80 Color Computer should be enough to give you an idea of what you can expect from the most inexpensive systems. Comments on the other computers in both categories are largely confined to notes relating specifically to software, modems, or the actual use of the computer as a terminal. If you are planning to get one of these systems, you should look at them primarily in terms of your other needs. If you already own one of them, the notes should help you get it up and running as a terminal.

INEXPENSIVE COMPUTERS

TRS-80 Color Computer

Manufacturer: Radio Shack
One Tandy Center
Fort Worth, TX 76102
Phone: (817) 340-3011

Availability: Radio Shack retail stores.

Support: Repaired through Radio Shack stores.

Price: $199.95 (16K system with standard Color Basic.)

Comes with RS-232 port as standard but uses a 4-pin connector rather than the standard DB-25 connector.

Baud rate limited to 600 baud maximum.

FIGURE 9. Radio Shack TRS-80 Color Computer. Photograph courtesy of Radio Shack, a division of TANDY Corporation.

Features: Stripped-down system contains 16K of internal memory (RAM), an RS-232 port, and an RF modulator for connection to a television set. (A 4K version used to be available but is no longer sold.)

Internal memory (RAM) can be expanded to 64K.

Full-stroke keyboard.

An optional cassette recorder is available for storage of information and programs.

Disk drives are also available for external storage.

Uses a standard television set as a screen. The display is 16 lines of 32 characters per line.

The Color Computer is about the size of a large portable electric typewriter.

Software: Radio Shack sells a Videotex cartridge that will turn the Color Computer into slightly more than a dumb terminal. This program has no provision for turning a printer on or off. (You can't use the printer and the modem at the same time anyway. See Printer note below.) Also, the program will not let you save information to disk or tape or send information from disk or tape. It will let you type information into the computer memory before going on-line though. You can then send the information from the computer's memory. This can be useful for electronic mail or bulletin boards.

Modems: The Color Computer can be used with any 300-baud RS-232 modem (see notes below).

Comments: The TRS-80 Color Computer is reasonably typical of computers costing less than $400. The "standard" system comes with 16K of memory, but you can upgrade it to 64K. The system comes without any form of external memory for storage of information, but you can add a cassette recorder or disk drives. And so on.

One comment in particular about the Color Computer's keyboard: The original version of the computer came with chicklet keys. These were surprisingly comfortable for typing. They were big enough and spread out far enough to allow for touch-typing. In late 1983 the outside of the computer was redesigned and the chicklet keys were replaced by a full-stroke keyboard. This new keyboard has an even better feel to it and is one of the best available on any inexpensive system.

Notes for Connecting to Printer: There is only one RS-232 port on this computer. You can use this for either a modem or a printer, but you cannot use both at the same time.

Notes for Connecting to Modem: The cabling for connecting the Color Computer to a modem can be a problem since the Color Computer uses a non-standard connector for the RS-232 port.

The easy way out of this problem is to get the Radio Shack Modem I or Modem II. Each of these 300-baud, 103-compatible modems has two RS-232 ports on it. One uses a standard DB-25 connector. The other uses the same four-pin connector that the Color Computer uses. Radio Shack also has a cable available for connecting the computer to the modem.

If you already have some other modem, you'll need a cable with the four-pin connector on one side to plug into the computer and a male DB-25 connector on the other side to plug into the modem. You can buy one of these from Radio Shack or make your own.

The cabling is simple enough since there are only four lines to worry about. You'll find a diagram of the Color Computer's RS-232 port in the specification section of the manual. The pins are numbered clockwise. Assuming that your modem is wired normally (as Data Communications Equipment), the lines should run as follows:

Computer	Function	DB-25
Pin 1	Carrier Detect	Pin 8
Pin 2	Receive Data from Modem	Pin 2
Pin 3	Ground	Pin 7
Pin 4	Transmit Data to Modem	Pin 3

Radio Shack is currently planning to sell a module that will fit into the ROM port of the Color Computer and provide an RS-232 connector with a DB-25 connector wired as DTE (for connection with a straight through cable to the modem). As of this writing, details are not available on which lines need to be connected, but judging by Radio Shack's other manuals, the instructions that come with the module should be clear enough. (You won't be able to use the Videotex cartridge with the module since the module already uses the ROM port. Other communications programs for the Color Computer are available on cassette tape though.)

Commodore VIC-20 and Commodore 64

Although the VIC-20 and the Commodore 64 are different machines with different capabilities, they also share many capabilities. Except where noted otherwise, the following comments apply to both systems.

The Commodore 64 and VIC-20 do not come with an RS-232 port as standard but an RS-232 terminal interface can be added. The current price is $49.50.

Either system can use a television set or monitor as a screen.

The display for VIC-20 is 23 lines of 22 columns each.

The display for Commodore 64 is 25 lines of 40 columns each.

Baud rate is under software control.

Modems: The Commodore VIC-20 and Commodore 64 can be used with any 300-baud or 1200-baud RS-232 modem but require purchase of the optional RS-232 Terminal Interface.

Commodore also sells the VICMODEM for $109.95. This 103-compatible, originate-answer, direct connect modem plugs directly into the computer's User's Port on the far left of the computer. This eliminates the need for the Terminal Interface. On the telephone side of the connection, the VICMODEM requires a modular plug phone. You take the plug out of the phone handset and plug it into the modem. Commodore also sells an optional modem adaptor for $19.95 that lets you plug the modem directly into the wall plug along with the phone, using a "Y" connector.

Commodore's Automatic Modem is similar to the VICMODEM except that it also has auto-dial and auto-answer capabilities. It sells for $149.95 list price.

Other modems for the VIC-20 and Commodore 64 include the Bizcomp 1080 VersaModem. The Commodore 64/VIC-20 version of the VersaModem comes with a cable that plugs into the VIC-20 or 64 User's Port. It also comes with a terminal program.

Software: The VICMODEM comes with VICTERM, a dumb terminal program supplied on cassette tape. It also comes with Term 64 (on the other side of the tape). This is the version of VICTERM that runs on the Commodore 64. The VICTERM/Term 64 program is also available separately.

The 1650 Automatic Modem comes with AUTOTERM 20 and AUTOTERM 64. These are similar to VICTERM and Term 64 except that they also allow for keyboard dialing through the modem.

VICTERM 40, which may be available by the time you read this, will be a smart terminal program for the VIC only. In addition to letting you send information to the printer or to disk or tape, this program changes the VIC display format to 40 characters per line. For most utilities, this 40-character format makes a much more readable display than does the VIC's standard 23 characters per line.

Features on VICTERM 40 will also include a protocol file-transfer capability (for use with CompuServe only) and keyboard dialing for use with the 1650 Automatic Modem.

EasyComm 64 is a smart terminal program for the Commodore 64 only. The program can capture information and save it to disk or tape, and can send information from disk or tape. Features also include auto-dial and auto-answer.

Notes for Connecting to Printer: The Commodore printers plug directly into the computer, using the computer's serial port. (This is *not* an RS-232 port.)

FIGURE 10. The Commodore 64.

Notes for Connecting to Modem: The VICMODEM, Automatic Modem, and Bizcomp VersaModem plug directly into the computer's User's Port, using an edge connector. The optional RS-232 interface (model VIC1011A) plugs into the same edge connector. The RS-232 interface uses a standard DB-25 connector wired as DTE. A straight-through connection of lines two, three, and seven will support most functions of most modems. A second RS-232 interface is currently under development for the Commodore 64 only. This will plug into the game port (on the right rear of the computer). It will also use a DB-255 connector wired as DTE.

Texas Instruments TI-99/4A

This comes without an RS-232 port as standard, but an optional RS-232 interface can be added at extra cost.

Baud rate: 300-baud maximum (using TI's Terminal Emulator II).

The TI-99/4A uses a television set for a screen.

The screen width is adjustable in several steps between 28 characters per line and 40 characters per line.

Software: TI's Terminal Emulator II cartridge turns the TI-99/4A into a reasonably smart terminal. The program will let you capture data in the memory buffer, then send it to the printer or to a file. It will also let you send a file directly from disk without first having to manually load it into memory. You cannot print data as you receive it.

In addition to turning the computer into a smart terminal, the program can also handle color, graphics, sound, and speech. (For "speech," your computer has to be hooked up to the TI speech synthesizer.) The transmission protocols for these additional capabilities are specific to the 99/4A. The only utility that makes use of them is TEXTNET, a Prestel-like system maintained by Texas Instruments and available through THE SOURCE.

The Terminal Emulator II cartridge is $49.95.

TI used to sell a Terminal Emulator I cartridge that turned the 99/4A into a dumb terminal. This program has been discontinued.

Modems: The TI-99/4A can be used with any 300-baud RS-232 modem with purchase of either of two RS-232 interfaces (see notes below).

TI sells an RS-232, 300-baud, acoustic modem for $99.

Others: TI sells a HEX-BUS modem for $99. This is a direct connect, 300-baud modem. It plugs directly into any HEX-BUS port on the system, eliminating the need for the RS-232 port. (The HEX-BUS ports on the TI-99/4A are similar in concept to the SIO connectors on Atari systems. If you're not familiar with that concept, take a look at the notes for the Atari 400.)

Notes for Connecting to Printer: Various printers can be connected to the computer through any RS-232 port, parallel port, or HEX-BUS port on the system, depending on which interface the printer itself uses.

As noted above, you cannot print incoming data with the Terminal Emulator program as it comes in, but you can capture data in the memory buffer, then send it to the printer at any time.

Notes for Connecting to Modem: If you want to use an RS-232 modem, you have two choices for how to get the RS-232 port.

If you have the Peripheral Expansion System (PES), you can add the RS-232 card. This fits into the PES. It has two RS-232 ports and one parallel Centronics port on it. Either of the RS-232 ports is suitable for use with any RS-232 modem.

If you have the HEX-BUS interface, you can get the HEX-BUS RS-232 interface. This plugs directly into the HEX-BUS interface and provides a single RS-232 port. Unless you already have an RS-232 modem, though, the easiest and cheapest way to get on-line is with TI's HEX-BUS modem. This plugs directly into any HEX-BUS port on the system.

Timex T/S 1000, Timex T/S 1500, Timex T/S 2068

The T/S 1000, T/S 1500, and T/S 2068 are three different machines with different capabilities. They have much in common, though, particularly when being used as terminals.

The differences first:

T/S 1000

Has a membrane keyboard and 2K RAM. List price is $49.95. Requires an additional memory pack for use as a terminal.
Uses a television set as a screen. Display is 32 characters by 24 lines.

T/S 1500

Similar in capabilities to the T/S 1000 but has 16K RAM and a chicklet keyboard with standard typewriter spacing. List price is $79.95.
Uses a television set as a screen. Display is 32 characters by 24 lines.

T/S 2068

Has the same chicklet keyboard as the Brother electric typewriter. Has color capabilities, 48K RAM, and 24K RAM.
Can use a color television, a color composite video monitor, a monochrome monitor, or an RGB color monitor for screen. Display can be set to either 32 characters by 24 lines or 64 characters by 24 lines, depending on the monitor being used.
All other comments apply to all three systems.
Comes without an RS-232 port but one can be added (see notes on page 109).
Baud rate: Can operate at 110, 300, or 1200 baud. Software-selectable.

Software: The Timex 2050 modem comes with a slightly more than dumb terminal program on cassette tape. This allows for keyboard dialing and auto-answer. It will also let you send information to your printer, but only a screenful at a time.

FIGURE 11. Timex Sinclair 2068. Photograph courtesy of Timex Computer Corporation.

As of this writing, a smart terminal program from Timex is actively under development. Check with Timex or your dealer for current availability.

Modems: Can be used with any RS-232 modem with the addition of an RS-232 port.

The Timex 2050 modem is a 300-baud, 103-compatible direct connect modem. Features include auto-dial, auto-answer, manual originate, and manual answer. This modem does not need an RS-232 port. It comes with a cable that plugs directly into any of the Timex computers. It also comes with a terminal emulator program on cassette tape.

Notes for Connecting to RS-232 Modem: Timex does not sell an RS-232 interface for its computers but attachments are available from others. Memotech, for example, has a complete line of Timex add-ons. They even have a modem package that includes the RS-232 port, built-in communications software, a Novation J-CAT modem, and all connecting cables. For further information, contact:

Memotech Direct Sales Division
7550 W. Yale Ave.
Denver, CO 80227
(800) 662-0949
(303) 986-1516 (in Colorado)

Atari 400

(Note: As of this writing, Atari is about to discontinue production of the Atari 400. There are plenty of 400s still around, though. If you have one, or run across a used one, you should find this information valuable. Also, much of the information here applies not just to the Atari 400 but to the 800 and to the new XL series as well. More on that later.)

The Atari 400 does not come with RS-232 port as standard, but one can be added with the purchase of an interface box (see notes below).

Baud rate: Can operate at 110, 300, or 1200 baud.

Typically uses a television set as a screen, but also comes with a port for a monitor. Display can be set to 24 lines of 40 characters each, 24 lines of 20 characters each, or 12 lines of 20 characters each.

Drawbacks: The Atari 400 has a membrane keyboard. This has the advantage of being peanut-butter-and-jelly-proof, but it is difficult to type on.

Software: Atari uses its own operating system, called the Atari Operating System, or Atari OS. (The disk version is Atari Disk Operating System, or Atari DOS.) When using Atari OS, the 400 can use only software written specifically for the Atari.

Atari sells two communications programs on plug-in cartridges: TeleLink I and TeleLink II. (See Chapter 4 for a description of TeleLink I.) TeleLink II is similar to TeleLink I but has additional capabilities. Where TeleLink I lets you store incoming information in memory, then send it to the printer, TeleLink II will let you print the information as it comes in. With TeleLink II, moreover, you can toggle the printer on or off at any time (using the START key as the toggle). TeleLink II also lets you store two phone numbers and log-on sequences.

Chameleon is another Atari program available through Apex (the Atari Program Exchange). This comes in both a disk version and a cassette tape version. Either one will let you send or receive files. Either version will also let the Atari emulate several specific terminals if the computer you are talking to can take advantage of the additional capabilities.

Other programs for the Atari include TSMART from Microperipheral Corporation and T.H.E. SMART TERMINAL from Binary Corporation. (See the review of T.H.E. SMART TERMINAL in Chapter 5.)

Modems: The Atari 400 can be used with any RS-232 modem with optional Interface Module.

Atari sells three modems: the 830 acoustic modem, the 835 direct connect modem, and the 1030 direct connect modem. All three are 300 baud. All allow full duplex or half duplex, originate mode or answer mode.

The 830 modem has a standard RS-232 port with a DB-25 connector.

The 835 modem (available only as part of Atari's Communicator II kit) and the 1030 modem both use Atari's SIO bus connector. (More on this shortly.)

Other modems specifically for the Atari include the Microconnection modem from Microperipheral Corporation (uses the SIO connector) and the Bizcomp 1080 from Bizcomp Corporation (comes with a cable for use with the Atari 850 Interface Module).

Any of the modems with an SIO bus connector can be plugged directly into the computer itself or into any of the SIO connectors on any of the Atari modules.

Making Connections on the Atari: The Atari Serial Input/Output connector, or SIO for short, is an Atari-specific connector; no one else uses it (except when designing something like the Microconnection which is meant to be used specifically with the Atari). Atari calls it the "Serial Input/Output bus connector" to distinguish it from RS-232 serial ports.

In any case, anything in an Atari system that uses the SIO connector can be plugged directly into the computer itself or into any of the SIO ports on any of the Atari modules.

This may need some explanation.

Each of the Atari modules is designed so that different kinds of connectors are shaped differently. This prevents you from plugging the wrong cable into the wrong place and destroying sensitive equipment by applying the wrong voltage somewhere. It also insures that anything you *can* plug in will automatically make the right connection. The rule of thumb for plugging things in on the Atari is, if it fits, it will work.

The Atari comes with one SIO bus connector on the computer. Plugging a cable into this port, though, does not necessarily mean that you can't plug anything else into the system. If you are using a disk drive, for example, you'll find another SIO port on the back of the drive. The Microconnection can plug into this port, or into any other SIO port on the system, and work just fine.

For RS-232 modems, Atari offers an optional 850 Interface Module. This contains seven ports: two SIO ports, four RS-232 compatible serial ports, and one Centronics-compatible parallel port. More about the 850 interface shortly.

Notes for Connecting to Printer: Various Atari printers use different connectors. Here again, the rule of thumb is, If it fits, it will work. Most Atari printers use the SIO connector.

Notes for Connecting to Modem: The Atari 400 cannot be connected directly to an RS-232 modem since the computer itself does not have an RS-232 port. You can, however, solve that problem by getting the 850 Interface Module. The current list price is $219.95. (This is widely available at a discount.) The four RS-232 ports on the Interface Module are labeled "Serial Interface." They do not use a DB-25 connector. Atari's 830 modem comes with the appropriate cable for connecting the modem to the Interface Module. The 835 and 1030 modems use the SIO bus.

The easiest way to get the Atari up and running as a terminal is to get Atari's Communicator II Kit. There used to be a Communicator I Kit that included the 850 interface, the TeleLink I cartridge, and the 830 Acoustic Modem. This has been discontinued.

The Communicator II kit includes TeleLink II and an 835 modem. It also includes one free hour on THE SOURCE and one free hour on CompuServe. It sells for $279.95.

If you have some other RS-232 modem, you'll have to create or buy your own cable. Atari sells a modem interface cable, item CX87, for $39.95.

If you'd rather, you can make your own cable. The four RS-232 ports on the 850 interface are numbered one through four. Each uses a standard DB-9 connector, but they do not all support the same functions. Port 1 is meant for the modem. The pin assignment on Port 1 is:

DB-9 (850)	Function	DB-25 (RS-232 Modem)
Pin 1	Data Terminal Ready	Pin 20
Pin 3	Send Data from 850	Pin 3
Pin 4	Receive Data at 850	Pin 2
Pin 5	Signal Ground	Pin 7
Pin 6	Data Set Ready	Pin 6

DB-9 (850)	Function	DB-25 (RS-232 Modem)
Pin 7	Request to Send	Pin 4
Pin 8	Clear to Send	Pin 5

One last comment. Although various Atari computers have different capabilities, they are mostly compatible when it comes to software and hardware. This means that many of the items that are now being produced for the new XL series, including the CP/M module, will also work with the 400. For more information, see the notes on the XL series.

SOME POPULAR SMALL COMPUTERS

Atari 800

As of this writing, Atari is about to discontinue the 800. As with other discontinued systems, if you already have one, or find a used one, this information should prove valuable.

An RS-232 port is not standard, but is available with purchase of the optional Atari interface box.

Comments: The Atari 800 is largely identical to the Atari 400 except for the keyboard. Where the 400 has membrane "keys," the 800 has real keys that give good tactile feedback and are suitable for touch-typing. (But it's still not a standard office keyboard). Other than that, all the notes about the 400 also apply to the 800.

There are two other differences worth mentioning. The 800 has four slots for internal expansion as opposed to one slot in the 400: This means that the 800, because

FIGURE 12. Atari 800 with Atari 850 Interface and Telelink I cartridge.

of its additional slots, can be expanded more than the 400 can be. This translates into being able to add more bells and whistles. The 800 also has room for two ROM (Read Only Memory) cartridges as opposed to one for the 400. When it comes to using the system as a terminal, though, these differences are minor.

For notes on software, connection to printer, and connection to modem, see Atari 400.

Atari XL Series—600XL, 800XL, 1400XL, 1450XLD

As of this writing, Atari is in the process of introducing a new line of computers. These all have a great deal in common. Unless specifically stated otherwise, each of the comments in this section applies to the entire XL series.

RS-232 Ports: None of the computers in the XL series comes with an RS-232 port. RS-232 ports can be added, however, with the purchase of the optional 850 Interface Box or the new Atari Expansion Box. The Expansion Box, which is not yet available at this writing, will eventually replace the 850.

Connector: Each of the computers in the XL series includes an Atari Serial I/O connector. (For further information on this, see the notes on the Atari 400.)

Baud Rate: Can operate at 110, 300, or 1200 baud.

Software: Operating systems: The operating systems for the XL series are called Atari XL OS and Atari XL DOS. These are only slightly different from the operating systems on the 400 and 800. Overall, the XL series is mostly software-compatible with the Atari 400 and 800, but there are some programs for each operating system that will not work on the other. All Atari communications software is upward-compatible. (So are most other Atari programs.) Before buying any third-party software, check with the

FIGURE 13. Atari 1450XLD. Photograph courtesy of Atari, Inc.

vendor to see if it works on the XL series. (If it works on the short-lived 1200XL, it will also work on the rest of the XL computers.)

Atari is releasing a CP/M module that will attach to any of these systems (or to the 400 or 800, I'm told). This CP/M module will let the Atari use virtually any off-the-shelf CP/M program, just like any other CP/M computer.

Modems: Can be used with any RS-232 modem if you have added an RS-232 interface.

Can also be used with any of the modems that plug directly into the Atari SIO bus. (Here again, see notes on the Atari 400 for details.)

The 1400XL and 1450XLD contain built-in 300-baud, direct connect modems and built-in communications software to go along with them.

Notes for Connecting to Printer: *See* Atari 400.

Notes for Connecting to Modem: *See* Atari 400.

Apple II, Apple II Plus, and Apple IIe

The Apple II does not come with an RS-232 port as standard, but one is available as an optional feature (see notes below).

The Apple II's ability to put its baud rate under software control is completely dependent on which peripheral cards happen to be plugged into the machine (see notes below). In any case, the hardware switch is easy to get to.

Software: Operating system: The Apple II runs three different operating systems: CP/M, Pascal, and Apple DOS.

Apple DOS revisions include 3.2, 3.3, and PRODOS. In general, software is upward compatible so that programs designed to work with 3.2 DOS will usually work with 3.3 DOS, and programs designed to work with 3.3 DOS will usually work with PRODOS. Still, it is important to double check that the software you're considering will work with your particular DOS. If you have 3.3 DOS, for example, and the software was written for 3.2 DOS, the program must first be "translated" to the correct disk format for 3.3 DOS. This is difficult to do if the program is copy-protected. Also, watch out for software written in Integer Basic. This version of Basic was originally available on the Apple in the form of firmware—that is, the program was written on ROM chips permanently in the machine. Most machines that run 3.3 DOS or PRODOS use Applesoft Basic instead. If the prompt sign on your Apple is], you have Applesoft Basic. If the prompt sign is >, you have Integer Basic. (Apples with 64K can have both languages, with the second language loaded in from disk when needed.)

Communications programs available for the Apple II include:

ASCII Express, "The Professional" (Apple DOS)
Data Trans
DataLink II (Pascal)
Dow Jones Software (Apple DOS—all three programs)
Hayes Terminal Program (Apple DOS, Pascal, or CP/M)

Micro Link II (CP/M)

MTERM (Apple DOS)

P-TERM (Pascal)

P.I.T.S. (Pascal)

Sci-Mate (CP/M)

Softerm (Apple DOS)

TELPAC (CP/M)

Transend (Apple DOS)

Z-TERM "The Professional" (CP/M)

If you are running CP/M on your Apple, you can add virtually any other CP/M program to the list as long as the program is available on an Apple format disk and as long as it can be installed both to use Apple screen-control codes and to work with the serial card in your system. What this translates to is: When it comes to CP/M programs, you can probably use it but check before buying.

Modems: Can be used with any RS-232 modem with purchase of the optional RS-232 port (see notes below).

There are several modems-on-a-board for the Apple II. These include:

TIMECOR The Operator

Transend Apple Modemcard

Hayes Micromodem II

Multi-Tech Multi-Modem II

Novation Apple-CAT II

Novation 212 Apple-CAT II

There are also several modems available that connect to the Apple II through the game port. These include:

Bizcomp 1080 VersaModem

MFJ Enterprises, Inc. MFJ-1232

Comments: Apples come in various varieties, notably the Apple II, the Apple II Plus, and the Apple IIe. For our purposes, there are no differences worth mentioning. (We'll cover the Apple III separately.)

Notes for Connecting to Printer: To use the Apple II with a printer, you need the optional printer card.

Notes for Connecting to RS-232 Modem: An optional RS-232 port is available for the Apple. This comes on a board that slips into one of the computer's slots.

Until late 1982, Apple had two boards available with RS-232 ports on them. One was called the "Communication Interface Card." This had one RS-232 port using a DB-25 connector wired as DTE. If you have this card in your computer, you can connect the computer to most modems with a straight through cable connecting lines two, three, and seven. This card, however, will only work at 300 baud and 110 baud.

(This is not precisely true; this board can be modified to work at 1200 baud. The modification is beyond the scope of this book, though, and voids the warranty.)

The other board was called the "High Speed Serial Card." This also had one RS-232 port on it using a DB-25 connector, but this was wired as DCE. If you have this card in your Apple, you can connect your computer to most modems by crossing lines two and three and connecting line seven straight through.

Both of these cards were discontinued in late 1982 and replaced with Apple's "Super Serial Card," which lists for $195. The Super Serial Card also has one RS-232 port on it using a DB-25 connector. This card, in the jargon, has "a user-selectable configuration of either DTE or DCE." In other words, you can choose between DTE and DCE wiring for the DB-25 connector. This card also allows for software-selectable baud rate if your program is set up for it.

If you already have one of these cards, by the way, and you're not sure which it is, take a look at the card itself. It should be labeled.

Finally, the Apple is popular enough so that many companies besides Apple supply accessories for the system. There's no point in listing the individual cards here, but you should be aware that other cards that supply an RS-232 port are available. The important point is that details on these connectors will vary. Find out what those details are *before* you buy the card.

Apple III

The Apple III comes with one RS-232 port as standard.

The baud rate in the Apple III is under software control.

Software: Communications software for the Apple III includes:

Apple Access III (Apple SOS)
DataLink III (See DataLink II)
MICRO/Terminal (Apple SOS)

Also, the Apple III has an Apple II emulation mode that lets it run virtually any program written for the Apple II. (It may have problems with some programs written for the IIe—unless Apple comes up with a IIe emulation mode.)

You can also run CP/M on the Apple III using the SOFTCARD III, available from Apple. This will let you run virtually any CP/M program.

Modems: Can be used with any RS-232 modem.

Notes for Connecting to Modem: The Apple III comes with one RS-232 port as standard. This uses a DB-25 connector wired as DTE. A straight through connection of lines two, three, and seven will support most functions of most modems.

If this connector is already tied up with a printer or the like, you can use Apple's Super Serial Card instead. For comments on using the Super Serial Card, see the notes under Apple II.

In addition, Apple's High Speed Serial Card and Apple's Communications Card will also work under Apple II emulation mode. They will not work under Apple III mode, however. For further information on the High Speed Serial Card and the Communications Card, see notes under Apple II.

Commodore PET/CBM

The Commodore PET and the CBM are essentially the same machine and are often referred to as the PET/CBM. There are different versions of each with differing screen widths, character sets, and so forth. All these variations have a cassette port, an IEEE 488 port, and a parallel User Port. (This User Port is *not* compatible with the User Port of the same name on the Commodore 64 or VIC 20.) Except where otherwise noted, the following comments apply to all versions of the machine.

Most versions of the PET/CBM come without an RS-232 port but adaptors are available (see notes below).

Baud rate is not under software control.

Software: Operating system: Uses Commodore's CBM OS.

CompuServe's smart terminal program, VIDTEX Executive, comes in a version for this system. Also the PET/CBM version of the Bizcomp 1080 VersaModem (see below) comes with communications software for the PET/CBM.

Finally, Small Systems of Mountain View, California, sells SOFTBOX. This will let you use most CP/M programs on the PET/CBM.

Modems: Can be used with any RS-232 modem but the RS-232 adaptor must be purchased separately (see notes below).

The Bizcomp 1080 VersaModem and the Anchor Signalman come in PET/CBM versions that do not need the RS-232 adaptor. They come equipped with cables and appropriate connectors for the system.

Notes for Connecting to RS-232 Modem: The PET/CBM does not have an RS-232 port. It does, however, have another standard port called the IEEE port (Read: I triple E port). Several companies sell adaptors that attach to this port and convert the signals to RS-232 standards. (This is vaguely similar to what Atari, for example, does with its interface box.) Two of these companies are:

Connecticut Microcomputer   TNW
34 Del Mar Ave.   3444 Hancock St.
Brookfield, CT 06804   San Diego, CA 92110
Phone: (203) 775-4595   Phone: (619) 296-2115

Prices for these adaptors start at about $140.

In most cases the adaptor comes with appropriate cables so that all you have to do is plug them into the computer on one side and into the adaptor on the other.

Typically these adaptors have RS-232 ports that use DB-25 connectors and are wired as DTE, but you'll have to double-check the particular adaptor.

IBM Personal Computer

The RS-232 port is optional at extra cost except for the PC XT, which includes the port as standard equipment.

Baud rate is under software control.

Software: Operating system: MS-DOS and CP/M-86. IBM-modified CP/M is available with additional electronics, but programs then need slight modification. Note: MS-DOS on the IBM is often referred to as PC-DOS.

Some programs that run on the IBM are:

ASCOM (CP/M-86, MS-DOS)
CROSSTALK (MS-DOS)
DataLink (See DataLink II)
Dow Jones Software (MS-DOS—all three programs)
INTELLITERM (MS-DOS)
InterLync (MS-DOS)
Lync (MS-DOS)
Micro Link II (MS-DOS)
Move-it (MS-DOS, CP/M-86)
MTERM (MS-DOS)
PC-Talk (MS-DOS)
PC/InterComm (MS-DOS)
Sci-Mate (CP/M-86)
Smartcom II (MS-DOS)
TELPAC (MS-DOS)
Transend/PC (MS-DOS)

Modems: The IBM PC can be used with any RS-232 modem, assuming the PC is equipped with the optional RS-232 port (see notes below).

There are also a growing number of modems-on-a-board for the PC. Three of these are the Hayes 1200B, the Bizcomp 2120, and Microperipheral's PConnection.

Notes for Connecting to Modem: The RS-232 port on the IBM PC is available as an optional feature in the form of a board that fits into the computer. (RS-232 ports are also available on combination boards available from other manufacturers.)

IBM's optional RS-232 port uses a DB-25 connector wired as DTE, which means that a straight through connection of lines two, three, and seven will support most functions of most modems. Whether this three-line cable will actually work, though, depends on the particular software you're using. Some software packages (notably CROSSTALK) will expect to see other lines connected and will not work consistently without them. In general, you are better off connecting all 25 lines straight through.

For reasons known only to IBM, the company chose to be different from everyone else and supply a male connector for the RS-232 port instead of a female connector. This means that the cable to your modem has to have a male plug on one end and a female plug on the other rather than having a male plug on both ends, which is the usual arrangement.

Watch out. The female DB-25 connector on the IBM is a parallel port, *not* a serial port. *Do not* plug your modem cable into this.

Osborne I, Osborne II

Comes with RS-232 port as standard, using a DB-25 connector.

Baud rate on the Osborne is under software control.

Software: The operating system is CP/M, which means that the computer will work with most CP/M programs. Still, it's best to double-check before buying.

The Password Modem (see below) comes with software for the Osborne.

Modems: Can be used with any RS-232 modem.

The communications port on the Osborne uses a DB-9 connector, not a DB-25. Password, a modem from U.S. Robotics, is available with a cable that plugs into this connector.

Notes for Connecting to Modem: The Osborne I and II come with an RS-232 port as standard equipment. This port uses a standard DB-25 connector wired as DTE, which means that to connect it to an RS-232 modem, you can use a straight through cable. Connecting lines two, three, and seven will support most functions of most modems.

As already noted, the Osborne also has a second connector labeled "Communications Port." This uses a DB-9 connector rather than a DB-25.

Osborne Executive

Comes with two RS-232 ports as standard. Both use a DB-25 connector.

Baud rate is under software control.

Software: As with the Osborne I and II, the operating system is CP/M, which means that the computer should work with most CP/M programs. (Translation: Once again, double-check before buying.)

Notes for Connecting to Modem: The Executive has two RS-232 ports. Both use a standard DB-25 connector.

One source of confusion: The "communications port," meaning the one that is meant for the modem, is wired DTE, which means that a straight through cable is all you need. (Here again, lines two, three, and seven should be sufficient for most modems.) The manual, I am told, identifies this as DCE wiring. No matter what they call it, though, it still works with a straight through cable. (The other DB-25 connector is wired as DCE, which the manual identifies as DTE wiring. At least it's consistent.)

KayPro II, 4, 10

The KayPro II and 4 are essentially the same machine. The major difference lies in disk capacity. Both have one RS-232 port and one Centronics-compatible parallel port. The KayPro 10 includes a ten-megabyte hard disk and a second RS-232 port. Comments here apply to all three machines.

Baud rate is under software control.

Software: The operating system on the KayPro is CP/M, which means that the computer will work with most CP/M programs.

Notes for Connecting to Modem: The RS-232 port on the KayPro II and 4 uses a standard DB-25 connector wired DTE. A straight through connection of lines two, three, and seven should be sufficient to support most functions of most modems.

One of the RS-232 ports on the KayPro 10 is labeled "Communications." KayPro tells me that this is also wired DTE, so that a straight through connection of lines two, three, and seven should be sufficient for most modems.

TRS-80 Model I

Comes without an RS-232 port as standard but there are interface boxes available that provide a port.

Baud rate is not under software control.

Software: Operating system: TRSDOS (The Radio Shack Operating System) and CP/M.

The Model I can be converted to use the CP/M operating system in either of two ways. One of these conversions is simple and inexpensive, but it will not run most off-the-shelf CP/M programs. (This is strictly for technical reasons that are not worth going into in detail. Briefly, the Model I's ROM occupies memory locations that are ordinarily used by programs written for CP/M. In order to run on the Model I, these programs must be revised so they no longer use those memory locations.)

The second method of converting the Model I to CP/M will allow it to use off-the-shelf CP/M programs, but this method requires extensive, and expensive, modifications.

Communications programs for the Model I include:

INTELLITERM (TRSDOS, LDOS)
Lync (TRSDOS)
MTERM (TDOS, TRSDOS, DOSPLUS IV, LDOS)
Omniterm (TRSDOS, LDOS)

ST80-III (TRSDOS, NEWDOS 80)
Uniterm/80 (TRSDOS, NEWDOS 80, LDOS)
Videotex (TRSDOS, LDOS)
Videotex Plus (TRSDOS, LDOS)

Modems: Can be used with any RS-232 modem with optional expansion interface (see notes below).

There are also several modems available that do not need an RS-232 port with the Model I. These include the Radio Shack Modem I and Microperipheral's Microconnection.

Comments: The TRS-80 Model I was replaced in Radio Shack's line by the Model III. There are plenty of Model I(s) still around, though, and they will work as terminals. The only special requirements are that, in general, they need to be running level 2 Basic and have 16K of internal memory. Even this is not strictly so, however. The Microconnection modem comes with a simple terminal program, S80. This program comes on cassette and will work with a system with Level I Basic and 4K memory.

Notes for Connecting to Modem: There are several ways to provide the Model I with an RS-232 port.

Radio Shack used to sell expansion interfaces. These interface boxes (Models 1140, 1141, and 1142) came with a 40-line ribbon cable that connected to the Model I. They had room for a serial card that provided an RS-232 port in the form of an edge connector. (The edge connector came on the box, the serial card converted it into an RS-232 port. The card was switch-selectable to be wired as either DCE or DTE.) Radio Shack also supplied a cable with the serial card. The cable had an appropriate connector for the edge connector on one end and a male DB-25 connector on the other end. The DB-25 connector plugged directly into the modem. If you have an expansion box with the serial card and the appropriate cables, all you have to do is set the serial card to match the wiring on the RS-232 cable and plug the cables in. (See Section I of this chapter for a discussion of wiring the cable.)

If you find yourself with a Model I and no expansion box, all is not lost. Even though Radio Shack no longer sells its expansion interface box, you can still get an equivalent interface elsewhere that will work with the Model I and provide an RS-232 port. LNW Research Corporation sells one for about $400. (This includes several additional enhancements for the Model I as well.) The address is:

LNW Research Corporation
2620 Walnut
Tustin, CA 92680
Phone: (714) 544-5744
        (714) 641-8850

As already noted, there are modems available for the Model I that do not need an RS-232 port. Radio Shack sells a cable, for example, that has a four-pin connector on one end to plug into the Modem I and a five-pin connector on the other end to plug into the five-pin cassette port on the computer. To use this set-up, though, you need a copy of the program CASCOM (also known as Cassette-Comm). This software lets the cassette port act as an RS-232 port.

TRS-80 Model III

The TRS-80 Model III is a direct descendant of the Model I. Not only did it replace the Model I in the Radio Shack line, but it is, for the most part, compatible with the Model I. The key phrase is "for the most part." There are just enough differences to warrant a separate listing here.

The Model III comes without an RS-232 port as standard. An RS-232 card with a DB-25 connector is available as an option at extra cost.

Baud rate is under software control.

Software: Most software available for the Model I is also available for the Model III. (This includes all software listed under the software notes for the Model I.) In addition, U.S. Robotics sells a version of TELPAC for the Model III.

Operating system: The standard operating system for the Model III is TRSDOS. Radio Shack also sells LDOS for Model IIIs with a hard disk. (TRSDOS programs can run under LDOS.)

As with the Model I, CP/M is available on the Model III in either of two ways. One requires the use of modified programs. The other uses standard CP/M programs but requires extensive and expensive modification to the computer.

Modems: The Model III can be used with any RS-232 modem but needs the optional RS-232 port.

Notes for Connecting to RS-232 Modems: The optional RS-232 card uses a standard DB-25 connector wired as DTE, which means that a straight through cable connecting lines two, three, and seven will support most capabilities of most modems. The 48K dual disk system comes with the RS-232 card as part of the package.

TRS-80 Model 4

The TRS-80 Model 4 has recently replaced the Model III in the Radio Shack line in much the same way that the Model III replaced the Model I. The Model 4 is mostly compatible with the Model III, and any software that will run on the III will also run on the 4. There is a complicating factor here though. The Model 4 uses LDOS for its operating system, masquerading under the name TRSDOS 6.0. There are some programs, ST80-III, for example, that will not run under TRSDOS 6.0. If you have an earlier version of TRSDOS on your Model 4, however, you will be able to run the program.

The Model 4 is available in three basic versions: 16K, 64K with one disk drive, and 64K (expandable to 128K) with two disk drives. An RS-232 port is standard on the two-drive version, optional on the others. For details on connecting the Model 4 to an RS-232 modem, see the notes under the Model III.

TRS-80 Model II and TRS-80 Model 12

The TRS-80 Model 12 has recently replaced the Model II in the Radio Shack line. Aside from styling considerations, the two systems are nearly identical. They are also fully compatible. The only important differences are that the Model 12 has a different keyboard and a larger disk capacity. All notes here apply to both systems.

The Model II/Model 12 comes with an RS-232 port as standard, using a DB-25 connector.

Baud rate is under software control.

Software: Operating system: TRSDOS. Standard CP/M is also available. Pickles and Trout sells a CP/M package that will run off-the-shelf CP/M software, meaning that you can use virtually any CP/M terminal program. Radio Shack's CP/M+ will also run virtually any off-the-shelf CP/M program.

The Model II/Model 12 comes with the utility TERMINAL on the TRSDOS disk.

Other communications software for the Model II/Model 12 includes:

MTERM
ST80-III (TRSDOS 2.0a or Lifeboat CP/M 2.2)
TELPAC (TRSDOS)
Videotex (TRSDOS)

Modems: Can be used with any RS-232 modem (see notes below).

Comments: Where the TRS-80 Model's I, III, and 4 serve as entry-level systems that come in extremely stripped-down versions, the Model II/Model 12 is clearly meant as a full-fledged, small business computer. One sign of this is that the system comes with two RS-232 ports as standard. One of these can be used conveniently for a printer, the other for a modem.

Notes for Connecting to RS-232 Modems: The DB-25 connector on the Model II/12 is wired as DTE. A straight through cable connecting lines two, three, and seven will support most functions of most modems.

CP/M COMPUTERS

There is no point in trying to list all the CP/M computers on the market, much less give detailed notes for each one. Most of these computers, though, have basic similarities.

The Vector 3 is reasonably typical of a large number of machines. These can be described collectively as Z80 systems built around an S-100 bus structure and using the CP/M operating system.

Virtually all of these systems come with at least one RS-232 port as standard and nearly all have a DB-25 connector. In the few cases where there is no RS-232 port or where the port is already tied up with a printer, there are standard boards available that will slip into the S-100 bus and provide the

123

needed RS-232 port. In addition, there are several S-100 modems available—modems built on an S-100 board. Any of these will slip into the standard S-100 bus card cage and automatically make the right electrical connections work properly.

Each of these computers can use virtually any software written for the CP/M operating system. But remember that there are slight variations from one computer to the next, and there is always the possibility that a piece of software that works well on one system will have problems running on another.

Here is a list of generic programs that can run on nearly any CP/M machine:

ASCOM
CROSSTALK
Lync
Move-it
Sci-Mate
Softcom
TELPAC

In addition to the above programs, Micro Link II and Smartcom II will run on various specific CP/M machines.

The Vector 3 is also reasonably typical of systems with baud rate under hardware control. In general, if you want to change the baud rate on one of these systems, you have to remove the computer's cover, take one of the computer boards from its card cage, and physically set a switch to the rate you want to use. This is easy enough to do if you have to do it only once and then forget it. But if you are using a 300/1200-baud modem, or if you want to use 300 baud for your modem and 1200 baud for your printer, switching from one speed to the other can be inconvenient, to say the least.

Other systems that fall into this general category—meaning Z80, CP/M systems built around an S-100 bus—include the NorthStar Horizon, the Cromemco, and the CompuPro.

Vector Graphic Vector 3

Comes with an RS-232 port as standard. This uses a DB-25 connector wired as DCE.

Baud rate is normally controlled by switches. (The Vector 3 also has an atypical, limited software-control capability, but this is not implemented in most terminal programs.)

Software: CONECT: written by Vector Graphic specifically for Vector Graphic systems.

The operating system is CP/M, which means that the Vector 3 can use essentially any CP/M software (see list under "CP/M Computers").

Modems: Can be used with any RS-232 modem (see notes below).

Others: The Vector can also use any modem built on a standard S-100 board, notably the Hayes Micromodem 100 (300-baud, 103-compatible), and the U.S. Robotics S-100 modem (300/1200-baud, 103/212-compatible).

Comments: Unlike most systems with a "hard wired" baud rate, the Vector 3 has a limited ability to put the baud rate under software control. Vector Graphic's program, CONECT, takes advantage of this. Few other programs do. This brings up an interesting point. Many computer companies write software for their own systems. Since these packages are designed to run on a specific system and only on that system, they are often tailored to the computer and take better advantage of that computer's capabilities. The Vector, for example, has something called a memory-mapped screen. With most terminal programs, this causes problems at 1200 baud (or higher) and results in lost characters. CONECT is written with this problem in mind. It works just fine at 1200 baud.

Notes for Connecting to a Printer: Vector includes a parallel interface for connection to a printer.

Notes for Connecting to Modem: The Vector 3 has a single RS-232 port that uses a standard DB-25 connector. This is wired as DCE, which means that pins 2 and 3 must be crossed in the cabling. If the RS-232 port is needed for a printer, Vector has boards available with additional RS-232 ports. Connecting lines two, three, and seven will support most functions of most modems.

OTHER CP/M COMPUTERS

There are also a number of Z80, CP/M computers that are not built around an S-100 bus structure. These are largely equivalent to those machines that are built around the S-100 bus except that you can't add an S-100 modem, or an S-100 board with extra RS-232 ports, simply because there is no bus in which to put the board. Virtually all these systems provide at least one RS-232 port, and most provide some way to let you connect both a printer and a modem at the same time. At the very worst, you can buy a transfer switch for your single RS-232 port and switch back and forth between your printer and your modem.

The Osborne, listed under "Popular Small Computers," is a good example of this sort of computer. Others include the ALTOS and the NorthStar Advantage.

DUAL PROCESSOR MACHINES

Finally, there are a number of computers that are built around two central processing units rather than one. These machines are, in effect, two computers housed in a single system. Such dual CPU computers are becoming more and more common; a good example is the DEC Rainbow.

DEC Rainbow 100 and Rainbow 100+

The DEC Rainbow 100 comes with a minimum of 64K memory and with either two or four disk drives with 400K per disk. The Rainbow 100+ comes with a minimum of 128K memory, dual disk drives with 400K per disk, and an internal 10-megabyte hard disk. The memory in the Rainbow 100 is expandable to 256K; the 100+ is expandable to 896K. Otherwise the two systems are substantially the same, and everything here applies to both.

Each system comes with two RS-232 ports as standard. Both use a DB-25 connector. One of these is labeled "Printer." The other is labeled "Comm," for "Communications," and is meant for the modem.

Baud rate is under software control.

Software: Operating system: The Rainbow gives you a choice of operating systems: CP/M or MS-DOS. The earliest Rainbows came with CP/M only. Later systems gave buyers a choice between CP/M or MS-DOS or both (at extra cost). Starting in late 1983, the standard package has included both operating systems at a lower cost than before.

The Rainbow runs two variations of the CP/M operating system. CP/M-80 is the eight-bit version. CP/M-86 is the sixteen-bit version. The CP/M operating system on the DEC is called CP/M-86/80. As the name implies, it functions as either eight-bit CP/M or sixteen-bit CP/M, as necessary. Simply load the program you want to use into the machine. The operating system will automatically test the program, then choose the eight-bit or sixteen-bit mode as appropriate. Most off-the-shelf, generic CP/M-80 programs will work with the Rainbow. See the list of communications programs under CP/M computers.

MS-DOS also runs on the Rainbow. This is not directly compatible with the IBM PC version of MS-DOS, which means that programs written specifically for the PC will not run on the Rainbow. (A note here to avoid confusion: The Rainbow can read *data* from IBM disks. Rainbow MS-DOS can read data files written by IBM MS-DOS, and Rainbow CP/M can read data files written by IBM CP/M. Version 2.0 and later of Rainbow CP/M, and version 2.05 and later of Rainbow MS-DOS, can not only read IBM data disks, but can also write data in IBM PC format. All this gives the Rainbow a certain degree of compatibility with the PC.)

As of this writing, MS-DOS is relatively new on the Rainbow, which means there are few programs available as yet. This should change quickly.

Finally, as pointed out elsewhere, the Rainbow is one of the very few systems that includes a built-in communications option. When booting up, you have the choice of going into the terminal-emulation mode rather than booting from a disk. If you choose the terminal-emulation mode, the system will emulate a DEC VT102 terminal. This gives you a slightly more than dumb terminal that will let you toggle your printer on and off but won't let you save information to disk.

Modems: Can use any RS-232 modem.

Comments: The Rainbow, as a dual CPU computer, is an example of a new generation of machines. One of the CPUs is a Z80, which is why the system can run the CP/M-80 operating system. The other CPU is an 8088, which is why the system can run the CP/M-86 and MS-DOS operating systems.

The reasoning behind having the two CPUs is simple. So far there is more software available to run on the older Z80 chip under the CP/M operating system. As time goes on, though, there promises to be more and more software for the newer, 8088 CPU using other operating systems (primarily MS-DOS). By having both CPUs in one computer, you can bridge the gap from old to new without having to buy a new system.

The Rainbow 100 has slots for three boards. (One of these is taken up in the 100+ by the disk controller board.) These slots use a Rainbow-specific bus structure. As of this writing, there are no modems-on-a-board designed for this system.

Notes for Connecting to Modem: The Rainbow's RS-232 "Comm Port" uses a standard DB-25 connector, which DEC tells me is wired DCE. Lines two and three must be crossed in going to the modem. DEC also tells me that, as with most systems, lines two, three, and seven will support most features of most modems.

SECTION III: MODEMS

In Chapter 3 we looked at two modems, one acoustic connect and one direct connect. Both of those modems, the Novation CAT acoustic and the Radio Shack Modem I, are examples of bare-bones devices. Either one will do a fine job of letting you communicate over the phone lines, but neither one provides such frills as automatic dialing, automatic disconnect, or choice of baud rates.

These are only a few of the additional features available in modems. Each increases the cost of the modem, but each also makes the process of communications easier. Whether the increased ease is worth the increased cost is up to you.

This section reviews several modems. They have been carefully selected to cover a wide range of possibilities—from the most basic bare-bones devices to the most sophisticated. Taken together, they provide a fair sampling of what is generally available. For convenience, the basic specifications on the Novation CAT and the Radio Shack Modem I are listed here as well.

Novation CAT Acoustic

Manufacturer: Novation, Inc.
　　　　　　　20409 Prairie St.
　　　　　　　Chatsworth, CA 91311
　　　　　　　Phone: (213) 996-5060

Price: $189.

Availability: Retail stores, direct order, discount houses.

Baud Rate and Compatibilities: 300 baud, 103-compatible.

Connection to Phone System: Acoustic.

Connection to Computer: RS-232.

Duplex: Full or half.

Modes: Manual answer or manual originate.

Indicator Lights: Power on, Ready (carrier detect).

Switches: Answer mode/originate mode/off.
Full duplex/half duplex/test.

Connectors: DB-25 connector on RS-232 port, power-cord connector.

Description of Use: See Chapter 3.

Notes for Connecting to Computer: Standard DB-25 connector wired as DCE. Connecting lines two, three, and seven will support all functions.

Radio Shack TRS-80 Modem I

Manufacturer: Radio Shack
One Tandy Center
Ft. Worth, TX 76102
Phone: (817) 390-3011

Price: $99.95.

Availability: Radio Shack stores.

Baud Rates and Compatibilities: 300 baud, 103-compatible.

Connection to Phone System: Direct connect.

Connection to Computer: RS-232.

Duplex: Full.

Mode: Answer or originate.

Indicator Lights: Power on, carrier detect.

Switches: Answer mode/originate mode/off.
Slide switch for choosing between RS-232 ports.

Connectors: Two RS-232 connectors (see notes below), one power-cord connector, one female connector for plugging a phone into the modem, one cord and connector for plugging the modem into the phone system.

Description of Use: See Chapter 3.

Notes for Connecting to Computer: This modem has two RS-232 connectors. One is a DB-25 connector wired as DCE. This allows the modem to be used as a standard RS-232 modem. Connecting lines two, three, and seven are sufficient to support all functions.

The other RS-232 port is a four-pin DIN connector. This is included specifically for connecting the Modem I to the Radio Shack Color Computer or Radio Shack Model I cassette port. If you are using the Modem I this way, appropriate cables are available from Radio Shack. (The Model I requires "Cassette-Comm" software for this to work, though. This is no longer sold by Radio Shack.)

Racal-Vadic VA212LC

Manufacturer: Racal-Vadic Inc.
  1524 McCarthy Blvd.
  Milpitas, CA 95035
  Phone: (408) 946-2227

Price: $495 suggested list. (Discounts are often available.)

Availability: Direct from any of several distributors. Call Racal-Vadic for the one closest to you.

Baud Rate and Compatibilities:
  0-300 baud, 103-compatible.
  1200 baud, 212-compatible.

Connection to Phone System: Direct connect.

Connection to Computer: RS-232.

Duplex: Full only.

Modes: Manual originate, automatic answer.

Indicator Lights:
  Transmit detect (TXD) indicates transmission of data.
  Receive detect (RXD) indicates reception of data.

FIGURE 14. Racal-Vadic 212LC. Photograph courtesy of Racal-Vadic Inc.

Carrier detect (CXD).

Data mode—indicates whether modem is set for data communications or voice communications.

Baud rate—indicates whether modem is set for high speed or low speed.

Switches: The VA212LC has two pairs of buttons.

One pair switches between high speed (1200 baud) and low speed (0-300 baud).

The other pair switches between voice communications and data communications.

Connectors: The VA212LC modem has one DB-25 connector for the RS-232 port and one connector for the power cord for plugging into a wall outlet. It also has two female (modular plug) phone connectors. One of these is used to plug a phone into the modem. The other is for a cable that goes from the modem to the phone system. (The cable comes with the modem.)

Description of Use: The VA212LC is extremely simple to use. This is largely because it offers you few choices beyond high speed or low speed.

To call an information utility, you first choose the speed you want. If the modem is set for 1200 baud, its high speed light will be on. If it is set for 300 baud, the light will be off. If the setting is correct, you leave it alone. Otherwise you push the appropriate button.

The second status light you need to look at is labeled "Data." If this light is on, it means that the modem is set to transmit data. The light should not be on until you're ready to do that. Here again, if the modem is set correctly—meaning that the light is off—you leave it alone. If it is not set correctly, you push the button labeled "Voice" and the data light will go out.

You then dial the utility. When you hear the modem on the other end squealing at you, you push the data button. At that point the data light goes on and the phone goes dead. Very quickly after that, the carrier detect light should come on as the modems establish communications. Meanwhile, you hang up the phone, turn to your keyboard, and carry on your conversation with the utility. When you're through, you log off. The modem automatically hangs up the phone when it loses the signal from the utility's modem.

The VA212LC modem has two additional status lights that we haven't run into before. These are "Transmit Detect" and "Receive Detect." They can be helpful under certain conditions if your system doesn't appear to be working. The transmit detect light flickers on and off each time a character is sent from your computer through the modem. The receive detect light flickers on and off each time a character is sent to your computer. When operating in full duplex, then, both lights should be flickering each time you type a character; the transmit detect light should flicker when the character is transmitted and the receive detect light should flicker when it is echoed back. If you find yourself typing and nothing is showing up on the screen, the presence or absence of flickering lights will help you determine where the problem is.

There are, finally, two minor complications with setting the modem for "data" or "voice." If the modem is set for voice and you push the data button, the phone will go dead. Once you've finished using the modem and the modem has hung up, you'll find that the phone will work normally again. This means that after you've logged off a utility, you can pick up the phone and use it even though the data light will still be on. The first complication comes when you try logging on to another utility. You will be able to dial easily enough, but you won't be able to establish communications between the modems unless you first push the voice button and then the data button to set the modem correctly.

The second complication comes if someone tries to call you. With the phone hung up and the data light on, the modem is in auto-answer mode. If the phone rings, the modem will pick up and start squealing into the phone line. This is useful if you've arranged with someone to call so you can exchange files. It is not useful if the person at the other end isn't expecting it. Unless your phone line is dedicated strictly to your computer, it's best to get in the habit of pushing the voice button whenever you finish using the modem.

The VA212LC has several other features worth mentioning. First, and possibly most important, its User's Guide is good. This is a rarity in this industry and deserves special mention. The manual tells you exactly what you need to know, using English rather than technobabble. The technical information is there too, but it's at the back of the guide where it won't get in the way if you don't need it.

Second, the VA212LC has both self-test and remote-test capabilities. The self-test runs automatically whenever the modem is on but not being used. Should the modem detect a problem, it flashes the carrier detect light.

The remote-test feature allows a Racal-Vadic service center to run a test of the modem over the phone lines. All you have to do is call them if you seem to be having problems.

The VA212LC also has an answer mode, but only automatic answer—meaning, you can use the modem in answer mode but there's no way to get it there manually. You have to let it answer the phone and establish the communications automatically. To do this, you must connect line twenty on the RS-232 cable.

Also, oddly absent is an on-off switch. When the modem is plugged in, it is on. Period. This means you either have to leave it on all the time or you need a convenient outlet where you can plug it in and unplug it as necessary. Racal-Vadic tells me it was designed that way and that it uses "only" six watts.

This lack of an on-off switch reflects a common attitude in the industry— especially among companies that sell modems primarily for commercial rather than home use. Even modems with on-off switches have transformers that are on whenever they are plugged in. I have yet to see an exception to this. The only convenient way to get around it is to plug the transformer into a power strip with its own on-off switch.

Notes for Connecting to Computer: The VA212LC has a standard DB-25 connector wired as DCE. Connecting lines two, three, and seven will support most functions and will be adequate for most purposes. If you need to use the auto-answer capability of this modem, you will also need to connect line twenty. Line one, the protective ground, is not used. One warning: Although the DB-25 connector on the VA212LC is wired as DCE, it is labeled DTE. I asked Racal-Vadic about this and was told that the label means "Connect this to a piece of equipment wired as DTE." Oh.

Final Comments: Racal-Vadic has a full line of modems to meet just about any need. The VA212LC is only one example. Other models are listed at the end of this chapter.

BIZCOMP 1012

Manufacturer: BIZCOMP Corporation
532 Weddell Drive
Sunnyvale, CA 94086
Phone: (408) 745-1616.

Price: $649.

Availability: Call Bizcomp for closest dealer.

Baud Rate and Compatibilities:
110–300 baud, 103-compatible.
1200 baud, 212-compatible.

Connection to Phone System: Direct connect.

Connection to Computer: RS-232.

Duplex: Full only.

Modes: Manual originate, auto-originate (with auto-dial and auto repeat dial), manual answer, auto-answer.

Indicator Lights: A single indicator light serves several functions, depending on what you're doing with the modem at any given instant.

It acts as a power-on indicator by lighting up when you turn on the modem.
It acts as an off-hook indicator by turning off when the modem "picks up" the phone to dial.
It acts as a carrier detect light by lighting up again when a connection is established.
It acts as a receive detect light by flickering during reception of data.
Finally, it acts as an error indicator by blinking when an error is detected when in self-test mode.

FIGURE 15. Bizcomp 1012.

Switches: The 1012 has a single on-off switch. The modem is controlled primarily through electronic "switches" that are toggled on and off by typing instructions on your keyboard.

The modem also has several "Option Switches" on the back that control the default settings for various options when the modem is turned on. These are relatively difficult to get to, however. The idea is to set them once when you install the modem and otherwise leave them alone.

Connectors: The 1012 has one DB-25 connector for the RS-232 port, one connector for the power cord, and one female modular phone jack for connecting the modem to the phone system. (An appropriate telephone cord, with a male connector on each end, comes with the modem.) Since the modem itself can dial a number, you can use it without a phone. If you want to keep a phone at the same location, you connect both at the wall module, using a "Y" connector.

Description of Use: The Bizcomp 1012 is a sophisticated device that is capable of handling just about any application that requires a modem. In spite of its range of capabilities, though, the 1012 is still easy to use.

Bizcomp calls the 1012 the "Intelligent Modem" because it contains its own dedicated microcomputer, or processor chip. This chip is programmed to obey the instructions that you type at your keyboard.

Basically, to use the modem, you put your terminal, or terminal-emulator program, into interactive mode, then type the instructions to the modem.

Because of the way the option switches are set when the modem comes from the factory, the 1012 will power up at 1200 baud. For most people, though, I suspect that the "Autobaud" setting will be more useful. In this setting, the modem expects to see a carriage return as the first character after power is turned on. When it receives the carriage return, it will automatically set itself to match the baud rate of the terminal. The one drawback is that if you accidentally send a different character, the modem will often set itself to the wrong rate. If that happens, you simply turn the modem off, then on again to reset it.

Once you've set the baud rate, you type a "T" for test. The modem will run through a testing routine and give the response, "Fully Functional," on your screen. (You can skip this step if you want to, but it's simple enough and fast enough to make it worth the time.)

Dialing is also simple. Type "D," for dial, followed by the number of the information utility. The phone number will show on your screen, giving you a chance to check it or start over again. When you're satisfied that you've typed the number correctly, simply hit RETURN and the modem will dial it for you.

The 1012 will also keep you posted on what's going on, putting a "Dial Tone" message on your screen when it detects a dial tone and a "C" when the connection has been established. (You can abort dialing any time before that by hitting any key.)

Once a connection is established, you pretty much ignore the modem until you've signed off the utility. Then you hang up the phone by sending the disconnect command to the modem.

The disconnect command can be a problem since Bizcomp chose to use the sequence ^P D. Many terminal-emulator programs use ^P as a toggle to turn the printer on and off. These programs will "intercept" the ^P rather than send it to the modem.

There are two ways out of this problem. Some programs have a command that will let you send control characters that would normally be intercepted by the program. This is often known as a "literal" command since the next character typed will be sent "literally" rather than being interpreted. If your program has such a command (^L for instance), you can tell the 1012 to hang up by typing ^L^P^D.

If your program does not have a literal command, you can reprogram the Bizcomp to hang up at some other command. The reprogramming is easy to do. Unfortunately, the Bizcomp will not remember the command once it has been switched off, which means you have to reenter this command each time you turn the modem on. You can do this more or less automatically, though, if your terminal program can handle an automatic log on sequence. Simply add a few extra lines at the beginning of each file to "log on" to the modem and reprogram it.

Other Features and Comments: The 1012 is capable of dialing by pulse (like a rotary phone) or by tone. This is important because some systems—including a few local phone-company systems—are not yet capable of handling tone dialing, while other systems—including some long-distance networks like Sprint and MCI—require tone dialing. Unfortunately, there is no simple way to switch from pulse to tone in midstream with the 1012. This presents a problem if you must use pulse dialing on local lines in order to get to a system like Sprint, which requires tone dialing. Default on the 1012 is pulse dialing.

Much less important, but nice nonetheless, is the redial command; if you don't get through to the utility the first time, you can redial the number without having to type it in again. Simply enter "D" followed by a carriage return.

There is also a repeat command that will automatically redial a number (without your telling it to each time) and will keep redialing until the modem detects a carrier on the other end. This feature can help avoid a great deal of frustration if you are trying to get through to a utility at a particularly busy time of day, but it is not as useful as it might be. You still have to keep an eye on the screen or the modem light to know when a connection has been established. Ideally, I'd like the modem to beep at me or somesuch to get my attention when it finally gets through. Bizcomp tells me that the modem sends a command to the terminal so that *it* will beep at you instead, but that doesn't help much if your computer or terminal can't beep either. Mine can't.

The 1012 has other capabilities that are largely irrelevant for our purposes but should still be mentioned in passing. Manual originate will let you dial a number manually, then turn the modem on in originate mode. Manual answer will do much the same for you in answer mode. Automatic answer, on the other hand, is something you might want to disable if you don't plan to use it. As shipped, the option switches are set so that the 1012 will pick up the phone and squeal into the phone line unless it's told otherwise. If you're not using this feature, you'll probably want to reset the switch so that the modem won't go into automatic answer mode unless you tell it to.

The 1012 is also capable of synchronous operation plus a number of sophisticated self-test procedures that can help track down any problems that show up.

Notes for Connecting to Computer: The Bizcomp's DB-25 connector is wired as DCE. As with nearly all modems, connecting lines two, three, and seven is usually sufficient to support most functions of the modem. The Bizcomp manual points out that some terminals and computers need to have lines five, six, and eight connected as well. It then goes on to warn against connecting any additional lines since "improper control of these leads will cause the 1012 to operate incorrectly." True enough, but I tested the modem with two different cables, including one with the full twenty-five lines connected, and had no problems. Line one, the protective ground, is not used.

Final Comments: The one real problem you may have with the Bizcomp is not with the modem itself but with the reference manual that comes with it. If this is your first modem, the manual is going to be tough reading. Not only is there too much unnecessary technical material mixed in with the information you need, but the whole thing is printed in a small, difficult-to-read typeface. Once you make it through the manual, however, you'll find that the modem itself is easy to use.

Finally, Bizcomp has several other modems available. Two of these in particular are worth pointing out:

- The 1080 VersaModem is available with interface kits for several specific, popular machines. Each of these kits contains an appropriate cable for the particular machine. Most of the kits contain software as well.
- The other modem is the 2120. This is similar in capabilities to the 1012 but comes on a board for the IBM PC. One additional feature on the 2120 is the ability to switch from pulse dialing to tone dialing in midstream.

For further details on these and other Bizcomp modems, see the listing at the end of this chapter.

Hayes Smartmodem 1200 and 1200B

Manufacturer: Hayes Microcomputer Products, Inc.
5923 Peachtree Industrial Blvd.
Norcross, GA 30092
Phone: (404) 449-8791

Price: $699.

Availability: Computer retail stores.
Also available through mail-order discount houses.

Baud Rate and Compatibilities:
0-300 baud, 103-compatible.
1200 baud, 212-compatible.

Connection to Phone System: Direct connect.

Connection to Computer: RS-232.

Duplex: Full or half.

Modes:

Manual originate.

Auto-originate (with automatic dial).

Manual answer.

Auto-answer.

"Reverse mode"—automatic dial, but comes up in answer mode. (This is useful for calling an originate-only modem.)

Indicator Lights:

High speed (HS)—indicates when modem is set at 1200 baud. (Smartmodem 1200 only.)

Automatic answer (AA)—indicates when modem is set to automatically answer the phone.

Off-hook (OH)—indicates when modem has "picked up" the phone.

Carrier detect (CD).

Receive data (RD)—indicates when modem receives data.

Send data (SD)—indicates when modem is sending data.

Terminal ready (TR)—indicates that the terminal is ready to send or receive data.

Modem ready (MR)—indicates that modem is on and ready.

Switches: The Smartmodem 1200 has a single on-off switch. As with the Bizcomp 1012, the Smartmodem is controlled by electronic "switches" that are toggled on and off by typing instructions on your keyboard.

As with the 1012 also, the Smartmodem 1200 has several option switches (Hayes calls them "configuration switches"). These are meant to be set once when you install the modem and otherwise left alone. On the Smartmodem 1200 these switches are located inside the modem. The manual gives clear, detailed instructions about them: where they are, how to get to them, and how to set them.

Connectors: The Smartmodem 1200 has one DB-25 connector for the RS-232 port, one connector for the power cord, and one female modular phone jack for connecting the modem to the phone system. (An appropriate telephone cord, with a male connector on each end, comes with the modem.) Since the modem itself can dial a number, you can use it without a phone, but as with the Bizcomp, if you want to keep a phone at the same location, you connect both at the wall module, using a "Y" connector.

Description of Use: If there is such a thing as *the* standard for modems in the personal computer market, the Hayes Smartmodem 1200 is it.

As the name implies, the Hayes Smartmodem, like the Bizcomp Intelligent Modem, contains its own dedicated microcomputer, or processor chip. Here again, the chip is programmed to obey instructions that you type in at the keyboard. The commands themselves are different, but the capabilities are much the same.

Using the Smartmodem is much like using the Bizcomp 1012; you put your terminal or terminal-emulator program into interactive mode, then type instructions to the modem.

To test the modem, for example, you type "AT" (for ATtention), followed by a return. The modem runs through a self-test. If there are no problems, it responds with "OK."

To dial, you enter "AT D" followed by the number to be dialed.

To use tone dialing rather than pulse dialing, you enter a "T" after the "D."

The Smartmodem keeps you posted during dialing not so much by putting messages on the screen as by letting you listen to what's going on. A built-in speaker lets you hear the dial tone, the number being dialed, the phone ringing on the other end, and—finally—the modems establishing communications. Normally the speaker cuts off at that point, but you can set the Smartmodem so that the speaker stays on. If you'd rather not hear the connection being made, you can also set the modem so the speaker never comes on.

When the connection is made, the modem puts the message "CONNECT" on your screen. If the connection is not established, it puts the message "NO CARRIER" on your screen.

Once you've established connection, you can, here again, pretty much ignore the modem. If you find that you have to talk to the modem, though—to change it from full duplex to half duplex for example—you can do it without hanging up. A special command (default is + + +) puts the modem in "local command state," meaning that it will interpret your commands instead of passing them through the phone line. You can make whatever changes you need to make, then go back on-line with the on-line command.

When you've signed off the utility, you tell the Smartmodem to hang up the phone by first putting it in the local command state and then sending the hang-up command.

Other Features and Comments: As you've probably gathered by now, the Bizcomp 1012 and the Hayes Smartmodem 1200 are comparable devices. Still, each has capabilities that the other lacks. The Smartmodem, for example, does not have an auto-repeat dial command and is not capable of synchronous communications.

On the other hand, the Smartmodem has the ability to switch from pulse dialing to tone dialing in midstream, which makes it easy to use when local lines require pulse but long-distance carriers like Sprint or MCI require tone dialing. It also sets itself automatically to the correct baud rate—meaning whatever your terminal or computer is set at. These are both valuable capabilities.

The Bizcomp 1012 and the Hayes Smartmodem also reflect different design philosophies. The Bizcomp 1012 was clearly designed for the user who isn't interested in, and may be confused by, extra lights on the modem. The Hayes Smartmodem was just as clearly designed for users who aren't scared away by the extra lights and, in fact, might miss the additional information they provide. The difference is a matter of individual preference—on about the same level as whether you prefer your car dashboard to have a tachometer or not.

There's one other advantage of the Smartmodem that should not be discounted. Because it is so popular, there are several terminal programs that are specifically designed to support it. If you're using one of these programs, you can pretty much forget about the commands for the modem and just follow the directions in the terminal program. The program itself will add the appropriate commands for dial, pulse, tone, or whatever.

Notes for Connecting to Computer: The Smartmodem's DB-25 connector is wired as DCE. Here again, as with nearly all modems, connecting lines two, three, and seven is usually sufficient to support most functions of the modem. The Smartmodem can also make use of other lines. In particular, it uses line one (the protective ground) and line twenty (data terminal ready). If you'd rather not bother with line twenty, you can set the appropriate configuration switch so that as far as the modem is concerned, the terminal is always on.

Hayes Smartmodem 1200B

The Hayes Smartmodem 1200B has all the capabilities of the Smartmodem 1200. The major difference is that it is mounted on a board that fits into the IBM PC. The 1200B comes with Smartcom II.

Hayes Smartmodem 300

The Hayes Smartmodem 300 and the Smartmodem 1200 are nearly identical in description and operation except that the Smartmodem is 300-baud, 103-compatible only. Except for comments relating to communications at 1200 baud, the above review applies to both the Smartmodem 300 and the Smartmodem 1200.

A SHORT CATALOG OF MODEMS

Here, finally, is a list of about 70 modems. As long as this list seems to be, it comes nowhere near covering every available 103- or 212-compatible modem. It does, however, cover modems in a wide range of capabilities and prices and should serve as a good starting point if you're shopping for a modem.

One comment about this list. With few exceptions, the 103-compatible modems here have a maximum speed of 300 baud. Many of these are limited to operating at 300 baud only. Others can operate at any speed between 0 and 300 baud. Still others can operate at some, but not all, of the standard speeds between 0 and 300 baud. Since there is no reason to communicate with an information utility at less than 300 baud, I've generally sidestepped the issue by listing the 103-compatible modems as "300 baud." The only exceptions to this are those few 103-compatible modems that have faster maximum baud rates. In those cases I have indicated the entire range.

Anchor   Signalman   Price: $99.

Manufacturer: Anchor Automation
6913 Valjean St.
Van Nuys, CA 91406
Phone: (213) 997-6493

Direct connect.
Modes: Answer, originate.
Duplex: Full only.
Compatibilities: Bell 103/113.
Baud rate: 300.
RS-232: Yes.
Comments: The RS-232 version of the Signalman comes with a ribbon cable ending in a male DB-25 connector. There are also versions available for the PET/CBM, TI-99/4A, Osborne I and II, IBM PC, and Atari. Each version comes with appropriate cable and connector for the specific machine.

Anderson Jacobson   AJ 247   Price: $295.

Manufacturer: Anderson Jacobson, Inc.
521 Charcot Ave.
San Jose, CA 95131
Phone: (800) 538-9721
(408) 263-8520 (in California)

Direct connect *and* acoustic coupler—switch-selectable.
Modes: Originate only.
Duplex: Full, half.
Compatibilities: Bell 103/113.
Baud rate: 0-450.
RS-232: Yes.

Anderson Jacobson   AJ 347   Price: $365.

Direct connect *and* acoustic coupler—switch-selectable.
Modes: Answer, originate, auto-answer.
Duplex: Full only.
Compatibilities: Bell 103/113.
Baud rate: 0-450.
RS-232: Yes.

Anderson Jacobson   AJ 1233   Price: $845.

Direct connect *and* acoustic coupler—switch-selectable.
Modes: Originate only.
Duplex: Full only.
Compatibilities: Bell 103/113, Bell 212, Racal-Vadic VA3400.
Baud rate: 300, 1200.
RS-232: Yes.

Anderson Jacobson   AJ 1235   Price: $795.

Direct connect *and* acoustic coupler—switch-selectable.
Modes: Originate only.
Duplex: Full only.
Compatibilities: Bell 103/113, Racal-Vadic VA3400.
Baud rate: 300, 1200.
RS-232: Yes.
Comments: Uses Racal-Vadic protocol at 1200 baud.

Anderson Jacobson   AJ 1259   Price: $695.

Direct connect.
Modes: Originate, auto-answer.
Duplex: Full only.
Compatibilities: Bell 103/113, Bell 212, Racal-Vadic VA3400.
Baud rate: 300, 1200.
RS-232: Yes.
Comments: Triple modem.

Anderson Jacobson   AJ 1259-AD   Price: $775.

Direct connect.
Modes: Originate, auto-answer, auto-dial.
Duplex: Full only.
Compatibilities: Bell 103/113, Bell 212, Racal-Vadic VA3400.
Baud rate: 300, 1200.
RS-232: Yes.

Atari   1030   Price: $199.95

Manufacturer: Atari
                1265 Borregas Ave.
                Sunnyvale, CA 94086
                Phone: (408) 745-2000
Direct connect.
Modes: Answer, originate. Also allows dialing from the keyboard.
Duplex: Full, half.
Compatibilities: Bell 103/113.
Baud rate: 300.
RS-232: No.
Plug-in: For all Atari computers. Comes with cable for Atari SIO bus connector.
Comments: The 1030 contains its own communications program (on a ROM chip).

Atari   830   Price: $199.95

Acoustic coupler.
Modes: Answer, originate.
Duplex: Full, half.
Compatibilities: Bell 103/113.
Baud rate: 300.
RS-232: Yes.
Comments: Comes with cable for attachment to Atari 850 interface. This has a DB-25 connector on one end and DB-9 on the other to plug into the 850.

Atari   835   Price: $279.95

Direct connect.
Modes: Answer, originate, auto-dial.
Duplex: Full, half.
Compatibilities: Bell 103/113.
Baud rate: 300.
RS-232: No.
Plug-in: For all Atari computers. Comes with cable for Atari SIO bus connector.
Comments: This is available only as part of Atari's Communicator II package.

Bizcomp   1012   Price: $649.

Manufacturer: Bizcomp Corporation
             532 Weddell Drive
             Sunnyvale, CA 94086
             Phone: (408) 745-1616
Direct connect.
Modes: Answer, originate, auto-answer, auto-dial, repeat dial.
Duplex: Full only.
Compatibilities: Bell 103/113, Bell 212.
Baud rate: 300, 1200.
RS-232: Yes.
Comments: For futher details, see the review earlier in this chapter.

Bizcomp   1022   Price: $249.

Direct connect.
Modes: Answer, originate, auto-answer, auto-dial, repeat dial.
Duplex: Full only.
Compatibilities: Bell 103/113.
Baud rate: 300.
RS-232: Yes.

Bizcomp   1080 VersaModem   Price: $139.

Direct connect.
Modes: Originate.
Duplex: Full only.
Compatibilities: Bell 103/113.
Baud rate: 300.
RS-232: Yes.
Comments: In addition to being available with a standard RS-232 interface, the 1080 is available with interface kits for the Atari 850 Interface Module, the Apple II game jack, the Commodore 64 or VIC-20 User Port, and the Commodore CBM or PET User Port. (This is a different User Port.) The Apple II interface kit and both Commodore interface kits come with communications software.

Bizcomp   2120   Price: $499.

Direct connect.
Modes: Answer, originate, auto-answer, auto-dial, repeat dial.
Duplex: Full only.
Compatibilities: Bell 103/113, Bell 212.
Baud rate: 300, 1200.
RS-232: No.
Comments: The 2120 is a modem-on-a-board for the IBM PC.

Commodore   VICMODEM   Price: $109.95

Manufacturer: Commodore Business Machines
               487 Devon Park Drive
               Wayne, PA 19087
               Phone: (215) 431-9100
Direct connect.
Modes: Answer, originate.
Duplex: Full, half.
Compatibilities: Bell 103/113.
Baud rate: 300.
RS-232: No.
Comments: The VICMODEM plugs directly into the User Port on either the VIC-20 or the Commodore 64.

Commodore   Automatic Modem 1650   Price: $149.95

Direct connect.
Modes: Answer, originate, auto-dial, auto-answer.
Duplex: Full, half.
Compatibilities: Bell 103/113.
Baud rate: 300.

Commodore   Automatic Modem 1650 (cont'd.)
RS-232: No.
Comments: The Automatic Modem plugs directly into the User Port on either the VIC-20 or the Commodore 64.

Hayes   Micromodem 100   Price: $399.

Manufacturer: Hayes Microcomputer Products
            5923 Peachtree Industrial Blvd.
            Norcross, GA 30092
            Phone: (404) 449-8791
Direct connect.
Modes: Answer, originate, auto-answer, auto-dial.
Duplex: Full, half.
Compatibilities: Bell 103/113.
Baud rate: 300.
RS-232: No.
Comments: This is a modem-on-a-board for S-100 systems.

Hayes   Micromodem IIe   Price: $329.

Direct connect.
Modes: Answer, originate, auto-answer, auto-dial.
Duplex: Full, half.
Compatibilities: Bell 103/113.
Baud rate: 300.
RS-232: No.
Comments: This is a modem-on-a-board for the Apple II, Apple II Plus, Apple IIe, and Apple III.

Hayes   Smartmodem 1200   Price: $699.

Direct connect.
Modes: Answer, originate, auto-answer, auto-dial, reverse auto-dial. (Dials, then goes to answer mode.)
Duplex: Full, half.
Compatibilities: Bell 103/113, Bell 212.
Baud rate: 300, 1200.
RS-232: Yes.
Comments: For details, see review earlier in this chapter.

Hayes   Smartmodem 1200B   Price: $599.

Direct connect.
Modes: Answer, originate, auto-answer, auto-dial, reverse auto-dial. (Dials, then goes to answer mode.)

Hayes   Smartmodem 1200B (cont'd.)

Duplex: Full, half.

Compatibilities: Bell 103/113, Bell 212.

Baud rate: 300, 1200.

RS-232: No.

Comments: The Smartmodem 1200B has the same capabilities as the Smartmodem 1200. The major difference is that the 1200B is mounted on a board for the IBM PC. Also, the 1200B comes with Smartcom II and with an optional phone jack.

Hayes   Smartmodem 300   Price: $289.

Direct connect.

Modes: Answer, originate, auto-answer, auto-dial, reverse auto-dial. (Dials, then goes to answer mode.)

Duplex: Full, half.

Compatibilities: Bell 103/113.

Baud rate: 300.

RS-232: Yes.

Comments: This has essentially the same capabilities as the Smartmodem 1200 except that it is limited to Bell 103-compatible, 300-baud operation.

Lexicon Corp.   Lex-11   Price: $175.

Manufacturer: Lexicon Corporation of Miami
             1541 Northwest 65th Ave.
             Ft. Lauderdale, FL 33313
             Phone: (800) 327-8913
                    (305) 822-6665 (in Florida)

Acoustic coupler.

Modes: Answer, originate.

Duplex: Full, half.

Compatibilities: Bell 103/113.

Baud rate: 300.

RS-232: Yes.

MFJ Enterprises, Inc.   MFJ-1232   Price: $129.95

Manufacturer: MFJ Enterprises, Inc.
             921 Louisville Rd.
             Starkville, MS 39759
             Phone: (800) 647-1800

Acoustic coupler.

Modes: Answer, originate.

Duplex: Full, half.

Compatibilities: Bell 103/113.

Baud rate: 300.

MFJ Enterprises, Inc.   MFJ-1232 (cont'd.)

RS-232: Yes.

  Can also use with Apple II without an RS-232 interface.

Comments: The MFJ-1232 is an RS-232 modem. An optional addition, MFJ-1231, includes software for the Apple II, and a cable that allows you to plug the modem into the Apple II game port. The MFJ-1231 modification costs $39.95.

Microcom   ERA 2 Communications Package   Price: See comments.

Manufacturer: MICROCOM, Inc.
              1400A Providence Highway
              Norwood, MA 02062
              Phone: (617) 762-9310

Direct connect.

Modes: Answer, originate, auto-answer, auto-dial, reverse dial.

Duplex: Full, half.

Compatibilities: Bell 103/113, Bell 212.

Baud rate: 300, 1200.

RS-232: No.

Comments: The ERA 2 Communications Package includes both a 300/1200-baud modem and a smart terminal program. Software features include auto-dial, auto-log on, protocol file transfer, and other, more sophisticated capabilities. (These include unattended operation and emulation of the VT100 series DEC terminals and the IBM 3101 terminal.) The package comes in various machine-specific versions for the Apple IIe, the IBM PC, and the new IBM home computer. As of this writing, plans are to make ERA 2 available for other machines "as demand warrants." Check with MICROCOM for the current list.

  Prices for the ERA 2 Communications Package vary, depending on the machine. The Apple IIe and IBM home computer versions are $399. The IBM PC version is $499.

Microperipheral   Microconnection   Price: See comments.

Manufacturer: The Microperipheral Corporation
              2565 152nd Ave., N.E.
              Redmond, WA 98052
              Phone: (206) 881-7544

Direct connect.

Modes: Answer, originate. (Auto-answer and auto-dial capabilities are also available at extra cost.)

Duplex: Full only.

Compatibilities: Bell 103/113.

Baud rate: 300.

RS-232: Yes.

Comments: The Microconnection comes in several variations besides the RS-232 version. These include versions for the Atari SIO bus connector, the

Microperipheral   Microconnention (cont'd.)

Commodore 64/VIC-20, the TRS-80 Model I, and the TRS-80 Color Computer. Most of these come with cables and an appropriate dumb terminal program. Prices begin at $149.95 and vary with the particular version.

Microperipheral   PConnection   Price: $170.

Direct connect.
Modes: Answer, originate, auto-answer, auto-dial, reverse dial.
Duplex: Full only.
Compatibilities: Bell 103/113.
Baud rate: 300.
Comments: This is a modem-on-a-board for the IBM PC only. It comes with a dumb terminal program.

Multi-Tech   FM-31   Price: $265.

Manufacturer: Multi-Tech Systems, Inc.
               82 Second Ave., SE
               New Brighton, MN 55112
               Phone: (612) 631-3550
Acoustic coupler.
Modes: Answer, originate.
Duplex: Full, half.
Compatibilities: Bell 103/113.
Baud rate: 300.
RS-232: Yes.

Multi-Tech   FM30   Price: $225.

Acoustic coupler.
Modes: Originate only.
Duplex: Full, half.
Compatibilities: Bell 103/113.
Baud rate: 300.
RS-232: Yes.

Multi-Tech   MT103J   Price: $295.

Direct connect.
Modes: Originate, auto-answer.
Duplex: Full, half.
Compatibilities: Bell 103/113.
Baud rate: 300.
RS-232: Yes.

Multi-Tech   MT113C   Price: $235.

Direct connect.
Modes: Originate only.
Duplex: Full, half.
Compatibilities: Bell 103/113.
Baud rate: 300.
RS-232: Yes.

Multi-Tech   MT113D   Price: $275.

Direct connect.
Modes: Auto-answer only.
Duplex: Full, half.
Compatibilities: Bell 103/113.
Baud rate: 300.
RS-232: Yes.

Multi-Tech   MT212A   Price: $670.

Direct connect.
Modes: Answer, originate, auto-answer, auto-dial.
Duplex: Full only.
Compatibilities: Bell 103/113, Bell 212.
Baud rate: 300, 1200.
RS-232: Yes.

Multi-Tech   MT212D   Price: $635.

Direct connect.
Modes: Answer, originate, auto-answer.
Duplex: Full only.
Compatibilities: Bell 212.
Baud rate: 1200.
RS-232: Yes.
Comments: Notice that this is strictly 1200-baud, 212-compatible.

Multi-Tech   Modem II   Price: $399.

Direct connect.
Modes: Originate, auto-answer, auto-dial.
Duplex: Full, half.
Compatibilities: Bell 103/113.
Baud rate: 300.
RS-232: No.

Multi-Tech   Modem II (cont'd.)

Comments: This is a modem-on-a-board for the Apple II. The board also contains a communications program as firmware—that is, written on a ROM chip.

Novation   103 SMART-CAT   Price: $249.

Manufacturer: Novation, Inc.
　　　　　　　20409 Prairie St.
　　　　　　　Chatsworth, CA 91311
　　　　　　　Phone: (800) 423-5419
　　　　　　　　　　　(213) 996-5060 (in California)

Direct connect.
Modes: Answer, originate, auto-answer, auto-dial.
Duplex: Full only.
Compatibilities: Bell 103/113.
Baud rate: 300.
RS-232: Yes.

Novation   103/212 SMART-CAT   Price: $595.

Direct connect.
Modes: Answer, originate, auto-answer, auto-dial.
Duplex: Full only.
Compatibilities: Bell 103/113, Bell 212.
Baud rate: 300, 1200.
RS-232: Yes.

Novation   Apple-CAT II   Price: $389.

Direct connect.
Modes: Answer, originate, auto-answer, auto-dial, redial.
Duplex: Full, half.
Compatibilities: Bell 103/113, Bell 202.
Baud rate: 300, 1200.
RS-232: No.
Comments: This is a modem-on-a-board for the Apple II. Notice that this is a 103-compatible and 202-compatible modem. A second board is available to add 212 compatibility, which turns this into the 212 Apple-CAT II. If purchased separately, the second board is also $389.

Novation   212 Apple-CAT II   Price: $725.

Direct connect.
Modes: Answer, originate, auto-answer, auto-dial, redial.
Duplex: Full, half.
Compatibilities: Bell 103/113, Bell 212, Bell 202.
Baud rate: 300, 1200.

Novation   212 Apple-Cat II (cont'd.)

RS-232: No.

Comments: This is a modem-on-a-board for the Apple II. (Actually on two boards. See the comments under the Apple-CAT II.)

Novation   212 AUTO-CAT   Price: $695.

Direct connect.
Modes: Answer, originate, auto-answer.
Duplex: Full only.
Compatibilities: Bell 103/113,, Bell 212.
Baud rate: 300, 1200.
RS-232: Yes.

Novation   CAT Acoustic   Price: $189.

Acoustic coupler.
Modes: Answer, originate.
Duplex: Full, half.
Compatibilities: Bell 103/113.
Baud rate: 300.
RS-232: Yes.

Novation   D-CAT   Price: $199.

Direct connect.
Modes: Answer, originate.
Duplex: Full, half.
Compatibilities: Bell 103/113.
Baud rate: 300.
RS-232: Yes.

Novation   J-CAT   Price: $149.

Direct connect.
Modes: Answer, originate, auto-answer, auto-dial.
Duplex: Full only.
Compatibilities: Bell 103/113.
Baud rate: 300.
RS-232: See comments.
Comments: The J-CAT uses something called TTL level signals, not RS-232 signals. These will work on some RS-232 ports but not on others, depending on the range of variation allowed in the design of the port. Novation says that the J-CAT will work with the Atari 850 Interface Module, some Apple boards (including the CCS 7710), some IBM boards, the Fortune, the Eagle II, the TI-99/4A RS-232 interface, the Radio Shack Color Computer, and the communications port on the Osborne I and II. (It will not work with the printer port on

Novation   J-CAT (cont'd.)

the Osborne I and II. The Osborne communications port uses the DB-9 connector.)

Novation also says that the J-CAT will work with the RS-232 ports on IBM PC boards from the following companies:

Personal Systems Technology
Apparat
Quadramn Corp.
AST Research
Seattle Computer
Chrislin Industries
PC Square
Tecmar, Inc.
STB Systems, Incorporated

It will not work with the boards from these companies:

Sigma Designs
Automated Business Machines, Inc.
Datamac Computer Systems
Alpha Byte

It also will not work with the standard RS-232 board from IBM.

Racal-Vadic   212LC   Price: $495.

Manufacturer: Racal-Vadic Inc.
              1524 McCarthy Blvd.
              Milpitas, CA 95035
              Phone: (408) 946-2227
Direct connect.
Modes: Originate, auto-answer.
Duplex: Full only.
Compatibilities: Bell 103/113, Bell 212.
Baud rate: 300, 1200.
RS-232: Yes.
Comments: See the review on the 212LC earlier in this chapter.

Racal-Vadic   212PA   Price: $695.

Direct connect.
Modes: Answer, originate, auto-answer, auto-dial.
Duplex: Full only.
Compatibilities: Bell 103/113, Bell 212.
Baud rate: 300, 1200.
RS-232: Yes.

Racal-Vadic   VA 3451   Price: $875.

Direct connect.
Modes: Answer, originate, auto-dial.
Duplex: Full only.
Compatibilities: Bell 103/113, Bell 212, Racal-Vadic VA3400.
Baud rate: 300, 1200.
RS-232: Yes.

Racal-Vadic   VA3413   Price: $695.

Acoustic coupler.
Modes: Answer, originate.
Duplex: Full only.
Compatibilities: Bell 103/113, Racal-Vadic VA3400.
Baud rate: 300, 1200.
RS-232: Yes.

Racal-Vadic   VA355   Price: $375.

Direct connect.
Modes: Answer, originate.
Duplex: Full only.
Compatibilities: Bell 103/113.
Baud rate: 300.
RS-232: Yes.

Radio Shack   DC-1200   Price: $699.

Manufacturer: Radio Shack
              One Tandy Center
              Forth Worth, TX 76102
              Phone: (817) 390-3011
Direct connect.
Modes: Originate, auto-answer. Auto-dial module available at extra cost ($149.95).
Duplex: Full, half.
Compatibilities: Bell 103/113, Bell 212.
Baud rate: 300, 1200.
RS-232: Yes.

Radio Shack   Modem I   Price: $99.95

Direct connect.
Modes: Answer, originate.
Duplex: Full only.
Compatibilities: Bell 103/113.

Radio Shack   Modem I (cont'd.)

Baud rate: 300.

RS-232: Yes.

Comments: The Modem I has two RS-232 ports. One of these is designed for use with the TRS-80 Color Computer. For more details, see the review of the Modem I in Chapter 3.

Radio Shack   Modem II   Price: $249.

Direct connect.

Modes: Answer, originate, auto-answer, auto-dial.

Duplex: Full, half.

Compatibilities: Bell 103/113.

Baud rate: 300.

RS-232: Yes.

Radio Shack   Acoustic Coupler   Price: $149.95

Acoustic coupler.

Modes: Answer, originate.

Duplex: Full, half.

Compatibilities: Bell 103/113.

Baud rate: 300.

RS-232: Yes.

Rixon   T103J   Price: $595.

Manufacturer: Rixon Inc.
2120 Industrial Parkway
Silver Spring, MD 20904
Phone: (301) 622-2121

Direct connect.

Modes: Answer, originate, auto-answer.

Duplex: Full only.

Compatibilities: Bell 103/113.

Baud rate: 300.

RS-232: Yes.

Rixon   R103J   Price: $249.

Direct connect.

Modes: Answer, originate, auto-answer.

Duplex: Full only.

Compatibilities: Bell 103/113.

Rixon   R103J (cont'd.)

Baud rate: 300.
RS-232: Yes.

Rixon   RA212A   Price: $499.

Direct connect.
Modes: Answer, originate, auto-answer, auto-dial.
Duplex: Full only.
Compatibilities: Bell 103/113, 212.
Baud rate: 300, 1200.
RS-232: Yes.
Comments: Uses pulse or tone dialing. Can change in midstream. Uses Hayes protocols, which means it will work with software designed for the Hayes Smartmodem.

Rixon   T212A   Price: $795.

Direct connect.
Modes: Answer, originate, auto-answer.
Duplex: Full only.
Compatibilities: Bell 103/113, Bell 212.
Baud rate: 300, 1200.
RS-232: Yes.

Rixon   TA-212   Price: $685.

Direct connect.
Modes: Answer, originate, auto-answer.
Duplex: Full only.
Compatibilities: Bell 103/113, Bell 212.
Baud rate: 300, 1200.
RS-232: Yes.

TIMECOR   The Operator   Price: $159.95

Manufacturer: The International Modem Exchange Corp.
            P.O. Box 8928
            Boston, MA 02114
            Phone: (617) 720-3600
Modes: Answer, originate, auto-answer, auto-dial.
Duplex: Full, half.
Compatibilities: Bell 103/113.
Baud rate: 300.
RS-232: No.

TIMECOR   The Operator (cont'd.)

Comments: Another modem-on-a-board for the Apple II. Comes with "start-up" communications programs on disk.

Transend Corporation   Apple ModemCard   Price: $325.

Manufacturer: Transend Corporation
2190 Paragon Drive
San Jose, CA 95131
Phone: (408) 946-7400

Direct connect.

Modes: Auto-answer, auto-dial.

Duplex: Full, half.

Compatibilities: Bell 103/113.

Baud rate: 300.

RS-232: No.

Comments: This is another modem-on-a-board for the Apple II. Features include tone and pulse dialing, audio monitor. Comes with a subscription to THE SOURCE.

U.S. Robotics   Auto Dial 212A   Price: $599.

Manufacturer: U.S. Robotics, Inc.
1123 West Washington
Chicago, IL 60607
Phone: (312) 733-0497

Direct connect.

Modes: Answer, originate, auto-answer, auto-dial.

Duplex: Full, half.

Compatibilities: Bell 103/113, Bell 212.

Baud rate: 300, 1200.

RS-232: Yes.

U.S. Robotics   Auto Link 212A   Price: $549.

Direct connect.

Modes: Answer, originate, auto-answer.

Duplex: Full, half.

Compatibilities: Bell 103/113, Bell 212.

Baud rate: 300, 1200.

RS-232: Yes.

U.S. Robotics   Auto Link 1200   Price: $499.

Direct connect.

Modes: Answer, originate, auto-answer.

Duplex: Full, half.

U.S. Robotics   Auto Link 1200 (cont'd.)
Compatibilities: Bell 212.
Baud rate: 1200.
RS-232: Yes.

U.S. Robotics   Micro Link 1200   Price: $449.

Direct connect.
Modes: Answer, originate.
Duplex: Full, half.
Compatibilities: Bell 212.
Baud rate: 1200.
RS-232: Yes.

U.S. Robotics   Auto Link 300   Price: $269.

Direct connect.
Modes: Answer, originate, auto-answer.
Duplex: Full, half.
Compatibilities: Bell 103/113.
Baud rate: 300.
RS-232: Yes.

U.S. Robotics   Micro Link 300   Price: $239.

Direct connect.
Modes: Answer, originate.
Duplex: Full, half.
Compatibilities: Bell 103/113.
Baud rate: 300.
RS-232: Yes.

U.S. Robotics   Phone Link   Price: $189.

Acoustic coupler.
Modes: Answer, originate.
Duplex: Full, half.
Compatibilities: Bell 103/113.
Baud rate: 300.
RS-232: Yes.

U.S. Robotics   Password   Price: $449.

Direct connect.
Modes: Answer, originate, auto-answer, auto-dial.
Duplex: Full, half.
Compatibilities: Bell 103/113, Bell 212.

U.S. Robotics   Password (cont'd.)

Baud rate: 300, 1200.

RS-232: Yes.

Comments: Comes complete with RS-232 cable. One nice touch is a switch on the modem to "cross" lines two and three to match the wiring in your computer's RS-232 ports. This frees you from having to worry about the cabling.

U.S. Robotics   S-100   Price: $499.

Direct connect.

Modes: Answer, originate, auto-answer, auto-dial.

Duplex: Full, half.

Compatibilities: Bell 103/113, Bell 212.

Baud rate: 300, 1200.

RS-232: No.

Comments: This is a 103/113, 212-compatible modem-on-a-board for any system with an S-100 bus structure.

UDS   103-O/A LP   Price: $145.

Manufacturer: Universal Data Systems
5000 Bradford Drive
Huntsville, AL 35805
Phone: (205) 837-8100

Direct connect.

Modes: Answer, originate.

Duplex: Full only.

Compatibilities: Bell 103/113.

Baud rate: 300.

RS-232: Yes.

UDS   103J LP   Price: $195.

Direct connect.

Modes: Answer, originate, auto answer.

Duplex: Full only.

Compatibilities: Bell 103/113.

Baud rate: 300.

RS-232: Yes.

UDS   212LP   Price: $445.

Direct connect.

Modes: Answer, originate.

Duplex: Full only.

Compatibilities: Bell 212.

UDS   212LP (cont'd.)
Baud rate: 1200.
RS-232: Yes.
Comments: Note that this is 1200 baud *only*.

UDS   212A   Price: $675.

Direct connect.
Modes: Answer, originate, auto-answer.
Duplex: Full only.
Compatibilities: Bell 103/113, Bell 212.
Baud rate: 300, 1200.
RS-232: Yes.

UDS   212A/D   Price: $745.

Direct connect.
Modes: Answer, originate, auto-answer, auto-dial, redial.
Duplex: Full only.
Compatibilities: Bell 103/113, Bell 212.
Baud rate: 300, 1200.
RS-232: Yes.

7

SEARCH STRATEGY

There's an old saw that time is money. When you're using a data base, that truism is compounded several times over. First, you are paying for the use of the phone, which is a time charge. Second, the cost for use of the data base itself is, with few exceptions, a time charge. Third, you are probably using either Tymnet, Telenet, or Uninet, which is also a time charge. (That's true whether you're paying for it directly or the utility is paying for it, in which case it has already been figured into the cost-per-hour of the utility.)

If you're playing a game or using CB emulation on one of the consumer-oriented data bases, you'll generally be paying between $5 and $10 an hour (at nighttime rates). This is not an overwhelming amount of money, and should come out of your entertainment budget in any case.

When you're looking for information, though, the price goes up. A common minimum price for information-oriented data bases on various utilities is $20 to $40 per hour. Rates can go over $100 an hour on some data bases. Even the "consumer-oriented" utilities like THE SOURCE or Delphi have daytime rates of $20 an hour and up.

Obviously, if you're searching for information, it pays to be efficient. In the information-retrieval business, this is known as developing a good search strategy.

"Search strategy" is one of those labels that sounds more meaningful than it is. Anytime you look for information, you are following a search strategy. If you look up a word in a dictionary, for example, you start with what you think is the right spelling. If you don't find it, the next step might be to look it up under another spelling, or to scan the words in the vicinity where you thought it should be, or to go to another dictionary. Each of these choices represents a different search strategy, and each is appropriate under certain conditions.

Developing a good search strategy is an individual achievement. It is based on your own mix of common sense, knowledge, and experience—all of which must be applied at every step in the process, starting with deciding where to look for the information.

To look up a word in a dictionary, for example, you have to know that a dictionary is an appropriate place to look. But if you are specifically checking for spelling, it helps even more if you know that there are special spelling dictionaries that list words without defining them. And if you can't find the word right away, it helps to have some sense of other possible spellings, based on rules of thumb about "ie" and "ei," or the knowledge that a word that sounds like "zylophone" can actually be spelled "xylophone."

The point is that search strategy is a skill that you keep improving each time you use it. More than that, since you will most likely be searching in subjects that you are familiar with, you already have much of the background you need: If you're a chemist, you already know what to expect from a data base labeled Chemical Abstracts. If you're not a chemist, there's not much reason to be looking there.

Still, no matter how individual each person's search strategy ultimately is, there are some general rules of thumb that apply to nearly everyone. Here are a few hints on how to save time and money.

BEFORE YOU GO ON-LINE

Start with the obvious. **Fees for many information systems vary with the time of day.** So do phone rates. Unless you absolutely must have the information immediately, wait until the rates are lowest. Checking the value of your stock on Dow Jones, for example, will cost you 90 cents a minute ($54 per hour) from 6:00 A.M. to 6:00 P.M., your local time. Wait until after 6:00 P.M., and it will cost only 15 cents a minute ($9 per hour).

The information you need may be available from more than one data base. If you're looking for more information on a news story that you just heard on the radio, you could probably find it on the AP data base *or* the UPI data base *or* on any of several electronic newspapars. In each case, you have to have an appropriate password beforehand, but in deciding which passwords to get and then determining which utility to use, take the time to figure out which data base is cheaper (or cheapest). And once you've figured out the costs, write them down so you won't have to do the calculation again next time.

While you're figuring out the cost of using a data base, don't forget to add in the communications cost—including the cost of the phone call.

This gets a little complicated, but you have to figure it out only once (or once for each rate change on each utility you use).

Some utilities let you call them direct, others do not. Small utilities, including bulletin-board systems, generally don't give you any other choice. Most large utilities let you call through one or more of the three major communications networks: Tymnet, Telenet, and Uninet. Some utilities have their own network as well.

If the utility you're using doesn't include a separate charge for the communications network, it doesn't matter how you call. You can base your choice strictly on the cost of the phone call itself. If the utility does charge separately for the communications network, though, the difference is often measured in several dollars per hour. On BRS, for example, the current charges vary from a low of $3 per hour for direct dialing to a high of $11 per hour for calling through Tymnet. The charges for Uninet and Telenet fall somewhere between these extremes. (These charges are specific to BRS. Other systems charge different amounts for the same networks.)

All other things being equal, you'll obviously want to call through the least expensive service available. Don't forget to include the cost of the phone call, though. You'll find a chart in the front of your phone book that will tell you exactly how much each local call will cost, depending on your exchange and the exchange you're calling. If you can't figure it out (it is not one of the easier rate computations I've ever seen), call your phone company business office and let them do it for you.

Pick an appropriate data base. This isn't as silly as it sounds. No one is going to make the mistake of looking for financial or business information on a data base called "Microcomputer Index," but picking the right financial or business-related data base is another matter altogether—at least until you're familiar enough with the data bases to have a sense of what you'll find in each one.

Later in this book you will find an "Index to On-Line Services." This index is meant as a starting point. Look up a subject and the index will give you a list of utilities with data bases relating to that subject. (Your search, of course, will be limited to the utilities you have passwords for, but we'll get to that in Chapter 8. For now, just assume you have the passwords you need.)

Once you have the list of the utilities that you may be interested in, you can take a look at the lists of the data bases themselves. You will find a separate data base list for each utility covered in Chapter 8. The data bases on these lists are grouped by subject. You should be able to eliminate several inappropriate choices just from the short comments you'll find there.

Once you have the list of possible data bases to search, the next step is to take a look at the descriptions for these data bases as given in the manuals from the various utilities. Here again you should be able to eliminate some obviously bad choices. You may find one or two obviously good ones.

At this point it's time to go on-line. If you're still left with too many data bases to search, you should be able to eliminate some of them fairly quickly. More often than not, several of the data bases you're interested in will be on a single utility. The large systems, notably DIALOG and BRS, will generally let you check across several data bases at once. You can't retrieve information this way, but you can see how many hits you'll get in each data base file. Once you see which file or files will give you the most hits, you know which one to go to for the information.

The same data base may be available from more than one utility. The Academic American Encyclopedia Database is available on BRS at $55 per hour, on Dow Jones at $36 per hour, and on BRS/AFTER DARK at $14 per hour. (These prices reflect the maximum charges for this data base on each utility.) If you check the "Index to On-Line Services" in Chapter 8, you'll find other examples of a given data base that's on more than one system. You will also find that the lists of data bases for each utility are cross-indexed to other utilities as appropriate. The point is, look up the data base on each system and check the prices before deciding which utility to use. Be aware, though, that some utilities have more powerful search capabilities than others. If you know how to take advantage of these capabilities, the "more expensive" utility may actually let you dig out the information faster and at a lower cost.

Decide what you want, and how you're going to ask for it, before you dial the phone. If you are very familiar with the particular data base, or if the subject you're searching is a simple one, it is probably enough to simply think the procedure through quickly. If you are *not* familiar with the data base, and particularly if you're not familiar with the utility in general, take the time to review any information you have about how to use it, then write down exactly the commands you plan to use—at least those you plan to start with. This will not only save you time once you get on the system, it will probably save you time overall because it will let you think about what you're doing without the additional pressure of being on-line.

While you're at it, take the commands you expect to use and enter them on disk beforehand if you have the capability. Then you can send the disk file as required and not worry about what a terrible typist you are.

Don't get too carried away with this off-line planning. One of the real benefits of working with an interactive data base is precisely that it is interactive. Don't just plod along in some predetermined direction. Read the information as it shows up on your screen and be willing to change your approach, depending on what you see.

ONCE YOU'RE ON-LINE

First, a word on searching in general. Different utilities have different search capabilities. Just about any system that lets you search for a key word, or key words, will also let you hook those words together with an "AND" or "OR."

The AND capability lets you search for items that contain both one phrase AND the other. If you're looking for information on computer-controlled robots, for example, you might search for "robots AND computers."

The OR capability lets you search for items that contain either one phrase OR the other. If you're looking for information on robots of all kinds plus information on computers of all kinds, you might search for "robots OR computers."

Many systems also use NOT. This lets you search for items that contain one phrase but not the other. If you want all articles on robots except those that deal with the computer control of robots, you might enter "robots NOT computer."

Many utilities also let you tell the system that you want to look for words that are next to each other. This is useful in searching for phrases like "artificial intelligence." For example, if you tell DIALOG to search for "artificial intelligence," it will retrieve those items where "artificial intelligence" was used as a "descriptor" by whoever indexed the item. If the indexer used "AI" or "machine intelligence" as the identifier, though, you won't find the item, even if the phrase "artificial intelligence" appears in the reference itself. One way around this limitation is to tell DIALOG to search for "artificial AND intelligence," but this will not only find items on artificial intelligence, it will also find items on the use of artificial flowers as bugging devices in the intelligence community. A better approach is to give the phrase to DIALOG as "artificial(w)intelligence," in which case the system will find only items that include the complete phrase. (The "(w)" is short for "with.")

Most search systems will also let you string phrases together. For example, if you are looking for items about the computer control of robots, you might also like to look for articles that discuss artificial intelligence as it applies to robots. The phrase you wind up with might be "robots AND (computer OR artificial(w)intelligence)."

The parentheses in this example tell the system which words to group together. In this case they tell it that you want to find items with the word "robots" *and either* "computer" *or* "artificial intelligence."

This is not a complete list of on-line searching capabilities by any means, but it does cover the most common features. Keep in mind that except for AND and OR, almost everything else about searching varies from one utility to the next. Even those utilities with similar capabilities usually have different commands for using those capabilities. This is one reason why you should take a moment before going on-line and review the commands for the utility you're about to use.

Searching Tips

Search for terms that are appropriate to the data base you are in. Searching for the word "patent" is appropriate if you're looking for an article on patents in an index to general-interest magazines. It is not appropriate if you're looking in a data base that is devoted to patents. This is a matter of common sense. The point is, take a minute to *think* before you go on-line. It's often worth taking time to put your search words on paper and play with alternate words before calling the utility.

Don't narrow the search too quickly. The most common mistake in searching a data base is trying to be too precise. If you're looking for information on young children, you may find it under "baby," or "infant," or "child," or "children." Include all these words in your search if the system allows for it. And don't forget variations on spelling. Were you looking for Videotex or Videotext? Make sure that the search is for both. Most systems let you truncate a word, usually with a question mark or asterisk. "Videotex?" would find "videotex" or "videotext." "Child?" would find "child" or "children."

As a general rule, you're better off casting a wide net, then narrowing it down if you've found too much. In particular, don't lock yourself un-necessarily into specific words or specific spellings.

The key word above is "unnecessarily." **If there are some specific words that must be just so, search for the specifics first.** If you're looking for an article about Isaac Asimov's two-hundreth book, "Asimov" and "two hundred" (or "200") should find it for you.

A related rule of thumb is: **Use what you know.** Usually you'll go into a search knowing something about it. You might be looking for a particular article, for example, and know the author's name. Anything that specific serves as a good starting point. (Unless, perhaps, the author is Asimov, in which case you're likely to retrieve entirely too many references.)

Sample as you go. When you're searching a data base, you generally are given a count of the number of hits you've made at each stage. Don't go too far down any given road without taking a look at some of what you have so far. If you have 500 hits, take a look at the first five; they may give you some hints about what to do next.

Doing something is better than doing nothing. If you're not finding anything with the strategy you're using or if you're coming up with the wrong kind of information, don't just sit there chewing your lip. Try something. You're paying for the time either way. If you're completely stumped and don't have any idea what to do, log off and think about it without having to pay for it.

Finally, here are two general hints about developing search strategies.

First, most utilities and most data base publishers will help you work out a strategy for a given search if you're stymied. More often than not you can reach the utility or publisher through a toll-free number, which means that the help is essentially free.

Second, the more expensive utilities tend to have more flexibility in their search techniques, but this flexibility makes them harder to learn and harder to use effectively. Typically these utilities offer training sessions to help you get started. Take advantage of them. There is a charge for these sessions, but it is much less than the cost of learning these things on your own through trial and error.

The dozen or so searching hints in this chapter will work for just about anyone on just about any searchable data base. As you become familiar with particular utilities and particular data bases, you'll be able to add your own individualized rules of thumb. Some of these will work on more than one utility; others will be specific to a single system or even to a single data base. In the meantime, think of this chapter as a starter kit—a bagful of hints that will get you going in the right direction.

8

THE UTILITIES
A Catalog

This chapter is a catalog of major on-line utilities, covering about a dozen systems in some detail. (The exact number depends on how you count them and whether you consider sister systems such as LEXIS and NEXIS to be one utility or two.) The major sections of the catalog cover BRS, BRS/AFTER DARK, CompuServe, Delphi, DIALOG, Dow Jones, KNOWLEDGE INDEX, Mead (LEXIS and NEXIS), NewsNet, THE SOURCE, and "Others."

The information on each utility is divided into three sections.

- The first section covers the basics: the cost of using the system, the phone number, the hours of operation, and so forth.
- The second section is a general description of the utility. The idea is to give you a feel for what the system is like: who it's aimed at, how hard or how easy it is to use, and what kinds of things you'll find on it.
- The third section is a list of the data bases and services on the system. For utilities with relatively few data bases (Dow Jones for example), you'll usually find a short description of each. For services with more than about 20 data bases, this section is limited to a list. In one or two cases, where the number of data bases is measured in the hundreds, this section is limited to a list of *subjects* covered rather than a comprehensive list of the data bases themselves.

The utilities covered in detail were chosen for a variety of reasons but mostly because each one, in its own way, is general enough to be interesting to a wide spectrum of people.

Some of the utilities on this list, Delphi being the prime example, are general both in terms of being inexpensive and in terms of being consumer-oriented to one degree or another. Others, DIALOG the principal example here, are general only in the sense that they contain data bases on a wide variety of subjects.

The difference between these two extremes is clear enough. Delphi is aimed at the "consumer" — the personal-computer user who may never have been on-line before. It is designed to be easy to use and costs well under $10 per hour (at evening rates). DIALOG, in contrast, is aimed primarily at research librarians and other "information specialists" who have invested time and effort in learning the most sophisticated state-of-the-art search techniques. It can also be expensive—as much as $300 per hour. (Or as little as $15 per hour; the price varies from data base to data base.) Still, with about 170 data bases on a wide range of subjects and with more data bases being added continually, DIALOG deserves a close look here.

Most general-interest utilities fall somewhere between these extremes. Dow Jones News/Retrieval is typical. It is a general-interest, business-oriented system available at a moderate price and designed for ease of use.

In addition to the utilities that are covered in detail, there is the section labeled "Others." This includes a less-detailed description of roughly half a dozen not quite general-interest utilities. It also includes a list of about 45 systems that are much more narrowly focused. The systems on this last list are too small or too specialized to warrant a close look in this book. You will find WESTLAW in this section, and AUTO-CITE—two systems that specialize in law-related information. You will also find Billboard Information Network (a utility that consists primarily of the Billboard Music Charts) and BRS/COLLEAGUE Medical, a new service from BRS tailored to the needs of doctors and medical researchers. I've given just enough information on these specialized systems to help you decide which ones you might like to learn more about.

SOME NOTES ABOUT THE CATALOG

One point you should keep in mind when reading this catalog: The only constant in this industry is change. Rapid change. On any given utility, data bases—and even services—are constantly being added, eliminated, restructured, or otherwise changed. There isn't a single utility covered here that isn't in the middle of some sort of change, major or minor. You will, therefore, find liberal use of two phrases throughout the catalog: "As of this writing..." and "Current plans are...." Things may settle down eventually, but for right now (and for several years to come certainly), the only way to get an up-to-the-minute picture of any given utility is to get on-line and take a look for yourself. Virtually all the systems covered here regularly send newsletters to their users for precisely that reason. And virtually all these systems also have an on-line update service, for the same reason.

The Index

The catalog of utilities is meant to serve double duty. It will both introduce you to the systems and serve as a reference guide. With that in mind, the systems are listed in alphabetical order.

At the end of this chapter you will find an "Index to On-Line Services." This is pretty much what it sounds like: an index to the services available through the utilities cataloged in the chapter. This index is designed to help you decide which utility or utilities you will find most useful. Look up the service or services you're interested in and you will find a list of the utilities that offer each service. The index is also designed to help you find an appropriate data base to search when looking for information. See the notes at the beginning of the index for details on how to use it.

Prices

One basic piece of information you will find for each utility is the price structure. For consistency's sake, I've listed all connect-time charges in terms of dollars per hour, which is the most common way that the utilities themselves list their prices. Keep in mind, though, that thinking in terms of dollars per hour may be useful for purposes of comparison but it is not always relevant—particularly in the case of an information search. Most utilities charge in increments of either minutes or hundredths of an hour. On-line searches, meanwhile, typically take anywhere from 5 to 15 minutes.

Telecommunications Networks

Another basic piece of information is a list of the communications networks through which each utility is available. The three most common networks are Telenet, Tymnet, and Uninet. Another common listing is Datapac, a Canadian network. You will also see a few networks that are specific to the particular utility: Sourcenet for THE SOURCE, Meadnet for Mead, and so on.

As I've mentioned elsewhere in this book, these networks are systems that provide a local number for calling an information utility, thereby saving you the cost of a long-distance call. That's only part of what they do, though.

The networks are known as "value-added carriers," which means they do more than simply substitute for the phone company. In particular, since they are designed to handle data rather than voice, they tend to be more reliable than standard phone lines in transmitting data long distance. Perhaps more important, you should be aware that there is at least one thing these networks can do that standard phone lines can't—namely, "translate" from one communications protocol to another. They can do that because when you call a network, it doesn't simply pass along the signals generated by your modem. Instead, your modem talks to the network's modem, and it's up to the network to talk to the utility.

What this adds up to is that if you have a modem that uses the Racal-Vadic protocol, for example, and there is a local network number that can also use that protocol, you can talk to any utility that's available though that network—including utilities that you would not be able to call direct. In short, it doesn't matter whether the utility itself can communicate with any given protocol as long as the network you're calling through can use that protocol.

There's a warning that goes along with this: Not all numbers on any given network can use all protocols. You will find that many network numbers can talk only to Bell 103-compatible modems. When you sign up with a utility, you usually get a list of network phone numbers that you can call for that utility. This list should tell you which numbers can talk to which modems. If it doesn't, call the utility (not the network) and ask about the numbers in your area.

That brings up another point. In Chapter 7, I mentioned that virtually all information utilities have a customer-service number, usually a toll-free 800 number that you can call if you get stuck. This applies to more than search strategies. If you're just getting started and you're having trouble understanding how the utility works, or you're having trouble logging on to it, or even if you're having trouble getting on to the communications network, call the customer-service number for help. That's what it's there for.

A final note on telecommunications networks and on telecommunications in general. The whole process of calling an information utility for the first time can be confusing. Typically, you're using your modem and your communications program for the first time; you're reading the phone numbers off a list that includes every network phone number in the country; and you're reading the log on procedure from two separate sheets of paper—one telling you how to talk to the network computer, the other telling you how to log on to the utility itself.

It may help to know that learning how to log on to a system is a minor skill, no more complicated than learning how to make a phone call. After you've done it a few times, you'll begin to feel comfortable with it. In six months you will be able to do it without a second thought.

Keep that in mind when you're dialing the phone with one hand, holding the handset with chin and shoulder, using your other hand to keep track of the phone number of the list, and using an elbow to hold the manual open to the first half of the log on procedure.

It helps.

CATALOG OF ON-LINE SERVICES

BRS

The Basics

Hours: On-line 22 hours a day, from 6:00 A.M. to 4:00 A.M. Eastern Time, seven days a week.

Command-based.

Baud rates: 300/1200 baud. (No extra charge at 1200 baud.)

Initial charge: Start-up fee of $50. This is applied against the first $50 of use if used within three months after receiving the password. (There is no start-up fee for users who subscribe to contracts with yearly minimum charges. See note below.)

No minimum monthly charge.

Training available at $70 per day or $35 per half day. (Training fee includes up to eight hours of search time. This must be used in a single day within one month of training.)

System reference manuals available at $18 each. Guides to individual data bases are additional at $3 each. A training workbook is also available for $15.

Updates: *BRS Bulletin,* a monthly newsletter, is sent free to all users. Update training sessions are available regionally twice a year at $70 per day.

Available through:

Direct dial	— $3 per hour
Uninet	— $8 per hour
Telenet	— $8 per hour
Tymnet	— $11 per hour
Telenet In-Wats	— $26 per hour (in cities without public dial access to Telenet)

For further information, contact:
BRS
1200 Route 7
Latham, NY 12110
(800) 833-4707
(800) 553-5566 (in New York)
(518) 783-1161

Price Structure

BRS has a price structure that defies simple description.

First, there is a telecommunications charge. This varies from $3 per hour (for direct dialing to BRS) on up to $26 per hour (for calling through Telenet In-Wats in cities without a public-access Telenet number).

Second, there is a charge for the time on BRS itself. This varies from $16 an hour to $35 an hour. The low figure is available if you are willing to guarantee a minimum of 240 hours of use over a year's time. (That translates to a minimum of $3,800 per year.) The high figure is for those who don't want to guarantee any given minimum number of hours per year. There are several other steps between these two extremes.

Third, there is a royalty charge that goes to the producer of the data base. This varies from a low of zero for a handful of data bases on up to a maximum of $70 per hour for the "American Men and Women of Science" data base. In addition, some data bases also add an "on-line citation royalty" for each search item found and read on-line. These vary from 5 cents to 40 cents per citation.

Fourth, there is an "off-line citation charge" for items you want to have printed and sent to you through the mail. This varies, depending on which of the nine formats you choose for the printed citations. The variation runs from half a cent per citation for the "accession number only" to ten cents per citation for "all paragraphs."

There is no additional charge for use at 1200 buad.

Description

BRS is a bibliographic information service aimed primarily at large users, meaning public libraries, universities, and business and professional offices. As of October 1983, there were slightly more than 70 data bases available on BRS. Some of them are also available elsewhere. Others are not. A more interesting development is that many of these data bases are now available on BRS/AFTER DARK, an off-hours service that is significantly cheaper and easier to use. (BRS/AFTER DARK is listed separately.)

Services Available

BRS has a limited electronic mail system for sending messages between users. Other than that, BRS provides information services only. These fall into two categories: on-line searching, with an option for off-line printing of items found, and a current awareness service, which is basically an electronic newsclipping service. As you would expect from a service aimed primarily at large information users, both of these services allow for sophisticated searching techniques.

On-Line Searching

The data bases on BRS cover subjects as widespread as agriculture, medicine, business, and religion. They also include standard reference works like *Books in*

Print. Some of these data bases contain references only; others contain abstracts of articles; still others include the full text of each item. BRS divides the data bases into six categories:

Sciences/Medicine
Business/Financial
Reference
Education
Social Sciences/Humanities
Energy/Environment

Each of these categories contains several distinct data bases, each of which must be searched separately. In ordering off-line prints of your search results, you can have BRS sort the hits from several different data bases into one alphabetized list.

In addition to the above categories, BRS provides several data bases that are concerned specifically with the BRS system. These include on-line updates about new data bases and an on-line version of the BRS monthly newsletter. BRS also has a data base called CROSS, which can be useful when you're not sure of which data base to look in for information. You can test your search strategy in CROSS and it will show you how many hits you'll find in each data base on the system.

SDI (Selective Dissemination of Information)

The BRS SDI service lets you store a search phrase in the system and have it automatically search for matches each time a specified data base is updated. The matches are then printed and mailed to you. This gives you a constant flow of new information on any subject as that information is added to the system.

DATA BASES AVAILABLE ON BRS

(LISTED BY CATEGORY)

SCIENCES/MEDICINE

ACS PRIMARY JOURNAL DATABASE Subject: Full text of 18 journals published by the American Chemical Society. Producer: American Chemical Society.

AGRICOLA Subject: Agriculture. Producer: National Agricultural Library. Also available on: BRS/AFTER DARK, DIALOG, KNOWLEDGE INDEX.

BIOSIS PREVIEWS AND BACKFILE Subject: Biological sciences. Producer: BioSciences Information Service. Also available on BRS/AFTER DARK, DIALOG, KNOWLEDGE INDEX.

CHEMICAL ABSTRACTS Subject: Chemistry. Producer: Chemical Abstracts Service. Also available on BRS/AFTER DARK.

CHEMICAL ABSTRACTS SEARCH TRAINING Producer: Chemical Abstracts Service.

COMPENDEX Subject: Engineering. This is the computer-readable form of *Engineering Index.* Producer: Engineering Information, Inc. Also available on DIALOG, KNOWLEDGE INDEX.

DISC   Subject: Microcomputing. Producer: BRS. Also available on BRS/AFTER DARK.

EPILEPSYLINE   Subject: Epilepsy and related issues. Producer: National Institute of Neurological and Communicative Disorders and Stroke.

HEALTH PLANNING AND ADMINISTRATION   Subject: Health economics, administration, and planning. Producer: National Library of Medicine. Also available on BRS/AFTER DARK, DIALOG.

INSPEC AND BACKFILE   Subject: Engineering, physics, and computer science. Producer: Institute of Electrical Engineers. Also available on DIALOG, KNOWLEDGE INDEX.

INTERNATIONAL PHARMACEUTICAL ABSTRACTS   Subject: Pharmaceutical and drug-related information. Producer: American Society of Hospital Pharmacists. Also available on DIALOG, KNOWLEDGE INDEX.

IRCS MEDICAL SCIENCE   Subject: Medical journals. Full text. Producer: IRCS.

KIRK-OTHMER ENCYCLOPEDIA OF MEDICAL SCIENCE   Subject: Medical reference work. Full text. Producer: John Wiley & Sons.

MATHEMATICAL REVIEWS ONLINE · Subject: Pure and applied mathematics. Producer: American Mathematical Society. Also available on BRS/AFTER DARK.

MEDLARS-ON-LINE AND BACKFILES   Subject: Medicine, nursing, dentistry. Producer: National Library of Medicine. Also available on BRS/AFTER DARK.

NTIS   Subject: Government reports. Various areas. Producer: National Technical Information Service. Also available on BRS/AFTER DARK, DIALOG, KNOWLEDGE INDEX.

NEW ENGLAND JOURNAL OF MEDICINE   Full text. Producer: *New England Journal of Medicine.*

PRE-MED   Subject: Clinical medicine. Producer: BRS. Also available on BRS/AFTER DARK.

BUSINESS/FINANCIAL

ABI/INFORM   Subject: Business. Producer: Data Courier, Inc. Also available on BRS/AFTER DARK, DIALOG, KNOWLEDGE INDEX.

FINTEL: FINANCIAL TIMES OF LONDON   Subject: Business. Producer: Information Industries, Inc.

HARFAX INDUSTRY DATA SOURCES   Producer: Harfax Database Publishing. Also available on DIALOG.

HARVARD BUSINESS REVIEW/ONLINE   Subject: Business and management. Full text. Producer: John Wiley & Sons. Also available on BRS/AFTER DARK, DIALOG.

INDEX TO FROST & SULLIVAN MARKET RESEARCH REPORTS   Subject: Market research. Producer: Frost & Sulllivan, Inc.

INDUSTRY AND INTERNATIONAL STANDARDS   Subject: Engineering standards. Producer: Information Handling Services.

MANAGEMENT CONTENTS   Subject: Index to and abstracts of worldwide English-language literature on business and management. Producer: Management Contents, Inc. Also available on BRS/AFTER DARK, DIALOG, THE SOURCE.

MILITARY AND FEDERAL SPECIFICATIONS AND STANDARDS Producer: Information Handling Services.

PATDATA   Subject: All patents registered through the U.S. Patent Office. Producer: BRS. Also available on BRS/AFTER DARK.

PREDICASTS ANNUAL REPORTS   Subject: Business and economics. Producer: Predicasts, Inc. Also available on DIALOG as PTS Annual Report Abstracts.

PREDICASTS F&S INDEX/FORECASTS   Subject: Business and economics. Producer: Predicasts, Inc. Also available on DIALOG as PTS F&S Indexes, PTS International Forecasts, and PTS U.S. Forecasts.

PREDICASTS PROMT/HISTORICAL TIME SERIES   Subject: Business and economics. Producer: Predicasts, Inc. Also available on DIALOG as PTS PROMT, PTS International Time Series, and PTS U.S. Time Series.

REFERENCE

ACADEMIC AMERICAN ENCYCLOPEDIA DATABASE   Subject: Multi-disciplinary. Full text. Producer: Grolier Electronic Publishing, Inc. Also available on BRS/AFTER DARK, Dow Jones News/Retrieval.

AMERICAN MEN AND WOMEN OF SCIENCE   Subject: Directory of scientists. Producer: R.R. Bowker. Also available on DIALOG.

BOOKS IN PRINT   Subject: U.S. books in print. Producer: R.R. Bowker. Also available on BRS/AFTER DARK, DIALOG, KNOWLEDGE INDEX.

BOOKSINFO   Subject: 800,000 books in print. Producer: Brodart, Inc.

CALIFORNIA UNION LIST OF PERIODICALS   Subject: California periodicals holdings. Producer: California Library Authority for Systems and Services.

DISSERTATION ABSTRACTS   Subject: Multi-disciplinary. Producer: University Microfilms.

GPO MONTHLY CATALOG   Subject: Index to government publications of all kinds, covering a wide range of topics. Producer: U.S. Government Printing Office. Also available on DIALOG.

ULRICH'S INTERNATIONAL   Subject: Directory of periodicals. Producer: R.R. Bowker. Also available on DIALOG.

USBE MOST-AVAILABLE TITLES   Subject: 10,000 serial titles available for distribution. Producer: Universal Series and Book Exchange, Inc.

EDUCATION

BILINGUAL EDUCATION BIBLIOGRAPHIC ABSTRACTS   Producer: National Clearinghouse for Bilingual Education. Also available on BRS/AFTER DARK.

ERIC   Subject: Education. Producer: National Institute of Education. Also available on BRS/AFTER DARK, DIALOG, KNOWLEDGE INDEX.

EXCEPTIONAL CHILD EDUCATION RESOURCES   Producer: Council for Exceptional Children. Also available on BRS/AFTER DARK, DIALOG.

NIMIS   Subject: Instructional materials for education of the handicapped. Producer: National Center for Educational Media and Materials for the Handicapped.

ONTARIO EDUCATION RESOURCES INFORMATION DATABASE   Subject: Education research, curriculum guidelines, educational reports. Producer: Ontario Ministry of Education.

RESOURCES IN COMPUTER EDUCATION   Subject: Computer applications in education. Producer: Northwest Regional Educational Laboratory.

RESOURCES IN VOCATIONAL EDUCATION   Subject: Vocational education. Producer: National Center for Research in Vocational Education.

SCHOOL PRACTICES INFORMATION FILE   Producer: BRS Education Service Group. Also available on BRS/AFTER DARK.

SOCIAL SCIENCE/HUMANITIES

ABLEDATA   Subject: List of commercially available products for the disabled. Producer: National Rehabilitation Information Center.

ALCOHOL USE/ABUSE   Producer: University of Minnesota College of Pharmacy.

CATALYST RESOURCES FOR WOMEN   Subject: Women and careers. Producer: Catalyst Library.

DRUGINFO   Subject: Drug abuse. Producer: University of Minnesota College of Pharmacy.

FAMILY RESOURCES   Subject: Marriage and family. Producer: National Council on Family Relations. Also available on BRS/AFTER DARK, DIALOG.

JOURNAL OF THE SOCIETY OF ARCHITECTURAL HISTORIANS   Producer: Society of Architectural Historians.

MLA BIBLIOGRAPHY   Subject: Language, linguistics and folklore. Producer: Modern Language Association of America. Also available on DIALOG.

NARIC   Subject: Rehabilitation. Producer: National Rehabilitation Information Center.

NATIONAL INFORMATION SOURCES ON THE HANDICAPPED   Subject: Physical and mental disabilities and related information. Producer: Clearinghouse on the Handicapped. Also available on BRS/AFTER DARK.

NIMH   Subject: Mental health and related information. Producer: National Institute of Mental Health.

PRE-PSYC   Subject: Clinical psychology. Producer: BRS. Also available on BRS/AFTER DARK.

PSYCHOLOGICAL ABSTRACTS   Formerly PSYCINFO. Producer: American Psychological Association. Also available on BRS/AFTER DARK, DIALOG, KNOWLEDGE INDEX.

PUBLIC AFFAIRS INFORMATION SERVICE   Subject: All social sciences. Producer: Public Affairs Information Service. Also available on BRS/AFTER DARK, DIALOG.

RELIGION INDEX   Subject: Religion. Producer: American Theological Library Association. Also available on BRS/AFTER DARK, DIALOG.

SOCIAL SCIENCE CITATION INDEX AND BACKFILE   Subject: Social science. Producer: Institute for Scientific Information. Also available on BRS/AFTER DARK, and on DIALOG as Social SciSearch.

SOCIOLOGICAL ABSTRACTS   Subject: Sociology and related disciplines. Producer: Sociological Abstracts, Inc. Also available on DIALOG.

ENERGY/ENVIRONMENT

EIS DIGESTS OF ENVIRONMENTAL IMPACT STATEMENTS   Subject: Environment. Producer: Information Resources Press.

ENERGY DATABASE   Producer: U.S. Dept. of Energy. Also available on BRS/AFTER DARK.

ENERGYLINE   Subject: Energy. Producer: Environment Information Center. Also available on DIALOG.

ENVIROLINE   Subject: Environment, conservation. Producer: Environment Information Center. Also available on DIALOG.

FEDEX: FEDERAL ENERGY DATA INDEX   Subject: Energy statistics. Producer: U.S. Dept. of Energy.

POLLUTION ABSTRACTS   Producer: Cambridge Scientific Abstracts. Also available on DIALOG.

BRS FILES

BRS BULLETIN ONLINE   Producer: BRS.

CROSS   Subject: Cross-file searching on BRS. Producer: BRS.

FILE   Subject: BRS data base directory. Producer: BRS.

NEWS   Subject: System updates. Producer: BRS.

TERM   Subject: Social-science thesauri on BRS. Producer: BRS.

New data bases are being added continually. For a current list, contact BRS.

BRS/AFTER DARK

The Basics

Hours: On-line 6:00 P.M. your local time through 4:00 A.M. Eastern Time, Monday through Friday; 6:00 A.M. to 4:00 A.M. Eastern Time, Saturday, Sunday, and Holidays.

Dual structure: You can use this as a menu-driven system, or you can bypass the menus and treat it as command-driven.

Baud rate: 300/1200 baud. (No extra charge for 1200 baud.)

Initial charge: One-time subscription fee of $50.

Minimum monthly charge: $12. (This does not include royalty charges. See "Price Structure.") Training not available and not necessary.

Reference manual: User's Manual comes as part of initial package. This manual deserves special praise for being both a well-designed introduction to and a useful reference for using this system.

Updates: A bi-monthly newsletter includes updates on new developments and contains articles that help teach search strategies. The newsletter also includes updated pages for the manual. An on-line version of the newsletter is available as a menu choice on the system.

Available through:
Uninet
Telenet
(at no additional charge)

For further information, contact:
BRS
1200 Route 7
Latham, NY 12110
(800) 833-4707
(800) 553-5566 (in New York)
(518) 783-1161

Price Structure

BRS/AFTER DARK has a relatively simple price structure.

On-line time is billed at a straightforward charge of $6 per hour to $20 per hour, depending on the data base.

One minor complication: Anything above $6 per hour is the royalty charge that goes to the producer of the data base. These royalty charges do not count as part of the $12-per-month minimum.

Description

BRS, which you'll find covered earlier in this chapter, is one of the bigger and better-known bibliographic information services aimed at large users. BRS/AFTER DARK is the "consumer-oriented" version of BRS. "Consumer-oriented" is in quotes because the nearly 30 available data bases are hardly what you would consider appropriate for the well-known "average" consumer. The target audience here is the information consumer (or end user, in industry jargon). This translates to business people, educators, attorneys, physicians, writers, and students. (Especially physicians. As of May 1983, fully 70 percent of BRS/AFTER DARK users were medical doctors. This may change though. BRS has started a new service, BRS/COLLEAGUE Medical, aimed specifically at doctors, medical researchers, and the like.)

BRS/AFTER DARK, quite simply, is aimed at individuals who are willing to (or forced to) dig out at least some information for themselves (at home, after business hours) instead of giving the job to their in-house or public library. With this user in mind, BRS/AFTER DARK has been designed to be easier to work with than its daytime sister utility. In being made easier than BRS, BRS/AFTER DARK has also been made more limited. You cannot, for example, order off-line prints of the items you find.

My own experience is that the system is extraordinarily easy to use. When Cathy Anderson at BRS first told me that "experienced searchers take about ten minutes to learn the system, others take about half an hour," I didn't quite believe it. It seems to be true though. I suppose I qualify as an experienced searcher. I gave the system the toughest test I know, which is to get on-line without so much as a glance at the manual. What I found was a self-explanatory series of prompts that guided me through every step. At no point did I feel lost or overwhelmed. And yes, I can honestly say that within ten minutes I had pretty well learned the system. When I finally went to the manual, it was to find out how to bypass some of the prompts that were slowing me down.

When BRS/AFTER DARK first came on-line, the only important problem with it was that in simplifying the search procedure, BRS also left out some useful capabilities that an experienced searcher would miss. (You could not, for example, tell the system to look for a key word in titles only.) Most of these more sophisticated capabilities have now been put into the system, though, adding considerably to its capabilities as a research tool.

In addition to ease of use and number of data bases, there are two other important differences between BRS and BRS/AFTER DARK: hours of operation and price.

BRS is on-line 22 hours a day, seven days a week. BRS/AFTER DARK is available only during off hours. This translates to evenings during the week plus all day on weekends and holidays. ("All day" in this case means 22 hours.)

As for price, BRS/AFTER DARK is much less expensive than BRS. Even better, where BRS has a price structure that is rivaled only by my local utility's billing system (which I gave up trying to understand long ago), BRS/AFTER DARK has a straightforward price-per-hour charge. This varies from data base to data base, but in each case it is a single charge rather than a convoluted combination of several charges.

Services Available

As of this writing, BRS/AFTER DARK is limited to information services only. This should change shortly. Both communications services and transaction services are planned for the near future. (Menu choices for electronic mail and software directories are already on the system. If you choose them, though, you're told they're not available yet.)

Information Services

BRS/AFTER DARK offers a carefully selected list of roughly 30 data bases from the regular BRS service. Most of these cover specialized areas from chemistry (Chemical Abstracts), to patent information (Patdata), to school administration (School Practices Information File). One or two are more general in scope, including the Academic American Encyclopedia Database and the Harvard Business Review/Online. Although the utility is planning to offer additional services in the near future, information retrieval is what BRS is about, and it remains the first priority in BRS/AFTER DARK.

Planned for the Near Future

Communications Services. *Electronic Mail* should be available by the time this book is published. Other communications services, including on-line conferences and CB emulation, may become available as well, but as of this writing, the final decision has yet to be made.

Transaction Services. BRS/AFTER DARK currently has a series of shop-at-home services under development. One of the earliest of these will be the "Swap Shop," basically a bulletin board for classified ads. "Swap Shop" will be for BRS users who want to buy, sell, and trade among themselves. It should be on-line by the time you read this.

Another shop-at-home service presently under development will sell micro-computer software—all kinds of software for all kinds of micros. Plans are for this to start as a catalog service. Eventually it should let you download software directly from the utility. Choices in protocols are currently being considered.

DATA BASES AVAILABLE ON BRS/AFTER DARK

(LISTED BY CATEGORY)

BUSINESS/FINANCIAL

ABI/INFORM   Subject: Business. Producer: Data Courier, Inc. Also available on BRS, DIALOG, KNOWLEDGE INDEX.

HARVARD BUSINESS REVIEW/ONLINE   Subject: Business and management. Full text. Producer: John Wiley & Sons. Also available on BRS, DIALOG.

MANAGEMENT CONTENTS   Subject: Business and management-related topics. Producer: Management Contents, Inc. Also available on BRS, DIALOG, THE SOURCE.

PATDATA   Subject: All patents registered through the U.S. Patent Office. Producer: BRS. Also available on BRS.

EDUCATION

BILINGUAL EDUCATION BIBLIOGRAPHIC ABSTRACTS   Producer: National Clearinghouse for Bilingual Educations. Also available on BRS.

ERIC   Subject: Education. Producer: National Institute of Education. Also available on BRS, DIALOG, KNOWLEDGE INDEX.

EXCEPTIONAL CHILD EDUCATION RESOURCES   Subject: Education of exceptional children. Producer: Council for Exceptional Children. Also available on BRS, DIALOG.

SCHOOL PRACTICES INFORMATION FILE   Producer: BRS Education Service Group. Also available on BRS.

ENERGY/ENVIRONMENT

ENERGY DATABASE   Subject: Energy and environment. Producer: U.S. Dept. of Energy. Also available on BRS.

REFERENCE

ACADEMIC AMERICAN ENCYCLOPEDIA DATABASE   Subject: Multi-disciplinary. Full text. Producer: Grolier Electronic Publishing, Inc. Also available on BRS, Dow Jones News/Retrieval.

BOOKS IN PRINT   Subject: U.S. Books in Print. Producer: R.R. Bowker. Also available on BRS, DIALOG, KNOWLEDGE INDEX.

SCIENCES/MEDICINE

AGRICOLA   Subject: Agriculture. Producer: National Agricultural Library. Also available on BRS, DIALOG, KNOWLEDGE INDEX.

BIOSIS PREVIEWS AND BACKFILE   Subject: Biological sciences. Producer: BioSciences Information Service. Also available on BRS, DIALOG, KNOWLEDGE INDEX.

CHEMICAL ABSTRACTS   Producer: Chemical Abstracts Service. Also available on BRS.

DISC   Subject: Microcomputing. Producer: BRS. Also available on BRS.

HEALTH PLANNING AND ADMINISTRATION   Subject: Health economics, administration, and planning. Producer: National Library of Medicine. Also available on BRS, DIALOG.

MATHEMATICAL REVIEWS ONLINE   Subject: Pure and applied mathematics. Producer: American Mathematical Society. Also available on BRS.

MEDLARS-ON-LINE AND BACKFILES   Subject: Medicine, nursing, dentistry. Producer: National Library of Medicine. Also available on BRS.

NTIS   Subject: Government reports. Various areas. Producer: National Technical Information Service. Also available on BRS, DIALOG, KNOWLEDGE INDEX.

PRE-MED   Subject: Current clinical medicine. Producer: BRS. Also available on BRS.

SOCIAL SCIENCES/HUMANITIES

FAMILY RESOURCES   Subject: Marriage and family. Producer: National Council on Family Relations. Also available on BRS.

NATIONAL INFORMATION SOURCES ON THE HANDICAPPED   Subject: Physical and mental disabilities and related information. Producer: Clearinghouse on the Handicapped. Also available on BRS.

PRE-PSYC   Subject: Current clinical psychology. Producer: BRS. Also available on BRS.

PSYCHOLOGICAL ABSTRACTS   Formerly PSYCINFO. Subject: Psychology. Producer: American Psychological Association. Also available on BRS, DIALOG, KNOWLEDGE INDEX.

PUBLIC AFFAIRS INFORMATION SERVICE   (PAIS) Subject: All social sciences. Producer: Public Affairs Information Service. Also available on BRS.

RELIGION INDEX   Subject: Religion. Producer: American Theological Library Association. Also available on BRS.

SOCIAL SCIENCE CITATION INDEX AND BACKFILE   Producer: Institute for Scientific Information. Also available on BRS.

New data bases are added continually. For a current list, contact BRS.

CompuServe Information Service

The Basics

Hours: On-line 8:00 A.M. to 5:00 A.M. Eastern Time, seven days a week. Between 5:00 A.M. and 8:00 A.M., the system is on an "as available basis."

Dual Structure: You can move around the system with commands, or you can use the menus.

Baud rate: 300/1200 baud. (Additional charge at 1200 baud.)

Initial charge: Starter's kits are available for suggested list prices ranging from $19.95 to $39.95. (These include User's Guide, ID, password, and varying amounts of connect time on "Standard Service.") These Starter Kits are available at retail computer stores. Call CompuServe for the closest dealer.

Minimum monthly charge: None.

Training not available and not necessary.

Reference manual: Basic reference manual comes with Starter Kit. Others are available at extra cost. The CompuServe reference manuals are divided into small units, which means you can buy the manuals for only those areas in which you're interested. This will keep you from being intimidated by the sheer size of the manual, but it often means that before you can try a new section of CompuServe, you have to order the manual, then wait for it before you can get started. This seems ironic in an on-line service. More important, the one manual you get when you sign up, the User's Guide, is really more of an overview of the system than an introduction to using it.

Updates: Subscribers also receive *Today* and *Update*.

Today is a monthly magazine that discusses computers and on-line services in general.

Update is a monthly customer newsletter describing new services, new offerings, and other changes on CompuServe. *Update* also includes hints on how to get the most out of CompuServe.

Available through:

CompuServe	—No additional charge
Tymnet	—Charge varies with time of day and location. (See "Price Structure.")
Telenet	—Surcharge is identical to Tymnet surcharge.
Datapac (in Canada)	—$8 per hour.

As of this writing, the CompuServe Network serves about 200 cities in the U.S. CompuServe is continually adding new numbers. For up-to-date information on areas served, call CompuServe directly.

For further information, contact:
CompuServe Information Service
5000 Arlington Centre Blvd.
Columbus, OH 43220
(800) 848-8199 (start-up information)
(614) 457-0802 (start-up information in Ohio)
(800) 848-8990 (customer service)
(614) 457-8650 (customer service in Ohio)

Price Structure

Not only is the basic CompuServe price structure simple but the rates are low enough to make this utility a bargain in many ways. "Standard Service" is $6.00 per hour at 300 baud.

If calling through a local CompuServe number, there is no communications surcharge. There is a surcharge if calling through Tymnet, Telenet, or Datapac.

The communications charges for Tymnet or Telenet are:

$2 per hour from the contiguous U.S.
$20 per hour from Alaska
$100 per hour from Hawaii
$8 per hour from Canada
$15 per hour from Puerto Rico

The communications charge for Datapac is $8 per hour.

Certain data bases available through CompuServe—notably COMP*U*STORE, the Official Airline Guide, and MicroQuote—are at additional charge. MicroQuote, for example, does not have an additional connect-time charge, but it does have a "transaction charge" that varies with the particular program you use, plus an information charge based on the number of items you retrieve and the kind of information requested (currently daily price and dividend of a stock, historical price and dividend, and so forth.) This is altogether too complicated to go into here. Details are available through CompuServe.

At 1200 baud, the basic charge per hour goes from $6 to $12.50. This is not an unreasonable jump by any means, but keep in mind that when dealing with something like an on-line conference or an SIG bulletin board, most of your time will be spent reading, typing, and thinking, not receiving information.

During prime-time hours (8:00 A.M. to 6:00 P.M. weekdays), basic connect charges are $12.50 per hour at 300 baud and $15 per hour at 1200 baud.

Communications charges for Tymnet and Telenet during prime time are also higher but only in the contiguous U.S., where they jump from $2 per hour to $10 per hour.

Charges on Datapac remain $8 per hour during prime time.

Other additional charges remain unchanged during prime time.

Description

CompServe is one of the larger general-interest systems, both in terms of the number of subscribers (currently measured in the tens of thousands) and in terms of the number of individual data bases on the system (currently measured in the hundreds). Services range from games to AP wire news, from on-line shopping to financial analysis, from CB emulation to organized Special Interest Groups. In addition, CompuServe provides access to something it calls a "Programming Area." This lets you write and store your own programs in any of several computer languages. It also gives you several other computer services, including limited text editing and access to business and educational programs.

There's enough on CompuServe so that you'll almost certainly find something of interest. In particular, you'll probably find something of business or professional interest—a financial information service, perhaps, or a Special Interest Group in your field.

If there is anything wrong with CompuServe, it is simply that there is too much there for the way the data bases are organized. When you first get on the system, you are likely to feel overwhelmed by the possibilities.

CompuServe divides its services into four categories. These are:

Services for Professionals
Home Services
Business and Financial Services
Personal Computing Services

As with any categories, these are somewhat arbitrary. At least it is not always easy to see the logic behind them. For example, if you're a lawyer or a doctor and you want to share information with others in your field or simply make contacts through a discussion group, you might reasonably look under Services for Professionals to see what's there. If you do that, you will, indeed, find a Special Interest Group, or SIG, for each of these categories. (They're called Forums rather than SIGs, but I'm told by CompuServe that there is no difference beyond the name change.)

If you're a writer or editor, or if you're a teacher or school administrator, you might just as reasonably look under Services for Professionals. If you do, you won't find anything. The Educator's SIG and the Literary SIG are both under Home Services, listed under Groups and Clubs (listed as SIGs, not Forums). And just to complicate matters for writers and editors, there's a separate Author's SIG under Personal Computing Services listed under Computer Groups and Clubs. (According to CompuServe, the Author's SIG was meant for software authors rather than word-smiths, but most of the people I've met on it have been writers, not programmers.)

If you're looking for the Fire Fighter's SIG or the Aviation SIG, you'll find them under Services for Professionals.

The apparent logic behind these classifications is that medicine, law, fire fighting, and flying are professions, but writing and teaching are hobbies of some sort. Or SIGs dealing with writing and education belong under Home Services because writing is something you do from a home office and education is something that parents are interested in. Or none of the above.

Whatever the logic behind the categories in CompuServe, it is not immediately obvious. This means that if you know a particular data base exists, you may have trouble finding it until you're familiar with the system. Much worse, if there's a data base that would interest you but you don't know about it already, you may never find it unless you accidentally trip across it or someone tells you about it.

This is one area where CompuServe can take lessons from Delphi, one of the newer information utilities. Delphi's data bases are arranged by function. If Compu-Serve followed this approach, it would group all SIGs together, probably as a single-menu choice under the category of Communications. That way, if you were looking for a Special Interest Group, you could go to a communications menu, pick Special Interest Groups, then ask to see a list of SIGs. (And they wouldn't complicate the issue by calling some of these "Forums" and some of them "SIGs.") All of this should improve with time. CompuServe is in the process of reorganizing its data bases to make the system easier to use.

One very nice feature on CompuServe, finally, is its dual structure. You can find your way around the system through the menus, but if you know where you want to go, you can get there directly by giving the command "GO," followed by the "page" number. This gives you the menus when you need them and lets you bypass them when you don't.

Services Available

CompuServe has services that fall in each of the major categories—information-based, transaction-based, and communications-based—plus a few services that can't be conveniently pigeonholed. Although CompuServe divides them differently, I've listed them here by functional category.

Communications Services

Communications services on CompuServe include electronic mail, on-line conferences, CB simulation, and bulletin boards. I've already mentioned seven Special Interest Groups, or SIGs (or Forums), that take advantage of these capabilities (Medical, Legal, Fire Fighter, Literary, Educator, Author, and Aviation SIGs).

In addition, there are SIGs organized around particular computers, or even around particular operating systems. (CP/M, certainly, but there's also an LSI TRS-80 group. This is organized around the LDOS operating system from Logical Systems Inc. You probably won't be interested in this SIG if you use TRSDOS on your TRS-80.) There are still other SIGs organized around cooking, golf, photography, and space. Typically, you'll find that the SIGs include bulletin boards, on-line conferences between members, and a library section where you can find information related to the subject of the SIG.

Transaction Services

Transaction services on CompuServe include electronic banking and a service that amounts to computerized classifieds; users can put items up for sale or post want ads. Less useful unless you happen to live near St. Louis is the classified advertising section from the *St. Louis Post Dispatch*.

CompuServe also serves as a gateway to COMP*U*STORE, a computerized home-shopping service that offers substantial discounts on its catalog of roughly 50,000 items.

Information Services

CompuServe's information services range from movie reviews to weather reports, from magazines to the AP wire services, from the Commodore Newsletter to the Stevens Business Report. The utility is particularly strong on business and financial information; it gives access to several "premium" (Read: extra cost) data bases that provide corporate financial information, quotes on stock or commodity prices, and so forth. Some of the information services, including MicroQuote, for example, let you search for the information you want. Others limit you to choosing from menus.

One of the newer "information services" available through CompuServe is InfoText. This lies somewhere between an information-based service and a transaction-based service. What you are doing with InfoText, really, is commissioning a research service to conduct an information search for you. InfoText can get expensive. First, you have to pay for the connect time on the utility being searched. Second, you have to pay for the researcher's time. Still, if it's a difficult search and you're not skilled in search techniques, it might be cheaper to pay someone else than to try it yourself.

Other Services

Some of the services that do not fall neatly into the three basic categories include Games (adventure, blackjack, bridge, chess, backgammon, and about two dozen more) and a few simple programs that CompuServe groups together under the heading Home Management ("Balance Your Checkbook," "Amortize A Loan," "Calculate Your Net Worth," and, optimistically, "Calculate Your Next Raise.")

In addition, there is the programming area of CompuServe, which, as already mentioned, opens the door to various word-processing and programming capabilities along with some business and educational programs. The programming area is strictly command-based, which means you have to know what you're doing before you can use it. There's no point in trying it until you have the appropriate manual in hand (CompuServe's *Personal Computing Guide*).

DATA BASES AVAILABLE ON COMPUSERVE

(LISTED BY CATEGORY)

DATA BASE LIST

CompuServe has a subject index that comes with the Starter Kit. It is also available on-line, which means that any time you want an updated version, you only have to go to CompuServe Page IND and print the new index. (You can get to the index by going to the main menu and choosing the "User Information" option or you can go there directly with the command "GO IND.")

Rather than try to duplicate CompuServe's index, I've limited this section primarily to listing categories of data bases along with a few examples in each category. The major exceptions are for magazines, newswires, and financial- and business-related data bases, where I have listed names of specific data bases in full. I've also included a short explanation and the name of the producer where appropriate. (Notice that you will not find communications services such as electronic mail here. I have listed only those categories that are built around a data base of some sort.)

Magazines

Better Homes and Gardens
Popular Science
Computers and Electronics

General News

Associated Press News Wire: Includes financial news, sports, U.S. news, Washington news, world news. (This carries current AP news only, holding stories for one or two days. A delayed version of the AP wire is available on NEXIS. The NEXIS version does not have the current day's stories but it does keep the stories on file.)

Newspapers: Currently two newspapers, *The Washington Post* and the *St. Louis Post Dispatch,* are available on CompuServe. The menu choice, "Middlesex Daily News," will take you to the AP wire.

Financial and Business Data Bases
(Includes Financial News Wires)

MicroQuote   Subject: Covers more than 40,000 stocks, bonds, and options, providing a range of statistical and descriptive information. Producer: Gregg Corporation.

Quick Quote   Subject: Covers current prices on New York, American, and OTC stock exchanges. Updated "periodically throughout the day."

Standard & Poor's General Information File   Subject: Descriptive and financial information on U.S. publicly held corporations. Producer: Standard & Poor's Corporation.

Value Line Data Base II   Subject: Provides both current and historical data on more than 1600 major industrial, transportation, utility, retail, banking, and insurance companies. Producer: Arnold Bernhard & Co.

Archer Commodities Report   Subject: Includes current reports on the commodities market plus commentary and "education and informational material." In addition, you can order charts, market newsletters, and quotations directly from Archer Commodities, Inc. Producer: Archer Commodities, Inc.

Commodity News Service   Newswire. Updated continuously. Subject: Contains news, prices, and information on the commodity market. Producer: Knight-Ridder Newspapers, Inc. Also available on THE SOURCE.

Business Information Wire   Subject: Covers 17 categories of business news. Producer: The Canadian Press (CP), a news-gathering cooperative of more than 100 Canadian daily newspapers.

Money Market Services Financial Analysis   Subject: On-line newsletter with money-market information. Focus is on forecasts of interest rates. Producer: Money Market Services.

Investor Protection Report   Subject: Biweekly newsletter. Covers underlying developments that affect the safety of investments.

Investment News and Views   Subject: Selected information taken from a variety of investment newsletters. Covers investment and trading opportunities, primarily in the stock market. Producer: Eric Balkan.

Raylux Investor's Report   Subject: Full text of *Raylux Business Outlook* and *Raylux Financial Commentary*, two financial newsletters. Producer: Raylux Associates, Inc.

GAMES

CompuServe's Games and Entertainment section includes about 35 games. (The section also includes Eliza, the computer program that plays the role of a non-directive, Rogerian psychotherapist.)

EDUCATION

CompuServe's education section consists of two subsections.

The College Board contains information on adult education, financial aid for college, and the like.

The Multiple Choice includes several multiple-choice tests, including an IQ test. Most of these tests are fun to play with but they probably should be listed under entertainment rather than education.

ON-LINE SHOPPING—TRANSACTION SERVICES

Computerized Classifieds—Bulletin Board
Software Exchange
COMP*U*STORE—Also available on THE SOURCE, Dow Jones News/Retrieval
Computer Art
Electronic Banking

SPECIAL INTEREST GROUPS, CLUBS, USER'S GROUPS

Computers: Apple, CP/M, Commodore VIC-20, DEC PDP-11, Heath, Pascal, RCA, TRS-80 Color Computer, TRS-80, LDOS TRS-80, Microconnection, VTOS ST-80, MCONN TRS-80.

Professional: Aviation, Fire Fighting, Medical, Authors, Literary, Educators.

Others: Ham Radio, Astronautics, Golf, Citizens Band Radio, Photography, Sports, Cooking, Space.

MICROCOMPUTER INFORMATION

Computer and computer-related newsletters from manufacturers, including RCA, Tandy, Microsoft, Commodore.

The Micro Advisor   Includes hardware and software reviews.

GENERAL INFORMATION

Pan Am Travel Guide
Official Airline Guide
Government Publications: An assortment of information from government pamphlets. Covers a wide range of subjects, including home canning, advice on buying used cars, and information about saving energy.

Weather: Weather reports on CompuServe are available from several sources and are suitable for a variety of uses. There is, for example, one menu choice for "Aviation Weather" and another for "Public and Marine Weather."

Movie Review
World Book Encyclopedia

This list is changing almost daily. For a current list, contact CompuServe.

DELPHI

The Basics

Hours: On-line 24 hours a day, seven days a week. Menu-based.

Baud rate: 300/1200 baud. (No additional charge at 1200 baud.)

Initial charge: $49.95.

Minimum monthly charge: None. (There was one when the system started but it has been dropped.)

Training not available and not necessary.

Reference manual: Comes with membership. Additional manuals are available for $19.95 each.

Updates: An on-line newsletter, Inside Delphi, is available as a menu choice on the system. This contains updates about changes on the system and hints on how to use Delphi.

Available through: Telenet. (Delphi was originally available through Tymnet but not Telenet. I mention this to avoid confusion in case you run across an earlier reference to Delphi elsewhere. Tymnet should have been available once again by the end of 1983. Check with Delphi for current availability and other details.)

For further information, contact:
General Videotex Corp.
3 Blackstone St.
Cambridge, MA 02139
(617) 491-3393

Price Structure

As with most information utilities, Delphi's cost varies with time of day and the particular service.

Home Time runs from 6:00 P.M. to 8:00 A.M. Monday through Friday, plus all day weekends and holidays. Cost for most services varies from $5 per hour to $16 per hour (plus $1 per hour for Telenet).

Office Time runs from 8:00 A.M. to 6:00 P.M. Monday through Friday except holidays. Cost for most services during office time varies from $13 per hour to $17 per hour (including the Telenet charge).

Whether dealing with Home Time or Office Time, the low price applies to the services that Delphi itself provides. This includes communications services and the Kussmaul Encyclopedia.

Higher rates are for the services that Delphi provides a gateway for. These include Dialcom Library and travel services.

DIALOG Information Services is a special case, with rates ranging as high as $300 per hour. These rates do not vary with time of day. They are adjusted so that calling through Delphi will cost the same as calling DIALOG directly. (For details on price, see DIALOG entry.)

Notice that there is no extra charge for using 1200 baud rather than 300 baud. There was an additional charge when the system started, but it has been dropped. Delphi deserves high praise for this move.

Description

Delphi has services that range from electronic mail, to on-line banking, to adventure games, to news, and to information services. Delphi, in short, is aimed at both the consumer and the business user. As such, it's the new kid on the block, challenging THE SOURCE and CompuServe, both of which have been around for some time. (Delphi was launched in February 1983.)

Wes Kussmaul, the major force behind Delphi and president of General Videotex Corporation, conceived and developed the utility originally as a consumer-oriented system. A major goal was (and is) to make the system as easy as possible to use. "The philosophy," he says, "was that friendliness builds subscribers among consumers and usage among business people." Kussmaul also feels that consumers are more "friendliness critical," so that a system designed to please consumers will please business users as well.

For the most part, Delphi succeeds in its goal of being easy to use. (There are one or two rough spots, but more on those later.) The menu-based structure is straightforward, self-explanatory, and unusually consistent throughout the system. In addition, there are several nice touches to help ease you into the system and make you feel comfortable with it even if you've never been on-line before. There is, in particular, the Guided Tour.

The first time you sign on to the system, you are automatically sent to the Guided Tour. Your tour guide, Max, welcomes you to the system, then takes you to "the security department," where you are asked to enter a password for future use. After that you can get off the tour or you can stay with it for a helpful introduction to the system's basic features. (Other utilities give you "introductions" to the system, but these generally throw so much information at you that you're more likely to be overwhelmed than enlightened.)

Once you've finished with the tour, you are sent to the main menu. The choices here are self-explanatory. If you want to use a bulletin board, you choose Bulletin-Boards. If you want to look up some information, you choose Library. If you want to arrange travel plans, you choose Travel.

As I've mentioned elsewhere, for me at least, when I'm looking for a particular data base, this division by function is much more useful than the division by category that you'll find on CompuServe and, to a lesser extent, on THE SOURCE. When I'm looking for a bulletin board on Delphi, I have to know only that it's a bulletin board. Once I get to Bulletin Boards, I can ask for a list. When I'm looking for a bulletin board on CompuServe, I have to start out by knowing which category it's in.

One other point about Delphi's ease of use: The manual is excellent, both as an introduction to Delphi and as a reference guide. It's helpful, it's readable, and with few exceptions, it tells you exactly what you need to know.

All this adds up to make Delphi impressively easy to use—as advertised. Even though Delphi has a variety of services available, it's not likely to overwhelm you when you first sign on to it.

I mentioned some rough spots. The fact is that Delphi has a few bugs in it. Some of them are fairly annoying. I managed to get into an infinite loop, for example, that I got out of only by hanging up the phone and calling back.

Any or all of these bugs may be cured by the time you read this. The point is that Delphi is a young service; it is still going through its shakedown period. I'm inclined to forgive these problems for now, because of the obvious effort that has already gone into making this system easy to use, and because—as best as I can tell—Delphi is still making that effort, actively soliciting suggestions from its users.

This brings up another point. Because Delphi is so new, it has relatively few users. Wandering around the system, looking at bulletin boards and such, gives me very much the same feeling as stalking the halls of a large, empty mansion. All of the rooms are there, but there's hardly anything in them. This has its disadvantages (there's almost no one to talk to), yet there is also something exciting about it. The relatively few people who are using Delphi now will help shape the directions the utility takes. They will do this both by their patterns of use and by giving suggestions that may actually be listened to. On THE SOURCE or CompuServe, where you're only one voice among tens of thousands, it's hard to feel like a pioneer.

Delphi is not really a consumer product—yet. But I still like it.

Services Available and List of Data Bases

Communications Services. Delphi provides electronic mail, bulletin boards, and on-line conferences. The value of these services may be questionable at the moment since the usefulness of communications is dependent on how many people you can communicate with. In browsing through the bulletin boards, for example, I've found relatively few messages and some boards that don't have any. As the number of subscribers on Delphi grows, that situation should change and the communications services should quickly become more important.

Bulletin boards on Delphi are divided into categories. Current bulletin boards include:

Computers: Apple, Atari, Commodore, CP/M, DEC, Heath/Zenith, IBM, NorthStar, Osborne, Other-Computers, S-100, Sinclair, TRS-80, Xerox.
General: Gossip, Miscellany, Personals.
Reviews: Books, Hardware, Software.
SIGs: Business Use, Games, Word Processing.
Delphi-related bulletin boards.

Electronic mail service on Delphi will let you send messages to subscribers on several other utilities. Be aware, though, that this is done as a two-step procedure. You're sending the mail to Delphi. Once a day (at night actually) Delphi runs a program that to other utilities and forwards them the same way you would: by calling the appropriate utility and sending the messages by electronic mail.

Transaction Services

Delphi Banking lets you pay your bills electronically, moving your money into your creditors' accounts almost as quickly as you can type in the information. The banking feature will also let you check your balance, look up transactions, balance your checkbook, and generally turn your computer into an automatic teller (without the cash-dispensing feature, as the Delphi manual points out). In order to use "Delphi Banking," you need an account at a Delphi-member bank. Check with Delphi for a current list.

Delphi also has several *shop-at-home services.*

Bazaar lets you list items for sale or auction, or bid on items that others have listed. If you wish, you can specify a minimum bid, a date to start and end bidding, and several other interesting possibilities. Delphi's manual also suggests that the service can be used for bidding on municipal or corporate contracts. This is another service that should become more interesting as Delphi's membership grows.

Catalog functions as a computerized equivalent of mail-order catalogs. Sellers can list their merchandise here and Delphi users can place orders.

Finally, you can call through Delphi to check airline schedules, the prices and availability of rental cars anywhere in the U.S., and the prices and availability of hotel rooms anywhere in the world. These services also let you make reservations for cars, planes, and hotel rooms.

Information Services

Information services on Delphi include the Kussmaul Encyclopedia. As of this writing, AP wire news is expected to be available shortly.

One nice touch here is that the Encyclopedia can be cross-indexed to AP news articles so that a search through the Encyclopedia will also turn up recent news stories on the same subject. Current plans are for this cross-indexing to be used with the AP wire as soon as AP is available on the system.

Delphi also offers access to DIALOG. This is basically equivalent to using DIALOG directly except that you go through Delphi to do it.

Plans are currently under way to "vastly increase the information-provider's area" in the Delphi library. This expansion "is expected to enhance the library and make it easier to use."

Other Services

Several services on Delphi do not fall neatly into the three basic categories of communications, transaction, or information. These include:

Scheduler. Essentially an electronic appointment diary.

Games. Adventure games (Colossal Cave, DND, Star Trek, and Zork); board games (backgammon, Othello, Hexapawn, and Qubic); gambling games (craps, darts, poker, Russian roulette, and Wheel of Fortune); logic games; and learning games for children.

Infomania. This is what you might call the participatory section of Delphi. It is also one of the most popular areas on the system, according to Glenn McIntyre, operations manager.

There are several menu choices within Infomania, but all have one thing in common: You as the user get to take part in them one way or another.

Members-Choice. Contains programs written by Delphi members and available for others to use.

Author. Contains poetry and prose also written by users and available for others to read.

Newsletter. Users can publish their own electronic newsletters "to be commented upon, savored, and vigorously discussed" by others. As of this writing, there are only two newsletters. "Inside Delphi" is about Delphi and is published by Delphi. The "National Club Circuit News" is published by PAN, the Performing Artists Network of North America. This deals primarily with the concerns of musicians. As with communications services, the usefulness of Newsletter should increase with time. The point for now is that the potential is there.

Collaborative-Novel. This is pretty much what it sounds like. Users take turns writing sections. (There are often several "novels" being written at any time.)

Poll. Once again, this is pretty much what it sounds like—a series of polls on questions that range from frivolous to "major questions of the day." Users not only get a chance to vote, they can make a short comment as well.

Dialcom-Library. You'll find this in Delphi's Library section, but it is less an information service than a library of about 120 computer programs.

Some of these serve financial or business needs. (BNDPRO "computes the price of accrued interest for a bond." SALES "generates a sales commission report.")

Other Dialcom programs provide engineering, scientific, mathematical, or statistical calculations. (LTORQ "computes the sum torque acting on lever." PROB "computes Binomial, Poisson, hypergeometric probabilities.")

Still other programs in Dialcom provide computing or editing functions. (XFTN is a computer language, Extended Fortran. SPELL is a spelling checking program.)

Librarian. This provides a trained researcher to conduct your on-line search for you, at a charge. The results are delivered by electronic mail. Like similar services on other utilities, this can quickly become expensive since you have to pay for the researcher's time plus the bill for the connect time that the researcher uses.

Future Services

Additional services currently being considered, or actively under development, include COMP*U*STORE. This, once again, is a shop-at-home service that offers a wide range of items, usually at a substantial discount.

DIALOG Information Services, Inc.

The Basics

Hours: On-line Monday through Thursday, midnight through 10:00 P.M.; Friday, midnight through 8:00 P.M. Saturday, 8:00 A.M. to 8:00 P.M. All times given in Eastern Standard Time.

Command-based.

Baud rate: 300/1200 baud. (No additional charge at 1200 baud.)

Initial charge: None. (Opening an account is not only free, it comes with up to $100 of free time for new customers if used during the first month of service.)

Minimum Monthly Charge: None.

Training: A one-and-one-half-day training session is available for new users. The current price is $135.

If you're an individual thinking about using DIALOG, $135 for training may sound expensive but it is probably one of the greatest bargains of all time. Unlike many computer courses, the training session goes far beyond hand-holding for nervous beginners. First, it will teach you the DIALOG commands. This by itself will save you from costly fumbling later when you're on-line and paying for the time. Even better, the training session is essentially a crash course in search strategies. There's probably nothing in it that you couldn't eventually work out on your own but your mistakes while you're learning will almost certainly cost you more than $135— probably much more. If you're still not convinced that it's worth the money, consider that in addition to teaching you how to use the system, the session includes several hours of free time on DIALOG to conduct any searches that interest you. This alone can be worth more than $135. (You also go home with a temporary password that's good for several hours of practice on DIALOG's ONTAP data bases. These are used for training. They normally cost $15 per hour.)

Reference manual: *The Guide to DIALOG Searching* is the basic reference manual for this system. This is a hefty (2½" thick) stack of pages that comes with a three-ring looseleaf binder. The current cost is $40 in North America. In addition to instructions about DIALOG in general, the guide contains a set of "bluesheets," with a separate bluesheet for each data base. More extensive information on each data base is available at $5 per data-base "chapter." Clearly, there is no point in paying for individual chapters except for the data bases you plan to use fairly often.

Updates: *Chronolog,* DIALOG's monthly newsletter, is sent automatically to all active subscribers. This contains hints on using the system and updated bluesheets when appropriate.

Available through:

Uninet	$6 per hour
Telenet	$8 per hour
Tymnet	$8 per hour
In-WATS	$18 per hour (for customers in outlying areas)
Datapac (in Canada)	$8 per hour

Users of dedicated Mead terminals can get to DIALOG through Mead. If you go through Mead, communications charges are $5 per hour. This is less than charges on any of the telecommunications networks. There is no additional charge from Mead.

For further information, contact:
DIALOG Information Services, Inc.
3460 Hillview Ave.
Palo Alto, CA 94304
(800) 227-1927 (except California)
(800) 982-5838 (toll-free in California)
(415) 858-3785

Price Structure

The concept behind DIALOG's price structure is reasonably simple, but prices vary from data base to data base, which complicates the issue.

First, there is the telecommunications charge. This varies from $5 per hour (if calling through Mead) to $8 per hour (if calling through Tymnet or Telenet), to $18 per hour (if calling on WATS lines from areas where the standard networks are not available).

Second, there is the on-line charge. This varies from data base to data base. The lowest "standard" charge is $15 per hour (for the training data bases only). The highest charge is $300 per hour (for one specialized data base). For most data bases the charge is under $100 per hour; for many it is well under. The vast majority range in price from $25 to $100, with most hovering around $65.

Third, a little under half the data bases have an additional charge for each record read while on-line. Where it exists, this charge is usually well under $1 per record, but be aware that it runs from a meager eight cents per record on up to a hefty $55 per record. Moral: Be careful which data bases you delve into.

Fourth, there is a charge for printing records off-line and having them sent to you. Here again the charges are generally well under $1 per record but they can run as high as $55 per record.

Finally, there is an automatic discount for more than five hours of use per month, and there are contracts available that give discounts in exchange for guarantees of minimum use.

The "average" search (if there is such a thing) is supposed to take 10 to 15 minutes and cost about $15.

There is no additional charge for use at 1200 baud.

Description

DIALOG is aimed mostly at large users, meaning public libraries, universities, and business and professional offices. Although DIALOG's data bases have been and still are primarily bibliographic files, the utility has lately been adding more non-bibliographic data bases. These include directory files (*Electronic Yellow Pages, Books in Print*), statistical files *(Bureau of Labor Statistics Consumer Price Index),* and even some full text files (*Harvard Business Review, Academic American Encyclopedia Database*).

As of October 1983, there were somewhat more than 170 data bases available on the system. DIALOG divides these into 17 major categories. As with all the large utilities, many of these data bases or their equivalents are also available elsewhere. Others are available only through DIALOG. The sheer number of data bases on DIALOG, however, gives it an edge over most competing services—unless, of course, you are looking for a specific data base that DIALOG does not have. In 1983, DIALOG initiated KNOWLEDGE INDEX, an "after-hours" service aimed at the small business, professional, and home-computer user. (KNOWLEDGE INDEX, which is significantly cheaper and easier to use, is listed separately.)

Services Available

Until recently DIALOG has offered information services only. These fall into two categories: On-line searching and a current awareness service. On-line searching has an option for off-line printing of the list of items found. It also has an option for ordering copies of the complete document or documents. The current awareness service is essentially an electronic newsclipping service with the clippings, or list or matches, delivered by (non-electronic) mail. Here again, as you would expect from a utility aimed primarily at large information users, both these services allow for sophisticated searching techniques.

As of this writing, DIALOG is about to add communications services to its repertoire. More on this later.

On-Line Searching

The data bases on DIALOG cover just about as wide a range as you can think of: agriculture, medicine, business, law, and more. They also include standard reference works like *Books in Print*. Some of these data bases contain references only. Others contain abstracts of articles. Still others include the full text of each item. DIALOG divides the data bases into 17 major categories. These are:

Chemistry
Agriculture and Nutrition
Medicine and Biosciences
Energy and Environment
Science and Technology
Materials Science
Patents
Business/Economics
Law and Government
Current Affairs
Directories
Social Sciences/Humanities
Multidisciplinary

Education
On-line Training and Practice (ONTAP)
Bibliography—Books and Monographs
Foundations and Grants

With more than 170 data bases to choose from, you may occasionally wonder which one, or which ones, to search in. One of DIALOG's data bases, DIALINDEX, solves the problem by giving you an index to the data bases on DIALOG. You can go to DIALINDEX, test a search strategy on one or more data bases and see how many hits you'll find in each data base on the system. You then go to the individual data bases to retrieve the records.

Once you've found what you're looking for, you can usually order copies of the item, or items, through DIALOG's DIALORDER, and have them sent by mail. Items ordered through DIALORDER are not computer printouts. They may come in the form of photocopies (as with magazine articles), the original material (as with books), or in other forms as appropriate.

SDI (Selective Dissemination of Information)

DIALOG also has an SDI service that lets you store a search phrase or phrases in the system. As with similar services on other systems, DIALOG will automatically search through new information every time a specified data base is updated, then print any relevant new references and mail them to you. This gives you a constant flow of new information on any subject you're interested in.

Currently Under Development

As of this writing, plans are afoot for adding communications services to DIALOG in the first half of 1984. This will include electronic mail, bulletin boards, and on-line conferences. Check with DIALOG for details.

DATA BASES ON DIALOG

(Listed by Category)

Agriculture and Nutrition

AGRICOLA   Subject: Agriculture. Producer: National Agricultural Library. Also available on BRS, BRS/AFTER DARK, KNOWLEDGE INDEX.

BIOSIS PREVIEWS AND BACKFILE   Subject: Biological sciences. Producer: BioSciences Information Service. Also available on BRS, BRS/AFTER DARK, KNOWLEDGE INDEX. Also listed in Medicine and Biosciences and in Energy and Environment categories on DIALOG.

CAB ABSTRACTS   Subject: Agricultural and biological abstracts. Producer: The Commonwealth Agricultural Bureaux.

CRIS/USDA   Subject: Current awareness data base for agriculturally related research. Producer: U.S. Dept. of Agriculture.

FOOD SCIENCE AND TECHNOLOGY ABSTRACTS   Producer: International Food Information Service.

FOODS ADLIBRA   Subject: Food technology and packaging. Producer: Komp Information Services. Also listed as an Industry Specific Business data base on DIALOG.

BIBLIOGRAPHY—BOOKS AND MONOGRAPHS

BOOK REVIEW INDEX   Subject: Published reviews of books and periodicals. Producer: Gale Research Company.

BOOKS IN PRINT   Subject: U.S. books in print. Producer: R.R. Bowker. Also available on BRS, BRS/AFTER DARK, KNOWLEDGE INDEX.

DIALOG PUBLICATIONS   Subject: On-line ordering of DIALOG publications. Producer: DIALOG.

LC MARC   Subject: Bibliographic records for all books cataloged by U.S. Library of Congress since 1968. Producer: U.S. Library of Congress.

REMARC   Subject: Cataloged collections of U.S. Library of Congress from 1897–1980. Producer: Carrollton Press.

BUSINESS/ECONOMICS—BIBLIOGRAPHIC DATA BASES

ABI/INFORM   Subject: Business. Producer: Data Courier, Inc. Also available on BRS, BRS/AFTER DARK, KNOWLEDGE INDEX.

ADTRACK   Subject: Index of ads in 148 major U.S. magazines. Producer: Corporate Intelligence, Inc.

ARTHUR D. LITTLE/ONLINE   Subject: Provides "broad coverage of industries, technologies, and management topics." Producer: Arthur D. Little Decision Resources.

ECONOMIC LITERATURE INDEX   Subject: Covers articles and book reviews from 260 economic journals and roughly 200 monographs each year. Producer: American Economic Association.

ECONOMICS ABSTRACTS INTERNATIONAL   Subject: Covers world literature on markets, industries, country-specific economic data, and research in economic science and management. Producer: Learned Information, Ltd.

FIND/SVP REPORTS AND STUDIES INDEX   Subject: Industry and market-research reports, studies, and surveys. Producer: FIND/SVP.

HARFAX INDUSTRY DATA SOURCES   Subject: Bibliographic sources of financial and marketing data for 65 major industries. Producer: Harfax Database Publishing. Also available on NEXIS.

HARVARD BUSINESS REVIEW   Subject: Full text of Harvard Business Review from 1977 to present. Producer: John Wiley & Sons. Also available on BRS, BRS/AFTER DARK.

INSURANCE ABSTRACTS   Subject: Life, property, and liability insurance. Abstracts from over 100 journals. Producer: University Microfilms International. Also listed as an Industry Specific Business data base on DIALOG.

MANAGEMENT CONTENTS   Subject: Business and management-related topics. Producer: Management Contents, Inc. Also available on BRS, BRS/AFTER DARK, THE SOURCE.

PHARMACEUTICAL NEWS INDEX   Subject: Covers pharmaceuticals, cosmetics, medical devices and related subjects. Producer: Data Courier, Inc. Also listed in Medicine and Biosciences category and as an Industry Specific data base on DIALOG.

PTS ANNUAL REPORTS ABSTRACTS   Subject: Covers annual reports of over 3,000 publicly held U.S. companies. Producer: Predicasts, Inc. Also available on BRS as Predicasts Annual Report.

PTS F&S INDEXES   Subject: Covers company, product, and industry information worldwide. Producer: Predicasts, Inc. Also available on BRS as Predicasts F&S Indexes.

PTS PROMT   Subject: Abstracts of business information from newspapers, business magazines, government reports, trade journals, and other sources. Covers a variety of industries. Producer: Predicasts, Inc. Also available on BRS as Predicasts Promt.

STANDARD & POOR'S NEWS   Subject: General news and financial information on more than 10,000 publicly owned U.S. companies. Covers 1979 through present. Producer: Standard & Poor's Corp. Also available on KNOWLEDGE INDEX. Also listed in Current Affairs category on DIALOG.

STANDARD & POOR'S NEWS DAILY   Subject: General news and financial information on more than 10,000 publicly owned U.S. companies. Covers current week only. Producer: Standard & Poor's Corp. Also listed in Current Affairs category on DIALOG.

TRADE AND INDUSTRY INDEX   Subject: Index to 275 major trade and industry journals in all Standard Industrial Classifications. Also indexes several newspapers, including *The New York Times* and *The Wall Street Journal*. Producer: Information Access Corporation. Also available on KNOWLEDGE INDEX.

BUSINESS/ECONOMICS—DIRECTORIES

COMMERCE BUSINESS DAILY   Subject: Products and services wanted or offered by U.S. Government. Producer: Commerce Business Daily, U.S. Dept. of Commerce. Also listed in "Law and Government" category on DIALOG.

D&B—DUN'S MARKET IDENTIFIERS   Subject: Information on more than 1,000,000 U.S. businesses with 10 or more employees. Producer: Dun's Marketing Services. Also available on Dow Jones News/Retrieval.

D&B—MILLION DOLLAR DIRECTORY   Subject: Business information on U.S. companies with a net worth of $500,000 or more. Producer: Dun's Marketing Services.

D&B—PRINCIPAL INTERNATIONAL BUSINESSES   Subject: Covers companies in 133 countries. Companies are chosen as "principal" businesses based on sales volume, national prominence, and "international interest." Producer: Dun & Bradstreet International.

EIS INDUSTRIAL PLANTS   Subject: U.S. Industrial Economy. Producer: Economic Information Systems, Inc.

EIS NONMANUFACTURING ESTABLISHMENTS   Subject: Contains location, name, percent of industry sales, and the like for more than 250,000 nonmanufacturing establishments. Producer: Economic Information Systems, Inc.

ELECTRONIC YELLOW PAGES—CONSTRUCTION DIRECTORY   Subject: Covers contractors and construction agencies. Producer: Market Data Retrieval, Inc.

ELECTRONIC YELLOW PAGES—FINANCIAL SERVICES DIRECTORY
Subject: Covers banks , savings and loan institutions, and credit unions in the U.S. Producer: Market Data Retrieval, Inc.

ELECTRONIC YELLOW PAGES—MANUFACTURERS DIREC-TORY   Subject: Covers manufacturing establishments in the U.S. Producer: Market Data Retrieval, Inc.

ELECTRONIC YELLOW PAGES—PROFESSIONALS DIRECTORY
Subject: Covers insurance, real estate, medicine, law, engineering, and accounting in the U.S. Also hospitals, medical labs, and clinics. Producer: Market Data Retrieval, Inc.

ELECTRONIC YELLOW PAGES—RETAILERS DIRECTORY   Subject: Covers retail businesses in the U.S. Producer: Market Data Retrieval, Inc.

ELECTRONIC YELLOW PAGES—SERVICES DIRECTORY   Subject: Covers services of all kinds in the U.S. Producer: Market Data Retrieval, Inc.

ELECTRONIC YELLOW PAGES—WHOLESALERS DIRECTORY   Subject: Covers wholesalers of all kinds in the U.S. Producer: Market Data Retrieval, Inc.

FOREIGN TRADERS INDEX   Subject: Directory of firms that either import goods from the U.S. or are interested in doing so as representatives of U.S. exporters. Covers 130 countries. Producer: U.S. Dept. of Commerce.

TRADE OPPORTUNITIES   Subject: Export opportunities for U.S. businesses. Producer: U.S. Dept. of Commerce.

TRADE OPPORTUNITIES WEEKLY   Subject: Export opportunities. Current information only. Producer: U.S. Dept. of Commerce.

BUSINESS/ECONOMICS—INDUSTRY SPECIFIC DATA BASES

COFFEELINE   Subject: All aspects of coffee production. Producer: International Coffee Organization.

BUSINESS/ECONOMICS—NUMERIC DATA BASES

BI/DATA FORECASTS   Subject: Market forecast reports for business activities in 35 countries. Producer: Business International Corporation.

BI/DATA TIME SERIES   Subject: Economic indicators in time-series records for up to 131 countries. Producer: Business International Corp.

BLS CONSUMER PRICE INDEX   Subject: Consumer price indexes by area, population category, and more. Producer: Bureau of Labor Statistics, U.S. Dept. of Labor.

BLS EMPLOYMENT, HOURS, AND EARNINGS   Subject: Employment, hours, and earnings broken down by industry and by national, state and local figures. Producer: Bureau of Labor Statistics, U.S. Dept. of Labor.

BLS LABOR FORCE   Subject: Employment/unemployment by a variety of demographic, social, and economic categories. Producer: Bureau of Labor Statistics, U.S. Dept. of Labor.

BLS PRODUCER PRICE INDEX   Subject: Producer price indexes for 2800 commodities. Producer: Bureau of Labor Statistics, U.S. Dept. of Labor.

DISCLOSURE II   Subject: Information on 8500 publicly held companies. SEC filings. Producer: DISCLOSURE. Also available on Dow Jones News/Retrieval. Also listed in Business/Economic Directory category on DIALOG.

PTS INTERNATIONAL FORECASTS   Subject: Abstracts of economic forecasts for all industries. Includes detailed statistics on products and end use. Producer: Predicasts, Inc. Also available on BRS as Predicasts Forecasts.

PTS INTERNATIONAL TIME SERIES   Subject: Demographic and economic data and projections for all countries of the world, with special emphasis on about 50 major countries. Producer: Predicasts, Inc. Also available on BRS as Predicasts Historical Time Series.

PTS U.S. FORECASTS   Subject: Abstracts of published forecasts for all industries in the U.S. Includes detailed data on products and end use. Producer: Predicasts, Inc. Also available on BRS as Predicasts Forecasts.

PTS U.S. TIME SERIES   Subject: Demographic and economic data and forecasts for the U.S. Producer: Predicasts, Inc. Also available on BRS as Predicasts Historical Time Series.

U.S. EXPORTS   Subject: Export statistics in dollar value and shipping weight. Includes all commodities. Producer: U.S. Dept. of Commerce.

Chemistry

CA SEARCH   Subject: Chemistry. Producer: Chemical Abstracts Service. Also listed in Medicine and Biosciences, Energy and Environment, Materials Science, and Patents categories on DIALOG.

CHEMICAL EXPOSURE   Subject: Covers chemicals that have been found in both human and animal tissues and body fluids. Producer: Chemical Effects Information Center. Also listed in Medicine and Biosciences category on DIALOG.

CHEMICAL INDUSTRY NOTES   Subject: Extracts from business-oriented articles covering the chemical industry. Producer: American Chemical Society. Also listed as an Industry Specific business data base and as a Business/Economics bibliographic data base on DIALOG.

CHEMICAL REGULATIONS AND GUIDELINES SYSTEM   Subject: Index to Federal regulatory material relating to the chemical industry. Producer: U.S. Interagency Regulatory Liaison Group. Also listed in Law and Government category on DIALOG.

CHEMLAW   Subject: Full text of Federal chemical regulations. Producer: Bureau of National Affairs. Also listed in Law and Government category on DIALOG.

CHEMNAME   Subject: Dictionary-type list of chemical substances. Producer: DIALOG. Also listed in Medicine and Biosciences and in Materials Sciences categories on DIALOG.

CHEMSEARCH   Subject: Companion file to Chemname on DIALOG. Covers the most recent citations. Producer: DIALOG. Also listed in Medicine and Biosciences and in Materials Sciences categories on DIALOG.

CHEMSIS   Subject: Part of DIALOG's Chemical Information System. Producer: DIALOG. Also listed in Medicine and Biosciences and in Materials Sciences categories on DIALOG.

CHEMZERO   Subject: DIALOG. Producer: DIALOG. Also listed in Medicine and Biosciences and in Materials Sciences categories on DIALOG.

CLAIMS COMPOUND REGISTRY   Subject: Dictionary of chemical compounds. Useful for searching Claims/Uniterm data base. Producer: IFI/Plenum Data Co. Also listed in Patents category on DIALOG.

PAPERCHEM   Subject: Index to and abstracts of scientific and technological literature on the paper industry. Producer: Institute of Paper Chemistry. Also listed in Materials Science category on DIALOG.

SCISEARCH   Subject: Multi-disciplinary index to scientific and technological literature. Producer: Institute for Scientific Information. Also listed in Medicine and Biosciences and in Science and Technology categories on DIALOG. Also available on: BRS and BRS/AFTER DARK as Social Science Citation Index.

TSCA INITIAL INVENTORY   Subject: Dictionary listing chemical substances in commercial use. Producer: DIALOG. Also listed in Law and Government category on DIALOG.

Current Affairs

CHRONOLOG NEWSLETTER   Subject: DIALOG's on-line newsletter with updates, search tips, and so forth. Producer: DIALOG.

MAGAZINE INDEX   Subject: Covers popular magazines in a broad range of subjects. Producers: Information Access Corp. Also available on KNOWLEDGE INDEX.

NATIONAL NEWSPAPER INDEX   Subject: Index to *The Christian Science Monitor, The New York Times, The Los Angeles Times, The Washington Post,* and *The Wall Street Journal.* Producer: Information Access Corp. Also available on KNOWLEDGE INDEX.

NEWSEARCH   Subject: Index to newspaper and magazine stories for current month only. Functions as a supplement to National Newspaper Index and Magazine Index for most current stories. Producer: Information Access Corp. Also available on KNOWLEDGE INDEX.

ONLINE CHRONICLE   Subject: The on-line industry. This is a full text data base, the on-line version of the News sections of *Online* and *Database* magazines. Producer: Online, Inc.

UPI NEWS   Subject: Full text of UPI wire starting from March 1983. There is a 48-hour lag between the time stories appear on UPI and the time they are entered in the DIALOG UPI data base. Producer: United Press International, Inc. A similar delayed version of UPI is available on NEXIS, going back to September 1980. The current UPI wire is available on Dow Jones News/Retrieval, THE SOURCE, and NewsNet.

Directories

AMERICAN MEN AND WOMEN OF SCIENCE   Subject: Directory of scientists. Producer: R.R. Bowker.

BIOGRAPHY MASTER INDEX   Subject: Index to over 600 sources of biographical information on scientists, celebrities, and others. Producer: Gale Research Co.

CAREER PLACEMENT REGISTRY/EXPERIENCED PERSONNEL   Subject: Resumés of individuals who are not recent college graduates. Producer: Career Placement Registry, Inc.

CAREER PLACEMENT REGISTRY/STUDENT   Subject: Resumés of recent college graduates. Producer: Career Placement Registry, Inc.

ENCYCLOPEDIA OF ASSOCIATIONS   Subject: Trade associations, professional societies, labor unions, and other groups with voluntary membership. Producer: Gale Research Co.

MARQUIS WHO'S WHO   Subject: On-line version of reference book by the same name. Contains bibliographies of 75,000 well-known individuals. Producer: Marquis Who's Who, Inc.

ULRICH'S INTERNATIONAL   Subject: Directory of Periodicals. Producer: R.R. Bowker.

EDUCATION

AIM/ARM   Subject: Index to materials on vocational and technical education, employment, and guidance. Producer: The Center for Vocational Education, Ohio State University.

ERIC   Subject: Education. Producer: National Institute of Education. Also available on BRS, BRS/AFTER DARK, KNOWLEDGE INDEX.

EXCEPTIONAL CHILD EDUCATION RESOURCES   Producer: Council for Exceptional Children. Also available on BRS, BRS/AFTER DARK.

IRIS   Subject: Educational materials on water quality and water resources. Producer: U.S. EPA Information Project, Ohio State University.

NICEM (NATIONAL INFORMATION CENTER FOR EDUCATIONAL ME-DIA)   Subject: Non-print educational material. Producer: National Information Center for Educational Media.

NICSEM/NIMIS   Subject: Media and devices for teaching handicapped children. Producer: National Information Center for Special Educational Materials.

U.S. PUBLIC SCHOOLS DIRECTORY   Subject: Covers public schools throughout the U.S. and territories. Producer: National Center for Education Statistics.

ENERGY & ENVIRONMENT

APTIC   Subject: Air pollution and its effects. Producer: Manpower and Technical Information Branch, U.S. EPA.

AQUACULTURE   Subject: Information on growing marine, brackish, and freshwater organisms. Producer: National Oceanic and Atmospheric Administration.

AQUALINE   Subject: Water, including waste water, and aquatic environment. Producer: Water Research Centre.

AQUATIC SCIENCES AND FISHERIES ABSTRACTS   Subject: Life science of seas and inland waters. Also covers related legal and political information. Producer: NOAA.

DOE ENERGY   Subject: All aspects of energy and related topics. Producer: U.S. Dept. of Energy.

ELECTRIC POWER DATABASE   Subject: R&D projects of interest to the electric power industry. Producer: Electric Power Research Institute.

ENERGYLINE   Subject: This is the machine-readable version of *Energy Information Abstracts*. Producer: Environment Information Center, Inc.

ENERGYNET   Subject: Dictionary of organizations and people in energy-related fields. Producer: Environment Information Center, Inc.

ENVIROLINE   Subject: Interdisciplinary index to and abstracts of worldwide environmental information. Producer: Environment Information Center, Inc.

ENVIRONMENTAL BIBLIOGRAPHY   Subject: Human ecology, atmospheric studies, energy, land resources, water resources, nutrition, and health. Producer: Environmental Studies Institute.

OCEANIC ABSTRACTS   Subject: Index to technical literature on marine-related subjects. Producer: Cambridge Scientific Abstracts.

POLLUTION ABSTRACTS   Producer: Cambridge Scientific Abstracts.

WATER RESOURCES ABSTRACTS   Subject: Covers water-related issues, including economics, to metropolitan water planning, management, and water-related questions of nuclear radiation. Producer: U.S. Dept. of the Interior.

WATERNET   Subject: Index to the publications of the American Water Works Association. Covers primarily technical reports and studies. Producer: American Water Works Assoc.

FOUNDATIONS AND GRANTS

FOUNDATION DIRECTORY   Subject: Descriptions of 3500 foundations that between them account for roughly 80 percent of all foundation-giving in the U.S. Producer: The Foundation Center.

FOUNDATION GRANTS INDEX   Subject: Covers grants awarded by more than 400 U.S. philanthropic foundations. Producer: The Foundation Center.

GRANTS   Subject: Lists 1500 grant programs available through government, commercial foundations, and private foundations. Producer: Oryx Press.

NATIONAL FOUNDATIONS   Subject: Covers all 22,500 U.S. foundations that award grants. Producer: The Foundation Center.

LAW AND GOVERNMENT

ASI   Subject: Index to statistical publications of agencies of the U.S. Government. Producer: Congressional Information Service, Inc.

CIS   Subject: Index to congressional publications. Producer: Congressional Information Service, Inc.

CONGRESSIONAL RECORD ABSTRACTS   Producer: Capitol Services International.

CRIMINAL JUSTICE PERIDOCALS INDEX   Subject: Index to 120 journals and periodicals dealing with justice and law enforcement. Producer: University Microfilms International.

FEDERAL INDEX   Subject: Index to proposed rules, regulations, bill introduction, speeches, hearings, roll calls, reports, vetoes, court decisions, executive orders, and contract awards. Producer: Capitol Services International.

FEDERAL REGISTER ABSTRACTS   Subject: Actions of Federal regulatory agencies as published in the *Federal Register*. Producer: Capitol Services International. The full text of the *Federal Register* is available on NEXIS.

GPO MONTHLY CATALOG   Subject: Index to government publications of all kinds. Producer: U.S. Government Printing Office. Also listed in Bibliography category on DIALOG.

GPO PUBLICATIONS REFERENCE FILE   Subject: Index of public documents currently for sale by the Government Printing Office. Producer: U.S. Government Printing Office. Also available on KNOWLEDGE INDEX. Also listed in "Bibliography" category on DIALOG.

LABORLAW   Subject: Labor relations, fair employment, occupational health and safety. References to and summaries of regulatory decisions in these fields. Producer: Bureau of National Affairs, Inc.

LEGAL RESOURCE INDEX   Subject: Indexing of 660 key law journals and five law newspapers, plus legal monographs and government publications. Producer: Information Access Corp. Also available on KNOWLEDGE INDEX.

NCJRS (NATIONAL CRIMINAL JUSTICE REFERENCE SERVICE)   Subject: All aspects of law enforcement and criminal justice—both U.S. and international. Producer: National Criminal Justice Reference Service.

Materials Sciences

METADEX   Subject: Metallurgy. Full title is METALS ABSTRACTS/ALLOYS INDEX. Producer: American Society for Metals.

NONFERROUS METALS ABSTRACTS   Producer: British Non-Ferrous Metals Technology Centre.

SURFACE COATINGS ABSTRACTS   Subject: Covers all aspects of paints and surface coatings. Producer: Paint Research Association of Great Britain.

TEXTILE TECHNOLOGY DIGEST   Subject: Covers world literature on aluminum, from processing of ore to end uses. Producer: American Society for Metals.

WORLD TEXTILES   Subject: Covers world literature on the science and technology of textile and related materials. Producer: Shirley Institute.

Medicine and Biosciences

EXCERPTA MEDICA   Subject: Medical abstracts and citations from over 3500 journals. Producer: Excerpta Medica.

HEALTH PLANNING AND ADMINISTRATION   Subject: Health economics, administration, and planning. Producer: National Library of Medicine. Also available on BRS, BRS/AFTER DARK.

INTERNATIONAL PHARMACEUTICAL ABSTRACTS   Producer: American Society of Hospital Pharmacists. Also available on BRS, KNOWLEDGE INDEX.

LIFE SCIENCES COLLECTION   Subject: Animal behavior, biochemistry, ecology, entomology, and more. Producer: Cambridge Scientific Abstracts.

MEDLINE   Subject: All aspects of health care. Producer: National Library of Medicine. Also available on KNOWLEDGE INDEX.

MENTAL HEALTH ABSTRACTS   Producer: National Clearinghouse for Mental Health Information.

TELEGEN   Subject: Genetic engineering and biotechnology—scientific, technical, and socioeconomic information. Producer: Environment Information Center.

ZOOLOGICAL RECORD   Subject: Zoological Literature. Producer: Bio-Sciences Information Service.

Multidisciplinary

COMPREHENSIVE DISSERTATION INDEX   Subject: Index to "virtually every American dissertation" accepted since 1861. Producer: University Microfilms International.

CONFERENCE PAPERS INDEX   Subject: Index to papers given in various hard sciences and engineering. Producer: Cambridge Scientific Abstracts.

DIALINDEX   Subject: Collection of indexes to all DIALOG data bases. Used within DIALOG to help decide which data base or data bases to search in. Producer: DIALOG.

Online Training and Practice

Each of the data bases in this category is extracted from the full data base by the same name. The co-producers in each cases are DIALOG Information Services and the producer of the full-scale version of the data base. Because the ONTAP data bases are only partial in nature, they are not adequate for information searching. They are on DIALOG to provide an inexpensive training ground for new searchers.

ONTAP ABI/INFORM
ONTAP CA SEARCH
ONTAP CHEMNAME
ONTAP COMPENDEX
ONTAP DIALINDEX
ONTAP ERIC
ONTAP INSPEC
ONTAP MAGAZINE INDEX
ONTAP MEDLINE
ONTAP PTS PROMPT

PATENTS AND TRADEMARKS

CLAIMS/CITATION   Subject: Index to later patents that cite any given patent. Producer: Search Check, Inc. and IFI/Plenum Data Co.

CLAIMS/CLASS   Subject: Code and title dictionary to U.S. patent classifications. Producer: IFI/Plenum Data Co.

CLAIMS/U.S. PATENT ABSTRACTS   Subject: Chemical, electrical, general, and mechanical patents. Producer: IFI/Plenum Data Co.

CLAIMS/U.S. PATENT ABSTRACTS WEEKLY   Subject: Chemical and chemically related U.S. patents. Producer: IFI/Plenum Data Co.

CLAIMS/UNITERM   Subject: Chemical and chemically related U.S. patents. Producer: IFI/Plenum Data Co.

PATLAW   Subject: Legal and administrative decisions relating to patents, trademarks, copyrights, and unfair competition law. Producer: Bureau of National Affairs, Inc. Also listed in Law and Government category on DIALOG.

TRADEMARKSCAN   Subject: Covers active Federal trademark applications. Producer: Thomson and Thomson.

SCIENCE AND TECHNOLOGY

BHRA FLUID ENGINEERING   Producer: BHRA Fluid Engineering.

COMPENDEX   Subject: This is the computer-readable form of *Engineering Index*. Producer: Engineering Information Inc. Also available on BRS, KNOWLEDGE INDEX.

THE COMPUTER DATABASE   Subject: Computers and all related subjects. Hardware, software, peripherals, published programs, telecommunications, and more. This data base contains an index to and abstracts of over 530 periodicals, plus books, conferences, and self-study courses. Producer: Management Contents.

Ei ENGINEERING MEETINGS   Subject: Index to published proceedings of engineering and technical conferences and meetings. Producer: Engineering Information, Inc.

GEOARCHIVE   Subject: Geological science. Producer: Geosystems.

GEOREF   Subject: Geological science. Producer: American Geological Institute.

INSPEC   Subject: Engineering, physics, and computer science. Producer: Institute of Electrical Engineers. Also available on BRS, KNOWLEDGE INDEX.

INTERNATIONAL SOFTWARE DATABASE   Subject: List of commercially available mini- and microcomputer software. Producer: Imprint Software Ltd. Also available on KNOWLEDGE INDEX.

ISMEC   Subject: Mechanical Engineering. Producer: Cambridge Scientific Abstracts.

MATHFILE   Subject: Index to and abstracts of mathematical literature. Producer: American Mathematical Society.

METEOROLOGICAL AND GEOASTROPHYSICAL ABSTRACTS   Producer: American Meterological Society.

MICOCOMPUTER INDEX   Subject: Index to magazine articles from microcomputer journals. Producer: Microcomputer Information Services. Also available on KNOWLEDGE INDEX.

NTIS   Subject: Government reports. Various areas. Producer: National Technical Information Service. Also available on BRS, BRS/AFTER DARK, KNOWLEDGE INDEX. Also listed in Law and Government and in Multidisciplinary categories on DIALOG.

SPIN   Subject: Physics. Producer: American Institute of Physics.

SSIE CURRENT RESEARCH   Subject: Smithsonian Science Information Exchange. Government and privately funded scientific research. All fields of basic and applied research. Producer: National Technical Information Service.

STANDARDS AND SPECIFICATIONS   Subject: Government and industry documents that specify terminology, performance testing, safety, and other standards. Producer: National Standards Assoc.

TRIS   Subject: Research information on all forms of transportation. Covers related regulations, legislation, energy and environmental concerns, and more. Producer: Dept. of Transportation and Transportation Research Board.

WELDASEARCH   Subject: All aspects of research on the joining of metals and plastics. Also covers related areas. Producer: The Welding Institute.

SOCIAL SCIENCE AND HUMANITIES

AMERICA: HISTORY AND LIFE   Subject: U.S. and Canadian history, ethnic studies, folklore, oral history, and the like. Producer: ABC-Clio, Inc.

ARTBIBLIOGRAPHIES MODERN   Subject: modern art and design. Producer: ABC-Clio, Inc.

CHILD ABUSE AND NEGLECT   Producer: National Center for Child Abuse and Neglect.

FAMILY RESOURCES DATA BASE   Subject: Covers psychological, sociological, educational, and medical literature relating to the family. Producer: National Council on Family Relations and Inventory of Marriage and Family Literature Project. Also available on BRS.

HISTORICAL ABSTRACTS   Subject: Covers world periodical literature in history and related subjects. Producer: ABC-Clio, Inc.

INFORMATION SCIENCE ABSTRACTS   Subject: Index to and abstracts of literature relating to information science. Producer: IFI/Plenum Data Co.

LANGUAGE AND LANGUAGE BEHAVIOR ABSTRACTS   Producer: Sociological Abstracts.

LISA (LIBRARY AND INFORMATION SCIENCE ABSTRACTS)   Subject: Library services, information storage and retrieval, abstracting and indexing services, and related fields. Producer: Learned Information Ltd.

MLA BIBLIOGRAPHY   Subject: Language, Linguistics and folklore. Producer: Modern Language Assoc. of America.

PHILOSOPHER'S INDEX   Subject: Index to and abstracts of books and journals in philosophy and related fields. Producer: Philosophy Documentation Center.

POPULATION BIBLIOGRAPHY   Subject: Index to information on abortion, demographics, family planning, fertility studies, and related areas. Producer: University of North Carolina, Carolina Population Center.

PSYCINFO   Subject: Psychology. Producer: American Psychological Assoc. Also available on BRS, BRS/AFTER DARK, KNOWLEDGE INDEX.

PUBLIC AFFAIRS INFORMATION SERVICE   (PAIS International) Subject: All social sciences, including political science, banking, public administration, international relations, economics, law, public policy, social wefare, and more. Producer: Public Affairs Information Service. Also available on BRS, BRS/AFTER DARK. Also listed in "Current Affairs" category on DIALOG.

RELIGION INDEX   Subject: Index to and abstracts of literature covering church history, biblical literature, and theology, as well as the history, sociology, and psychology of religion. Producer: American Theological Library Assoc. Also available on BRS.

RILM ABSTRACTS   Subject: Abstracts of all significant literature on music. (*Repertoire International de Litterature Musicale*). Producer: City University of N.Y., International RILM Center.

SOCIAL SCISEARCH   Subject: Index to 1000 journals in all fields of social science. Producer: Institute for Scientific Information.

SOCIOLOGICAL ABSTRACTS   Subject: Sociology and related disciplines. Producer: Sociological Abstracts, Inc.

UNITED STATES POLITICAL SCIENCE ABSTRACTS   Subject: Index to and abstracts of 120 major U.S. political science journals. Producer: University of Pittsburgh, University Center for International Studies.

WORLD AFFAIRS REPORT   Subject: Digest of worldwide news as seen from Moscow. Producer: California Institute of International Affairs. Also listed under "Current Affairs" category on DIALOG.

New data bases are continually being added. Check with DIALOG for a current list.

Dow Jones News/Retrieval

The Basics

Hours: On-line 22 hours a day from 6:00 A.M. to 4:00 A.M. Eastern Time. Menu-based.

Baud rate: 300/1200 baud.

Initial charge: $50 sign-up fee.

Minimum monthly charge: None (except for Executive Membership monthly fee).

Training: In-house training classes are available for large users by special arrangement but they are not really needed. The system is simple enough to learn on your own.

Reference manuals:

The Dow Jones News/Retrieval Fact Finder (comes free with password).
An Introduction to Free Text Search of the Dow Jones News Database (available free on request)

Updates: *Dowline* is automatically sent to all Dow Jones subscribers. This includes how-to articles for using the utility and announcements of new data bases and services as they become available. On-line updates are also available through the INTRO data base.

Available through:

Telenet
Tymnet
Uninet
Datapac (in Canada)
There is no additional charge for any of these communications networks.

Protocol Notes: This utility is notorious for sending control codes that confuse various pieces of software. If you plan to use Dow Jones, you should get a communications program that lets you filter out incoming control codes. If you'd rather not spend the time figuring out which control codes you need to filter out, you can get one of the program sold by Dow Jones. (You'll find them in the list at the end of Chapter 5.)

For further information, contact:
Dow Jones & Company, Inc.
PO Box 300
Princeton, NJ 08540
(800) 257-5114
(609) 452-1511 (in New Jersey)

Price Structure

The basic Dow Jones price structure is fairly simple, although there are some complications.

Standard membership is on a strictly pay-as-you-go basis. The cost ranges from $9 per hour to $144 per hour, depending on the data base, time of day, and baud rate.

Prime time is from 6:00 A.M. Eastern Time through 6:00 P.M. your local time, Monday through Friday.

Non-prime time is from 6:01 P.M. your local time through 4:00 A.M. Eastern Time, Monday through Friday and all day Saturday, Sunday, and designated holidays.

Baud Rate Charge: Communication at 1200 baud is charged at twice the 300-baud rate.

Data Base Charge: The data bases are divided into four categories, priced as follows:

	300 Baud	1200 Baud
Dow Jones Business and Economic News		
Prime time:	$1.20 minute ($72 per hour)	$2.40 minute ($144 per hour)
Non-prime time:	$ .20 minute ($12 per hour)	$ .40 minute ($24 per hour)
Dow Jones Quotes		
Prime time:	$ .90 minute ($54 per hour)	$1.80 minute ($108 per hour)
Non-prime time:	$ .15 minute ($ 9 per hour)	$ .30 minute ($18 per hour)
Financial and Investment Services		
Prime time:	$1.20 minute ($72 per hour)	$2.40 minute ($144 per hour)
Non-prime time:	$ .90 minute ($54 per hour)	$1.80 minute ($108 per hour)
General News and Information Services		
Prime time:	$ .60 minute ($36 per hour)	$1.20 minute ($144 per hour)
Non-prime time:	$ .30 minute ($18 per hour)	$ .60 minute ($36 per hour)

Two other categories of membership are available: Blue Chip and Executive.

Blue Chip Membership requires an annual fee of $100. This buys a one-third savings in the cost of *non-prime time* use and a guaranteed minimum of six hours each year on new or selected data bases.

Executive Membership requires a $50 monthly fee per location. (Multiple floors in the same building count as one location.) This buys a one-third savings in the cost of all use and a guaranteed minimum of six free hours each year on new or selected data bases.

Description

Dow Jones News/Retrieval is usually mentioned as a "general" utility, in the same category as THE SOURCE, CompuServe, and the like. It's not. If you think of it that way, you'll probably be disappointed by what you find here—or what you don't find. There are no games, no CB emulation, and no Special Interest Groups or bulletin boards. That's not what this utility is about.

There are a few general-information services available—weather reports, movie reviews, and sports reports, to name three—but these are essentially extras, nice to have but not the reason for signing up on this system.

Among other things, Dow Jones News/Retrieval features an on-line version of *The Wall Street Journal,* updated throughout the day. This is indicative of the real strength of this utility.

A quick glance through the Dow Jones list of more than 20 data bases shows a definite leaning toward news in general and business and financial news and information in particular. This is only to be expected, coming as it does from the same company that publishes *The Wall Street Journal, Baron's National Business and Financial Weekly,* and the *Dow Jones News Service,* not to mention the Dow Jones market quotes.

This is a good utility to look to for current news or for researching past news. It is also a prime source for business and financial information.

If you are new to using information utilities, you will find that it is much easier to start with a system like Dow Jones, which concentrates on one or two services instead of overwhelming you with possibilities. Before you can quickly and comfortably find your way around any given utility, you have to construct a mental map of how the system is structured. The relative simplicity of Dow Jones makes that job a little easier and prepares you for other, more complicated systems. (As time goes on, Dow Jones will undoubtedly add more services and become a more complicated system itself. But as time goes on, we'll all be better prepared to handle the complications.)

Services Available and a List of Data Bases

Dow Jones News/Retrieval is limited primarily to information services of varying kinds, with emphasis on business and financial information.

These are divided into five categories.

INTRO

There is no charge for browsing through INTRO. It's there, basically, to keep you up to date on the utility. It includes announcements of new data bases, hints on how to use the service, announcements of new guides as they become available, and so forth.

DOW JONES BUSINESS AND ECONOMIC NEWS

Wall Street Journal Highlights Online: This is just what it sounds like: an on-line version of *The Wall Street Journal,* updated throughout the day. It includes front-page news, front- and back-page features, market pages, editorial columns, and commentary from the print edition of the paper. Producer: Dow Jones.

Dow Jones News: This data base lets you search through headlines and retrieve stories from *The Wall Street Journal, Barron's,* and *Dow Jones News Service.* Stories are available for retrieval almost immediately after being loaded into the system (90 seconds). They are kept for varying lengths of time, up to 90 days, depending on the nature of the story. You can ask for stories by company name or by category. (Some categories are: Advertising, Aerospace, Africa, the Supreme Court, and Computers.) You can also ask for the most recent story or you can ask for a list of headlines. If you get the headlines, you can pick the stories you want from that list. Producer: Dow Jones.

Free Text Search: (Available only Monday through Friday, from 6:00 A.M. to midnight, Eastern Time.) Free Text Search on Dow Jones is an important supplement to the News Search capability. Where News Search covers stories that are anywhere from 90 seconds to 90 days old, Free Text Search can be used with stories one day old or older—back to June 1979. Where News Search will search only by company name or a predetermined category, Free Text Search will search the full text of the data base by date or by any word or words you care to look for.

This is a fairly sophisticated searching system. You can join search words together with AND (Japan AND Computers), OR (Japan OR Computers) or NOT (Japan NOT Computers). You can string these possibilities together in any combination (Japan AND Computers NOT Sony). You can restrict your search to those articles where the desired words are in the same paragraph, the same sentence, or even in a specific order (Japanese ADJ Computers—ADJ meaning adjacent to). None of this is difficult to do, but before trying it, make sure to read the manual, *An Introduction to Free Text Search of the Dow Jones News Database*.

Weekly Economic Update: A review of the week's economic events and a look at upcoming possibilities. Producer: Dow Jones.

FINANCIAL AND INVESTMENT SERVICES

Corporate Earnings Estimator: Forecasts for 2400 companies. Producer: Zacks Investment Research, Inc.

DISCLOSURE II: Detailed information on 8500 publicly held companies from information filed with the Securities and Exchange Commission. In addition to the on-line time charge, there is an extra charge of $4 for each company record looked at during prime time, or $2 per record during non-prime time. Producer: Disclosure. Disclosure II is also available on DIALOG.

Media General Financial Services: Corporate financial information on 3150 companies and 170 industries. Producer: Media General Financial Services.

Weekly Economic Survey (formerly Money Market Services): Economic survey of 40 to 50 top financial institutions. Compiled weekly. Producer: Money Market Services.

The Forbes Directory: Rankings of the largest U.S. corporations by sales, profits, assets, and market values. Updated yearly. Producer: Forbes.

DOW JONES QUOTES

Current Quotes: With a minimum 15-minute delay during market hours. Producer: Dow Jones.

Historical Quotes: Daily volume, high, low, and close for one year, with monthly summaries back to 1979 and quarterly summaries back to 1978. Producer: Dow Jones.

Historical Dow-Jones Averages: By date for one year back. Producer: Dow Jones.

GENERAL NEWS AND INFORMATION SERVICES

Master Menu: The menu for moving through the system also contains help messages, or instructions, for each data base.

Symbol Directory: This on-line directory of company symbols is updated daily. The symbols are needed for searching the news data bases.

Academic American Encyclopedia: Contains 28,000 articles on various subjects, updated twice a year. Producer: Grolier Electronic Publishing, Inc. Also available on BRS, BRS/AFTER DARK.

News/Retrieval World Report: An on-line "newspaper." Foreign and national news, updated throughout the day. (Contains current information only. See UPI note below.) Producer: Dow Jones. Excerpted from UPI Wire.

News/Retrieval Sports Report: Covers professional, college, and "top amateur" sports. Includes stories, stats, scores, and standings for "most major sports." (Contains current information only. See UPI note below.) Producer: Dow Jones. Excerpted from UPI Wire.

News/Retrieval Weather Report: National weather summary and forecast, but only by region. Weather tables for over 50 cities. Useful if you're on the way to the airport and are wondering what the weather's like at your destination. Producer: Dow Jones. Excerpted from UPI Wire and U.S. Weather.

UPI NOTE: The News/Retrieval categories are all based, at least in part, on the UPI Wire Service. Each carries current stories only. Similar current UPI coverage is available on THE SOURCE. "Newsclipping" of the current UPI wire is available on NewsNet. In addition, delayed versions of UPI are available on DIALOG and NEXIS. These delayed versions do not include the current day's stories, but once on the system all stories are kept "forever."

Cineman Movie Reviews: Includes reviews of both current and past movies—as far back as 1930. Producer: Cineman Syndicate. Also available on THE SOURCE.

Wall $treet Week Online: Transcripts from the four most recent programs of the PBS television show. Producer: PBS.

COMP*U*STORE: Dow serves as a gateway to COMP*U*STORE, the on-line shopping service. Charges are billed separately by COMP*U*STORE.

KNOWLEDGE INDEX

The Basics

Hours: On-line 6:00 P.M. to 5:00 A.M. your local time Monday through Thursday.
6:00 P.M. to 12 midnight your local time on Friday.
8:00 A.M. to 12 midnight on Saturday.
3:00 P.M. Sunday to 5:00 A.M. Monday.

Command structure (with help screens available).

Baud rates: 300/1200 baud. (No additional charge at 1200 baud.)

Initial charge: One-time subscription fee of $35 (includes two hours of on-line time).

Minimum monthly charge: None.

Training not available and not necessary.

Reference manual: User's Workbook comes as part of initial package.

Updates: Updates to the manual are sent automatically at no charge.

KNOWLEDGE INDEX News, a quarterly newsletter, covers new data bases and changes to the system. The newsletter also includes articles on search strategies and hints on how to get the most out of KNOWLEDGE INDEX.

Available through:
Telenet
Tymnet
Uninet
Datapac (in Canada)
(There is no extra charge for any of these.)

For further information, contact:
KNOWLEDGE INDEX
3460 Hillview Ave.
Palo Alto, CA 94304
(800) 227-5510
(415) 858-3796 (in California)

Price Structure

KNOWLEDGE INDEX has a straightforward $24-per-hour charge. There is no additional charge for telecommunications, no additional charge for "premium" data bases, and no additional charge for use at 1200 baud.

There is an additional charge for copies of documents. As with DIALORDER on DIALOG, full text items ordered through KNOWLEDGE INDEX are *not* computer printouts. They come as photocopies, or original material, or whatever form is appropriate. The charge is currently $4.50 per document plus $.20 per printed page. This will have gone up by the time you read this but as of this writing, the new price has not yet been established.

Billing on KNOWLEDGE INDEX is strictly through credit cards: Visa, Master-Card, or American Express. The utility will not bill you directly.

Description

KNOWLEDGE INDEX is another "consumer-oriented" version of a large information utility. In this case the parent is DIALOG.

Once again, "consumer-oriented" goes in quotes because the target audience is not the general consumer but the information consumer. This includes business people, professionals, and students.

The relationship between KNOWLEDGE INDEX and DIALOG is much the same as the relationship between BRS/AFTER DARK and BRS. In each case the consumer version of the utility gives access to a selected group of data bases taken from the main utility. In each case also, the consumer version costs less and has more limited hours of access. Most important, perhaps, in each case the consumer version is much easier to use.

Barbara Gersh at DIALOG says that "the better searchers" on DIALOG have been through the system seminar and have been using DIALOG for several months. In contrast, she says, it takes most people about two hours to learn how to use KNOWLEDGE INDEX. The cost for this ease of use is a loss of some of the more powerful search techniques. For the casual user, this should not be a problem. In fact, for a new user the more powerful techniques are more likely to be confusing than helpful—especially if you use the system only occasionally.

My own experience is that KNOWLEDGE INDEX is both easy to use and powerful enough to leave me without wishing for more capabilities. Coming onto this system as I did, already familiar with DIALOG, I felt comfortable almost immediately. Even without that background, though, most people will probably find KNOWLEDGE INDEX easy enough to learn. The User's Workbook includes a carefully designed tutorial that will take you step by step through everything you need to know about the system—from logging on, to advanced search techniques, to ordering documents. The tutorial is intelligently divided into sections on basic, intermediate, and advanced searching. This means you can learn the simple, less-powerful techniques first, use them until you feel comfortable with them, and only then go on to more advanced techniques.

In addition to the tutorial, the workbook includes information on the specific data bases and a useful reference card that contains a summary of the search commands. Even better, once you get on-line, you can get help from the system at any time simply by entering "?" and a carriage return.

Services Available

KNOWLEDGE INDEX began with information services only. Communications services should also be available by the time you read this. As of this writing, the system includes about 20 of DIALOG's more than 170 data bases. New data bases are continually being added.

Communications Services

As of this writing, communications services are expected to be added in 1984. These will include electronic mail, bulletin boards, and on-line conferencces. Check with KNOWLEDGE INDEX for details.

DATA BASES ON KNOWLEDGE INDEX

(Listed By Category)

Agriculture

AGRICOLA Subject: Agriculture. Producer: National Agricultural Libary. Also available on BRS, BRS/AFTER DARK, DIALOG.

Books

BOOKS IN PRINT Subject: U.S. books in print. Producer: R.R. Bowker. Also available on BRS, BRS/AFTER DARK, DIALOG.

Business

ABI/INFORM Subject: Business. Producer: Data Courier, Inc. Also available on BRS, BRS/AFTER DARK, DIALOG.

TRADE AND INDUSTRY INDEX Subject: Index to 275 major trade and industry journals in all Standard Industrial Classifications. Also indexes several newspapers, including *The Wall Street Journal* and *The New York Times* Financial Section. Producer: Information Access Corp. Also available on DIALOG.

Computers and Electronics

INSPEC AND BACKFILE Subject: Engineering, physics, and computer science. Producer: Institute of Electrical Engineers. Also available on BRS, DIALOG.

INTERNATIONAL SOFTWARE DATABASE Subject: List of commercially available mini- and microcomputer software. Producer: Imprint Software, Ltd. Also available on DIALOG.

MICROCOMPUTER INDEX   Subject: Index to magazine articles from over 21 microcomputer journals. Producer: Microcomputer Information Services. Also available on DIALOG.

CORPORATE NEWS

STANDARD & POOR'S NEWS   Subject: General news and financial information on more than 10,000 publicly owned U.S. companies. Covers 1979 through present. Producer: Standard & Poor's Corp. Also available on DIALOG.

EDUCATION

ERIC   Subject: Education. Producer: National Institute of Education. Also available on BRS, BRS/AFTER DARK, DIALOG.

ENGINEERING

COMPENDEX   Subject: This is the computer-readable form of *Engineering Index*. Producer: Engineering Information, Inc. Also available on BRS, DIALOG.

GOVERNMENT PUBLICATIONS

GPO PUBLICATIONS REFERENCE FILE   Subject: Index of public documents currently for sale by the Government Printing Office. Producer: U.S. Government Printing Office. Also available on DIALOG.

NTIS   Subject: Government reports in various technical areas. Producer: National Technical Information Service. Also available on BRS, BRS/AFTER DARK, DIALOG.

LEGAL

LEGAL RESOURCE INDEX   Subject: Indexing of 660 key law journals and five law newspapers, plus legal monographs and government publications. Producer: Information Access Corp. Also available on DIALOG.

MAGAZINES

MAGAZINE INDEX   Subject: Index to 370 popular magazines in a broad range of subjects. Producer: Information Access Corp. Also available on DIALOG.

MEDICINE

BIOSIS PREVIEWS AND BACKFILE   Subject: Biological sciences. Producer: BioSciences Information Service. Also available on BRS, BRS/AFTER DARK, DIALOG.

INTERNATIONAL PHARMACEUTICAL ABSTRACTS   Producer: American Society of Hospital Pharmacists. Also available on BRS, DIALOG.

MEDLINE   Subject: All aspects of health care. Producer: National Library of Medicine. Also available on DIALOG.

NEWS

NATIONAL NEWSPAPER INDEX   Subject: Index to *The Christian Science Monitor, The New York Times,* and *The Wall Street Journal,* beginning in 1979. Producer: Information Access Corp. Also available on DIALOG.

NEWSEARCH   Subject: Index to newspaper and magazine stories for current month only. Functions as a supplement to National Newspaper Index and

Magazine Index for most current stories. Producer: Information Access Corp. Also available on DIALOG.

Psychology

PSYCINFO   Subject: Psychology. Producer: American Psychological Association. Also available on BRS, BRS/AFTER DARK, DIALOG.

New data bases are continually being added. For a current list, contact KNOWLEDGE INDEX.

Mead Data Central (LEXIS and NEXIS)

Mead Data Central provides full text retrieval of various kinds of information on two different but related systems.

NEXIS is Mead's utility for business and general news.

LEXIS is a sister utility for legal research.

The price structures on these two utilities are similar, although monthly charges on LEXIS are higher. Both systems are aimed primarily at large users: news organizations, corporate libraries, public-relations firms, advertising companies, commercial banks, brokerage houses, accounting firms, and, of course, law firms. As of this writing, LEXIS has taught roughly 200,000 lawyers how to use the system. The LEXIS brochure quotes one lawyer's opinion that computerized legal research becomes "economically feasible" in firms with six or more lawyers.

The Basics

Hours: On-line 23 hours per day Monday through Friday. (3:00 A.M. through 2:00 A.M. Eastern Time.) On-line 7:00 A.M. through 10:00 P.M. Eastern Time on weekends.

The system is neither command-based nor menu-based in the usual sense. Instead, it relies heavily on labeled function keys for giving commands. Prompts and help messages are available when needed.

Baud Rate: 1200 baud only.

Initial charge:
$400 for installation of first NEXIS deluxe terminal.
$200 for installation of first UBIQ terminal.
$200 for installation of first stand-alone printer.

Additional equipment for the same building is at no additional charge. This applies to both LEXIS and NEXIS.

Minimum monthly rates: NEXIS subscription charge is $50 per month. This is *not* chargeable against use. It covers the basic equipment rental and the dedicated line for the Mead terminal.

The LEXIS monthly subscription charge gets a little complicated. For the first building location it is $100 plus an additional charge for each "professional" (Read: lawyer) using the system. There is also an additional but reduced charge for additional locations. Check with Mead for details.

Training on LEXIS is available at $75 per person. This covers an unlimited amount of training in-house or at seminars as needed.

Training on NEXIS is free (or covered in the basic charge). Here again, this includes an unlimited amount of training in-house or at seminars as needed.

Reference manuals: Handbooks are provided at no extra charge.

Available through:
Meadnet
Telenet

Meadnet consists of dedicated data lines, which translates to high-speed (1200 baud) service with little or nothing in the way of garbage (or "noise") mixed in with the information. This makes it the preferred, and until recently, the only choice. Mead is in the process of expanding now, however, and is considering using Telenet also, as necessary.

In either case, there is no additional communications charge.

Protocol note: Meadnet can communicate only with a 1200-baud, 212-compatible modem.

For further information, contact:
Mead Data Central
P.O. Box 933
Dayton, OH 45401
Phone: (800) 543-6862 (this number works in Ohio also)

Price Structure

The price structures on NEXIS and LEXIS are somewhat complicated.

First, there is the monthly subscription charge: $50 for NEXIS, $100 and up for LEXIS.

Second, there is a monthly equipment charge if you are renting equipment. On NEXIS there is no charge for the terminal, but there is a $150-per-month charge for the stand-alone printer. On LEXIS the charge is $150 per month for a deluxe terminal, $55 per month for a UBIQ terminal, and $150 per month for a stand-alone printer. (Additional equipment is "at reduced prices.")

Third, there is the connect-time charge. At peak time (7:30 A.M. to 7:30 P.M. your local time), this can be anywhere from $90 per hour to $30 per hour, depending on how many hours per month you use the service. Off-peak rates are $45 per hour, or for large users, the peak-time rate if it is lower.

Finally, there are additional search surcharges on both systems and off-line printing charges on LEXIS.

Description

LEXIS is organized into a series of law "libraries." Some of the specific data bases or their equivalents are also available on-line elsewhere, but the LEXIS data bases include information that is not typically available on other systems. LEXIS also includes Mead's LEXPAT, the only full text patent data base available on-line.

As of this writing, NEXIS offers full text retrieval from about 90 different sources, including newspapers, magazines, wire services, and newsletters. (The number is growing rapidly though. It should soon go over 100.) NEXIS also includes the full text of the *Encyclopaedia Britannica* and its various yearbook updates. NEXIS has recently absorbed the New York Times Information Service as well, which, among other things, includes the complete text of *The New York Times* starting with June 1980.

Both LEXIS and NEXIS offer access to DIALOG.

Until recently LEXIS and NEXIS were available only through Mead's own terminals. As this book was being finished, Mead announced a decision to make both systems available on other terminals and computers, beginning with the IBM Displaywriter, the IBM 3101 terminal, the IBM PC, the Hazeltine 1520 and Televideo 950. Other terminals and computer should follow, but no decisions have been made as yet.

As of this writing, many of the particulars surrounding the new availability of LEXIS and NEXIS are somewhat up in the air. Software for the IBM PC, for example, is expected to cost "in the range of $150 to $250."

In any case, for the moment, Mead remains an expensive utility, still aimed at large (or at least rich) users.

Services Available

Both LEXIS and NEXIS provide strictly information services, primarily in the form of full text retrieval.

NEXIS covers such diverse sources as *Newsweek, Business Week, Christian Science Monitor,* and *Aviation Week and Space Technology.* In addition to these full text data bases, NEXIS also offers INFOBANK and TODAY, two data bases produced by *The New York Times.* (These were taken over from the New York Times Information Service.)

TODAY contains daily summaries from *The New York Times* and amounts to a short, on-line version of *The Times.* INFOBANK contains abstracts of articles from more than 60 newspapers, magazines, and journals. It also contains two other data bases: Advertising & Marketing Intelligence (AMI), and Deadline Data on World Affairs. Each of these is searched separately from the INFOBANK abstracts.

LEXIS is divided into "Libraries." Some of the major categories for these libraries are Federal law, state law, United Kingdom law, and French law. These major categories are further divided into more specific areas.

DATA BASES ON LEXIS AND NEXIS

Here is a list of NEXIS data bases. All are available through LEXIS as well. The LEXIS-specific data bases are not listed here since they are all strictly related to legal research. Information on LEXIS is available from Mead.

NEWSPAPERS

American Banker
BBC Summary of World Broadcasts and Monitoring Report
The Bond Buyer
The Christian Science Monitor
ComputerWorld and ComputerWorld Extra
Facts on File World News Digest
Harfax Database of Industry Data Sources (also available on DIALOG)
The Japan Economic Journal
Legal Times
Manchester Guardian Weekly
The New York Times
The Washington Post (also available on CompuServe)

MAGAZINES

ABA Banking Journal
Aviation Week & Space Technology
Business Week
Byte
Chemical Engineering
Chemical Week
Coal Age
Congressional Quarterly Weekly Report and **Editorial Research Reports**
Data Communications
Defense and Foreign Affairs
Dun's Business Month (Dun's Review)
The Economist
Electronics
Engineering News-Record
Engineering and Mining Journal
High Technology
Inc.
Industry Week
Issues in Bank Regulation
Journal of Bank Research
The Magazine of Bank Administration
Mining Annual Review
Mining Journal
Mining Magazine
National Journal
Newsweek
Offshore

Oil & Gas Journal
U.S. News & World Report

NEWSLETTERS

Advertising Compliance Service
Banking Expansion Reporter
Coal Outlook
Coal Week
Coal Week International (McGraw-Hill)
Defense & Foreign Affairs Daily
Defense & Foreign Affairs Weekly
The Dorvillier News Letter
East Asian Executive Reports
Economic Week
Electric Utility Week
Enhanced Recovery Week
Financial Times
Forbes
Inside Energy/with Federal Lands
Inside FERC
Inside NRC (McGraw-Hill)
Latin America Commodities Report
Latin America Regional Reports
Latin America Weekly Report
Legal Times of Washington
McGraw-Hill's Biotechnology Newswatch
Metals Week
Middle East Executive Reports
The Morgan Guaranty Survey
Nuclear Fuel
Nucleonics Week
Platt's Energy Litigation Report (McGraw-Hill)
Platt's Oil Policy Letter (McGraw-Hill)
Platt's Oilgram News
The RayLux Financial Service Newsletter
Securities Week
Synfuels (McGraw-Hill)
Synfuels Week
Update/The American States (also available on NewsNet)
Washington Quarterly
Wharton News Perspectives
World Financial Markets

WIRE SERVICES

Wire services on NEXIS are available only on a delayed basis. Depending on the particular wire service, the stories show up on NEXIS anywhere from 12 to 48 hours after first appearing on the wire. Once on the system, the stories stay there. (Most systems remove old stories as the news wire is updated.)

Jiji Press Ticker Service

Kyodo English Language News Service

PR Newswire (also available on NewsNet).

Reuters General News Report

Reuters North European News Service

The Associated Press World, National, and Business Wire (The AP wire is also available on CompuServe, for current stories only.)

United Press International States Wires

United Press International World, National, Business, and Sports Wires (The UPI wires are also available on THE SOURCE and NewsNet for current stories. Dow Jones also uses extracts from UPI wires in its News/Retrieval sections. Backfiles of UPI wire stories are also available on DIALOG.)

Xinhua (New China) News Agency

GOVERNMENT DOCUMENTS

Federal Reserve Bulletin

Weekly Compilation of Presidential Documents

Code of Federal Regulations (Issued annually. Covers Federal regulations in force on date of publication.)

Federal Register (Issued daily. Covers Federal regulations and legal notices. Also includes proposed and temporary regulations. A related data base, **Federal Register Abstracts,** is available on DIALOG.)

OTHER

INFOBANK

The Abstracts   Abstracts from 60 magazines, newspapers, and other periodicals

Advertising & Marketing Intelligence (AMI)

The New York Times

TODAY   (On-line abridged version of *The New York Times)*

National Automated Accounting Research System   Contains annual reports of corporations listed on the New York, American, and OTC stock exchanges. Also, "Authoritative accounting materials...statements of auditing standards, industry accounting guides."

The Associated Press Political Service   Contains in-depth information about political candidates, issues, campaigns, and elections)

Forensic Services Directory

Encyclopaedia Britannica

New data bases are being continually added. Check with Mead for the current list.

NewsNet

The Basics

Hours: On-line 24 hours each day, seven days each week. Menu-based.

Baud rate: 300/1200 baud. (1200 baud is at additional charge.)

Initial charge: None. (Not only is there no initial charge, but the password comes with a coupon worth $24 of connect time.)

Monthly minimum: $15. Training not available and not necessary.

Reference manual: None available, and for the most part, you won't miss it. If you really want a "manual," you can print the various help screens from the system and put them in a looseleaf binder.

Updates: NewsNet's monthly newsletter (on-line and in print) includes helpful hints about how to get more out of the system.

Available through:
 Direct dial (Washington, D.C. area only)
 Telenet
 Tymnet
 Uninet
 Datapac (in Canada)

There is no communications surcharge for any of these.

For further information, contact:
 NewsNet
 954 Haverford Road
 Bryn Mawr, PA 19010
 Phone: (800) 345-1301
    (215) 527-8030 (in Pennsylvania)

Price Structure

The concept behind NewsNet's price structure is reasonably simple but it gets a little complicated in practice.

 The basic rate at 300 baud is $24 per hour from 8:00 A.M. to 8:00 P.M., Monday through Friday.

 This rate applies to time spent scanning, looking for key words, reading sample copies of newsletters in the library, and so on. The complications show up when you actually read the newsletters.

 Most newsletters have two rates: a validated rate and a non-validated rate. The validated rates are for those who subscribe to the print edition of the particular newsletter. The non-validated rates are for non-subscribers. As of this writing, validated rates run from a low of $24 per hour to a high of $48 per hour. Non-validated rates run from $24 per hour to $120 per hour, with most of them at $48 per hour or less.

On evenings, weekends, and holidays there is a $6-per-hour savings from the daytime rates. (This represents a 25 percent savings on the basic connect time. Additional royalties for the various newsletters remain unchanged.)

At 1200 baud, all rates are doubled.

You can get a complete list of current daytime rates from the "Prices" choice on the main menu.

Finally, if you don't have a terminal or computer, NewsNet will rent you one. The current choices as of this writing are:

- Scanset at $39 per month.
- Teleprinter add-on at $39 per month. (This not only gives printing capabilities to the Scanset, it has other possibilities that we'll get to shortly.)
- Teleprinter with keyboard at $59 per month.

The minimum rental for any of these systems is three months. There is also a one-time handling fee of $50 to $75, depending on the system.

Description

Whenever I discuss NewsNet, I find myself using the word "impressive" a lot.

Started in April 1982, NewsNet is one of the newer information utilities. It is also one of the most impressively useful systems available, particularly when it comes to business news and information (as opposed to financial news). Given the connect charge ($18 per hour and up), it would be misleading to think of this as a general-interest utility, but it would probably be fair to call it a business-oriented general-interest utility.

The core of NewsNet is the on-line newsletter—electronic editions of dozens of different newsletters in about 35 different fields. Some of these are updated monthly, some biweekly, some weekly, some daily, and some "as news develops."

You can read these newsletters all the way through as they come out, or scan the headlines and decide which to read, or search for key words when looking for background on some particular subject. The most exciting feature of NewsNet, though, and the one that makes the utility so useful, is NewsFlash. This lets you enter up to ten key words or phrases and have NewsNet search any or all incoming newsletters for matches. NewsNet, in effect, becomes an electronic clipping service tailored to your exact needs. More on this later.

NewsNet bills itself as being "For the Business Information Edge," and indeed most of its newsletters are clearly aimed at those who need to keep up with one industry or another—*Energy and Minerals Resources* for the energy industry, for instance, or *Hazardous Waste News* and the *Sludge Newsletter* for the chemical industry. Still, with this many newsletters to choose from, the odds are pretty good that you'll find something that interests you. If not, wait a while; the system is still growing. As of this writing, the number of newsletters on the system hovers at about 150, with another 50 or so planned for the near future. You can check with NewsNet for the current count.

The newsletters on NewsNet cover a wide range of topics, including environment, investment possibilities, politics and legislation, and social sciences. You'll even find a newsletter called *Micro Moonlighter* that will give you tips on how to use your microcomputer to run a business out of your house. If you're interested in computers as computers, moreover, you should find one or more of the computer newsletters worth looking at.

There are indications that NewsNet is broadening its scope somewhat. One of the more recent additions to the system is *The Computer Cookbook,* an on-line version of the book by the same name. A related data base consists of updates to the book. This particular cookbook gives recipes for putting a computer system together. If you have an Apple II, for example, and are thinking of adding a board to get 80 characters per line, you can search for the key words "Apple" and "80 column" and *The Cookbook* will give you information on 80-column cards and their prices. Very often you'll find specific recommendations as well.

Another recent addition is the UPI newswire, which gives you general news on NewsNet also but not as an on-line service—meaning that you cannot do an on-line search of the UPI wire.

This needs a little explaining. NewsNet processes the UPI information, taking current wire stories and making them available through NewsFlash. The stories are updated throughout the day but with a four-hour delay. (This is due to the contractual arrangement with UPI.)

The entire UPI wire is searched by NewsFlash so that UPI stories are part of NewsNet's electronic clipping service. Keep in mind, though, that when you change your NewsFlash key words, the changes do not become effective until midnight. This means that the newsclipping service may not be appropriate for stories of only transient interest.

One of the most impressive things about NewsNet is that the system is easy to use. (Not as easy as the people I've spoken to at NewsNet seem to think it is, but easy enough.) To run a search, for example, you go to the Command Menu and pick "Search." The system then prompts you for the newsletter or newsletters to search for, the dates to limit the search to, and for the key words to search for. You answer the prompts as appropriate and the system does the search. When it's through, it tells you the number of hits. If it's a manageable number, you can either read them or go through the headlines first to weed out the ones you don't need. If it is not a manageable number, you can start the search over again, making it more restrictive this time.

There are a few things NewsNet could do to make the system easier to learn. Ideally, I'd like to see an on-line introduction—something along the lines of Delphi's Guided Tour.

Ideally also, I'd like the password to come with a short written introduction to the system. A few pages would be enough. Something of this sort is currently under development, I'm told, and may be available by the time you read this. Right now the password comes with a short sample search showing you how to use the system and with instructions that carefully explain the procedure for logging on to the system through Tymnet, Telenet, or Uninet. You also get a list of available newsletters and a

"System Overview," which amounts to a flowchart with some notes. This is useful once you have at least a vague idea of how the system works, but I suspect that as an introduction to NewsNet, most people will find it more intimidating than helpful.

Even as it stands, NewsNet is reasonably easy to learn. My own experience, jumping into it cold—without even the flowchart or the list of newsletters—was that it took me about an hour to understand how to use the system. This is not an unreasonable investment of time.

One of NewsNet's most impressive tricks is the automatic programming of their rental terminals. When you first get the terminal, you plug it in and call NewsNet's computer. The computer asks you a few questions and then proceeds to program the auto-dial and auto-log on commands—everything up to but not including your password. From then on you can reach NewsNet by making a simple menu choice, then typing your password. Some people might dismiss this as a gimmick, and I suppose that in some sense it is—but it is a most impressive gimmick. It is even a useful one. Odds are, moreover, that anyone who rents a terminal knows little or nothing about using it and would not find it easy to program one.

Services Available

As of this writing, NewsNet deals almost entirely in information services, and within information services, almost entirely with newsletters.

Communication Services

The one communication-based service is a limited kind of electronic mail. It lets you send questions, letters, press releases, or whatever, but only to NewsNet or to newsletter publishers. This can be useful, of course (especially the press-release possibility), but it is not the kind of full-fledged electronic mail service that you'll find on THE SOURCE, for example, or even the more limited electronic mail service that you'll find on CompuServe.

Information Services

When it comes to information-based services, NewsNet is in its element.

The most obvious (and least-inspired) way to use NewsNet is to read the on-line editions of newsletters as soon as they are available rather than to wait for the print versions to show up in your mailbox. This has its advantages, but in most cases it probably won't be worth the additional cost just to be able to read a newsletter one or two days earlier than otherwise.

The real value of the system is in its search capability.

You can search by key words to find a specific article that you vaguely remember reading several weeks or several months ago.

You can use key words to gather background information on a field that you need to get caught up on quickly.

You'll find, also, that in doing a key word search, you will automatically turn up sources of information that you may never have considered using or may never even have heard of before.

Searching by key word on NewsNet is both a useful feature and one that is easy to learn. The price you pay for ease of learning, though, is that it's also limited.

You cannot, for example, specify that words must be next to each other. If you're searching for articles on artificial intelligence, your search phrase will be "Artificial AND Intelligence," and you will turn up some articles that have nothing to do with artificial intelligence but happen to contain both words. (NewsFlash searching, which we'll get to shortly, will let you specify that words must be next to each other.)

Another feature lacking in NewsNet's on-line search function is the ability to exclude words. In searching for references to artificial intelligence, you may want to ignore the subject as it applies to robots, for example. But there's no way to tell the system that.

Neither of these features is all that important. They are both fairly sophisticated refinements; you can get along without them quite easily.

There is one feature that I badly miss. Although you can join key words together with AND or with OR, you cannot use both terms at the same time. This means that if you're looking for articles on artificial intelligence in robots, you can look for "Artificial AND Intelligence AND Robots," or you can look for "AI AND Robots," but you cannot look for "((Artificial AND Intelligence) OR AI) AND Robots." (Read: Find all articles that mention Artificial AND Intelligence AND Robots, AND find all articles that mention AI AND Robots.)

Of course you can get much the same list by running two searches: one for "Artificial AND Intelligence AND Robots" and one for "AI AND Robots." The problem is, the two lists will overlap, which means you then have to run through them manually to eliminate the duplications.

The absence of this feature is intentional; it is a direct result of a design philosophy that favors ease of use over additional capability. You can expect features like this to creep into the system over time as more users become more sophisticated searchers.

The most impressive feature on NewsNet—the most exciting, and potentially the most useful—is the NewsFlash service, which we've already touched on. This lets you enter up to ten key words and phrases and have NewsNet automatically search for matches whenever new information is added to the system. You can tailor these phrases to your general business or personal interests or to particular projects. If you find that you're getting too many hits or too few, you can tinker with the phrases, adding a word or removing one until you start getting exactly the information you want and need.

NewsFlash comes in two varieties. One will show you your hits whenever you sign on to the system. You can then read through them, print them out, or save them to disk on your own system. The other version, Outcall service, will call you up and print out an article each time it finds one. To take advantage of this, you need a dedicated phone line with a modem and printer attached at all times. The Outcall service is relatively new. As of this writing, you can use it only with a NewsNet Teleprinter. It may become available for other systems in the future.

The NewsFlash service, not so incidentally, is part of the basic NewsNet service; there is no additional charge. It not only works as an electronic newsclipping service, it works well, and it works at a reasonable price. There is a surcharge for Outcall service.

Finally, one specific data base that deserves special mention is PR Newswire. This contains the full text of news releases from about 7500 corporations, government agencies, labor unions, public-relations agencies, and just about anything else you can think of. No matter what your business interests, you're likely to find out about new developments from PR Newswire faster than anyplace else. This is where newspapers and trade journals often get information themselves. Combine PR Newswire and the UPI wire with the NewsFlash feature, and you have a powerful personal news system indeed.

NEWSLETTERS AND NEWSWIRES ON NEWSNET

(LISTED BY CATEGORY)

Items in bold are on-line editions of printed newsletters. Other entries exist only in electronic form.

ADVERTISING AND MARKETING

Media Science Reports. Publisher: Unlimited Publishing, Inc. Also listed under Publishing and Broadcasting and under Electronics and Computers categories on NewsNet.

Source. Subject: Business and business management. Producer: Newsletter Management Corp. Also listed under Management and under General Business categories on NewsNet.

AEROSPACE

Defense Industry Report. Publisher: Industry News Service, Inc. Also listed under Electronics and Computers and under Research and Development categories on NewsNet.

Defense R&D Update. Publisher: Industry News Service, Inc. Also listed under Electronics and Computers and under Research and Development categories on NewsNet.

Satellite Week. Subject: Satellite communications and related space technology. Producer: Television Digest, Inc. Also listed under Telecommunications and under Electronics and Computers categories on NewsNet.

AUTOMOTIVE

Electric Vehicle Progress. Producer: Alexander Research & Communications, Inc. Also listed under Research and Development and under Manufacturing categories on NewsNet.

Runzheimer on Automotive Alternatives. Subject: Alternative energy sources for automobiles. Producer: Runzheimer and Co., Inc. Also listed under Energy and under Transportation categories on NewsNet.

Building and Construction

Construction Computer Applications Newsletter. Subject: Computer applications in the construction industry. Producer: Construction Industry Press. Also listed under Electronics and Computers and under General Business categories on NewsNet.

Chemical

Hazardous Waste News. Subject: Regulation of hazardous wastes. Producer: Business Publishers, Inc. Also listed under Environment and under Government and Regulatory categories on NewsNet.

Sludge Newsletter. Subject: Management, treatment, use, disposal, and regulation of sludge. Producer: Business Publishers, Inc. Also listed under Environment and under Government and Regulatory categories on NewsNet.

Toxic Materials News. Subject: EPA's toxic substances control program. Producer: Business Publishers, Inc. Also listed under "Government and Regulatory" and under "Environment" categories on NewsNet.

Corporate Communications

The Corporate Shareholder. Subject: Relations between corporations and the financial community, including individual investors. Producer: Corporate Shareholder, Inc. Also listed under Finance and Accounting and under Management categories on NewsNet.

Education

Campus Exchange.   Publisher: Interrobang, Inc. Also listed under Politics and under Research and Development categories on NewsNet.

Electronics and Computers

Annex Computer Report. Publisher: Annex Holdings Corp. Also listed under Finance and Accounting and under Investment categories on NewsNet.

The Business Computer. Publisher: P/K Associates, Inc. Also listed under General Business and under Corporate Communications categories on NewsNet.

Communications & Distributed Processing Resources Report. Subject: The computer industry. Producer: International Data Corp. Also listed under Telecommunications and under Office categories on NewsNet.

The Computer Cookbook. Producer: William Bates. Also listed under Telecommunications and under Publishing and Broadcasting categories on NewsNet.

The Computer Cookbook Update.   Producer: William Bates. Also listed under Telecommunications and under Publishing and Broadcasting categories on NewsNet.

Computer Market Observer.   Subject: Marketing, financial news, and personnel in computer industry. Producer: Auerbach Publishers, Inc. Also listed under General Business and under Investment categories on NewsNet.

IBM Watch.   Producer: Enterprise Information Systems, Inc. Also listed under Telecommunications and under Office categories on NewsNet.

Interactive Video Technology. Subject: Interactive video industry: new products and services and a calendar of conferences and seminars. Producer: Heartland Communications. Also listed under Education and under Telecommunications categories on NewsNet.

Micro Moonlighter. Subject: Information on how to manage a business out of your home, using a personal computer. Includes case studies and business news. Producer: J. Norman Goode. Also listed under General Business and under Advertising and Marketing categories on NewsNet.

Mini/Micro Bulletin. Subject: The mini- and microcomputer industry, with emphasis on new hardware and software. Producer: Auerbach Publishers, Inc. Also listed under General Business and under Investment categories on NewsNet.

Modem Notes. Producer: Modem Notes, Inc. Also listed under Telecommunications and under Publishing and Broadcasting categories on NewsNet.

Personal Computers Today. Subject: All aspects of the personal computer industry. Producer: Phillips Publishing, Inc. Also listed under Telecommunications and under Office categories on NewsNet.

Robotronics Age Newsletter. Subject: Robotics. Producer: Twenty-First Century Media. Also listed under Research and Development category on NewsNet.

S. Klein Newsletter on Computer Graphics. Producer: Technology & Business Communications, Inc. Also listed under Manufacturing and under Research and Development categories on NewsNet.

The Seybold Report on Professional Computing. Producer: Seybold Publications, Inc. Also listed under Office and under General Business categories on NewsNet.

two/sixteen Magazine. Producer: Richard H. Young. Also listed under Research and Development and under Telecommunications categories on NewsNet.

UNIQUE: Your Independent UNIX/C Advisor. Subject: UNIX operating system and C language. Producer: InfoPro Systems. Also listed under Telecommunications and under Research and Development categories on NewsNet.

ENERGY

Daily Petro Futures. Subject: Opening and closing prices and chart analysis for futures of heating oil, gasoline, and propane traded on the New York Mercantile Exchange. Producer: News-a-tron. Also listed under "International" and under "Investment" categories on NewsNet.

Energy and Minerals Resources. Subject: All aspects of fossil fuels, uranium, and industrial, strategic, and precious metals, from exploration to end use, to national and international policy. Producer: Business Publishers, Inc. Also listed under Metals and Mining and under Power Generation categories on NewsNet.

International Petroleum Finance. Producer: Petroleum Analysis Limited. Also listed under International and under Finance and Accounting categories on NewsNet.

Petroleum Information International. Subject: The international oil and gas industry. Producer: Petroleum Information Corp. Also listed under Finance and Accounting and under International categories on NewsNet.

Solar Energy Intelligence Report. Subject: The solar-energy industry, with particular emphasis on various solar-based, alternate-energy technologies. Producer: Business Publishers, Inc. Also listed under Power Generation and under Research and Development categories on NewsNet.

ENTERTAINMENT AND LEISURE

The Fearless Taster. Subject: Wines, and recipes that complement the wines described. Producer: Resources for Communication. Also listed under Farming and Food and under Publishing and Broadcasting categories on NewsNet.

The Gold Sheet. Subject: Scores, point spreads, and other statistics for college and professional football and basketball. Producer: Nation-Wide Sports Publications. Also listed under Investment and under Publishing and Broadcasting categories on NewsNet.

Hollywood Hotline. Subject: The entertainment industry. Producer: Eliot Stein. Also listed under Telecommunications and under Publishing and Broadcasting categories on NewsNet.

Video Week. Subject: All video technology industries, from videocassettes, to broadcast TV, to satellite transmissions. Producer: Television Digest, Inc. Also listed under Publishing and Broadcasting and under Electronics and Computers categories on NewsNet.

ENVIRONMENT

Air/Water Pollution Report. Subject: Air and water pollution, with special attention to environmental laws and regulations. Producer: Business Publishers, Inc. Also listed under Government and Regulatory and under Law categories on NewsNet.

Land Use Planning Report. Subject: Public land management, community development, and regional planning and zoning. Includes news on government legislation. Producer: Business Publishers, Inc. Also listed under Government and Regulatory and under Real Estate categories on NewsNet.

Nuclear Waste News. Producer: Business Publishers, Inc.

World Environment Report. Subject: Environmental issues and trends in both developing and industrialized countries. Producer: Alexander Research & Communications, Inc. Also listed under Energy and under Government and Regulatory categories on NewsNet.

FARMING AND FOOD

Agricultural Research Review. Subject: Research studies in the agricultural sciences. Producer: Lloyd Dinkins. Also listed under Electronics and Computers and under Advertising and Marketing categories on NewsNet.

Agri-Markets Data Service. Subject: Contains data on the production and marketing of food commodities. Also commentary on and analyses of world agricultural markets and export trade. Producer: Capitol Publications.

Computer Farming Newsletter. Subject: Applications of microcomputers in farming and ranching. Includes hardware and software reviews. Producer: Lloyd Dinkins. Also listed under Electronics and Computers and under Advertising and Marketing categories on NewsNet.

Farm Exports. Producer: Lloyd Dinkins. Also listed under Electronics and Computers and under General Business categories on NewsNet.

Farm Software Developments. Subject: Microcomputer software applications in agriculture. Includes software reviews. Producer: Lloyd Dinkins. Also listed under Electronics and Computers and under Advertising and Marketing categories on NewsNet.

FINANCE AND ACCOUNTING

Bank Network News. Subject: Bank networks designed for electronic funds transfer. Includes coverage of home banking terminals and automatic tellers. Producer: Barlo Communications Corp. Also listed under Electronics and Computers and under Telecommunications categories on NewsNet.

Banking Regulator. Subject: Federal legislation and policies that affect commercial banks. Producer: Reports, Inc. Also listed under Government and Regulatory and under Law categories on NewsNet.

Credit Union Regulator. Subject: Federal policies and regulations that affect credit unions. Producer: Reports, Inc. Also listed under Government and Regulatory and under Law categories on NewsNet.

Federal Reserve Week. Producer: Business Publishers, Inc. Also listed under Investment and under Government and Regulatory categories on NewsNet.

Financial Management Advisor. Subject: Financial management for privately owned businesses. Producer: Newsletter Management Corp. Also listed under Management and under Investment categories on NewsNet.

Fintex All-Day Foreign Exchange Monitor. Producer: Fintex, Inc. Also listed under International and under Investment categories on NewsNet.

Fintex All-Day U.S. Money Market Monitor. Producer: Fintex, Inc. Also listed under International and under Investment categories on NewsNet.

Washington Credit Letter. Producer: Business Publishers, Inc. Also listed under Advertising and Marketing and under Government and Regulatory categories on NewsNet.

GENERAL BUSINESS

International Intertrade Index. Subject: Products that are newly imported to the U.S. Includes name and address of manufacturer and wholesale prices. Producer: International Intertrade Index. Also listed under Research and Development and under International categories on NewsNet.

Update/The American States. Subject: Business climate, economic forecasts, data, trends, and business profiles in all states in the U.S. Producer: Tower Consultants International, Inc. Also listed under Advertising and Marketing and under Management categories on NewsNet. Also available on NEXIS.

GOVERNMENT AND REGULATORY

Access Reports/Freedom of Information. Producer: The Washington Monitor, Inc. Also listed under Law category on NewsNet.

Grants and Contracts Alert. News Bulletin Service. Subject: Federal funding of non-defense projects. Producer: Capitol Publications, Inc. Also listed under Health and Hospitals and under Research and Development categories on NewsNet.

Grants and Contracts Weekly. Subject: Announcements of opportunities for non-defense Federal grant funding. Producer: Capitol Publications, Inc. Also listed under Health and Hospitals and under Research and Development categories on NewsNet.

PACS & Lobbies.   Subject: Federal laws and regulations that affect lobbying and the financing of political campaigns. Producer: Amward Publications, Inc. Also listed under Politics and under Public Relations categories on NewsNet.

U.S. Census Report.   Producer: Business Publishers, Inc. Also listed under Social Sciences and under Advertising and Marketing categories on NewsNet.

The Weekly Regulatory Monitor.   Producer: The Washington Monitor, Inc. Also listed under Environment and under Energy categories on NewsNet.

HEALTH AND HOSPITALS

Diack Newsletter.   Producer: Diack, Inc. Also listed under Research and Development category on NewsNet.

Health Benefit Cost Containment Newsletter.   Subject: Programs, methods, and relevant legislation and industry news. Producer: Information Services Inc.

International SOS Newsletter.   Producer: Information Services Inc. Also listed under General Business and under Management categories in NewsNet.

INSURANCE

Weekly Marketeer.   Producer: Insurance Marketing Services, Inc. Also listed under Finance and Accounting and under Investment categories on NewsNet.

INTERNATIONAL

Africa News.   Subject: Political, economic, cultural, and social developments in nations throughout Africa. Producer: Africa News Service, Inc. Also listed under Politics and under General Business categories on NewsNet.

Business Opportunities Australia.   Producer: Chronicle Publications Pty., Ltd. Also listed under Investment and under Real Estate categories on NewsNet.

The Exporter.   Producer: Trade Date Reports. Also listed under Finance and Accounting and under General Business categories on NewsNet.

Fintex International Economic Summaries.   Producer: Fintex, Inc. Also listed under International and under Investment categories on NewsNet.

Latin American Energy Report.   Subject: Latin American energy industry. Producer: Business Publishers, Inc. Also listed under Energy and under Power Generation categories on NewsNet.

Tax Notes International.   Producer: Tax Analysts. Also listed under Taxation and under law categories on NewsNet.

INVESTMENT

Biotechnology Investment Opportunities.   Producer: High Tech Publishing Company. Also listed under General Business and under Farming and Food categories on NewsNet.

Daily Industrial Index Analyzer.   Subject: Industrial averages of stocks on New York Stock Exchange. Includes commentary on and analysis of current and future market conditions. Producer: News-a-tron. Also listed under General Business and under Finance and Accounting categories on NewsNet.

Energies, Trends, Cycles.   Producer: Pat Esclavon. Also listed under Metals and Mining and under Finance and Accounting categories on NewsNet.

Executive Investing.   Gryphon Asset Management Corp. Also listed under Finance and Accounting and under General Business categories on NewsNet.

Fedwatch.   Producer: Money Market Services, Inc. Also listed under Finance and Accounting and under Government and Regulatory categories on NewsNet.

Ford Investment Review.   Subject: Investment newsletter. Producer: Ford Investor Services. Also listed under Finance and Accounting and under General Business categories on NewsNet.

Howard Ruff's Financial Survival Report.   Producer: Target, Inc. Also listed under Taxation and under General Business categories on NewsNet.

Insight.   Producer: Money Market Services. Also listed under Finance and Accounting and under Government and Regulatory categories on NewsNet.

Low-Priced Stock Alert.   Producer: Idea Publishing Corp. Also listed under Finance and Accounting and under General Business categories on NewsNet.

Market Consensus Alert.   Producer: Idea Publishing Corp. Also listed under Finance and Accounting and under General Business categories on NewsNet.

Market Digest.   Producer: Gryphon Asset Management Corp. Also listed under Finance and Accounting and under General Business categories on NewsNet.

Penny Stock Preview.   Producer: Idea Publishing Corp. Also listed under Finance and Accounting and under General Business categories on NewsNet.

The Stranger Report.   Producer: Robert A. Stranger and Co. Also listed under Taxation and under Finance and Accounting categories on NewsNet.

Stock Advisors' Alert.   Producer: Idea Publishing Corp. Also listed under Finance and Accounting and under General Business categories on NewsNet.

Tax Shelter Insider.   Producer: Newsletter Management Corp. Also listed under Taxation and under General Business categories on NewsNet.

Trude Latimer's Stock Traders' Hotline.   Producer: Trude Latimer. Also listed under Finance and Accounting and under General Business categories on NewsNet.

Wall St. Monitor: Weekly Market Digest.   Producer: Karen Lazarovic Publications, Inc. Also listed under Metals and Mining and under Finance and Accounting categories on NewsNet.

MANAGEMENT

Altman & Weil Report to Legal Management.   Subject: Services, products, and trends relating to the management of law offices and similar businesses. Producer: Altman & Weil Publications, Inc. Also listed under Office and under Law categories on NewsNet.

The Entrepreneurial Manager.   Producer: The Center for Entrepreneurial Management, Inc. Also listed under General Business and under Finance and Accounting categories on NewsNet.

Executive Productivity.   Subject: Techniques for increasing executive productivity. Producer: Newsletter Management Corp. Also listed under General Business and under Office categories on NewsNet.

Management Contents Preview.   Producer: Management Contents. Also listed under Finance and Accounting and under General Business categories on NewsNet.

Office Automation Update.   Subject: News, reports, and trends in office automation. Producer: Newsletter Management Corp. Also listed under Electronics and Computers and under Office categories on NewsNet.

RIA Executive Alert.   Producer: The Research Institute of America, Inc. Also listed under Office and under General Business categories on NewsNet.

METALS AND MINING

Daily Metals Report.   Subject: A daily analysis of market conditions for metals. Based on prices on the London Metal Exchange. Producer: News-a-tron. Also listed under Investment and under International categories on NewsNet.

OFFICE

Advanced Office Concepts.   Subject: Office automation, personal business computers, word processors, and the like. Producer: Advanced Office Concepts. Also listed under Electronics and Computers and under Telecommunications categories on NewsNet.

The Seybold Report on Office Systems.   Producer: Seybold Publications, Inc. Also listed under Electronics and Computers and under General Business categories on NewsNet.

POLITICS

F&S Political Risk Letter.   Subject: Risk of doing business in about 70 countries. Producer: Frost & Sullivan, Inc. Also listed under Government and Regulatory categories on NewsNet.

Legislative Intelligence Week.   Producer: Communications Services, Inc. Also listed under Government and Regulatory and under Law categories on NewsNet.

PUBLIC RELATIONS

Cable Hotline.   Producer: Larimi Communications Associates, Ltd. Also listed under Advertising and Marketing and under Publishing and Broadcasting categories on NewsNet.

Contacts Daily Report.   Producer: Larimi Communications Associates, Ltd. Also listed under Advertising and Marketing and under Publishing and Broadcasting categories on NewsNet.

Contacts Weekly.   Producer: Larimi Communications Associates, Ltd. Also listed under Advertising and Marketing and under Publishing and Broadcasting categories on NewsNet.

Public Relations Newswire.   Newswire Service. Subject: Public relations releases of all kinds from industry, government, labor unions, and others. Producer: Public Relations Newswire Association, Inc. Applies to all other categories on NewsNet as well.

Trade Media News.   Producer: Larimi Communications Associates, Ltd. Also listed under Advertising and Marketing and under Publishing and Broadcasting categories on NewsNet.

PUBLISHING AND BROADCASTING

Editors Only.   Producer: Editors Only. Also listed under Public Relations and under Advertising and Marketing categories on NewsNet.

IIA Friday Memo.   Producer: Information Industry Association. Also listed under Electronics and Computers and under Telecommunications categories on NewsNet.

Link News Briefs.   Producer: Link Resources Corp. Also listed under Telecommunications and Electronics and under Computers categories on NewsNet.

NA Hotline.   Subject: Covers various aspects of the publishing industry from electronic publishing, to editorial techniques, to postal regulations. Producer: The Newsletter Association. Also listed under Advertising and Marketing and under Public Relations categories on NewsNet.

NewsNet Action Newsletter.   Subject: NewsNet. Producer: NewsNet, Inc. Also listed under Electronics and Computers and under Telecommunications categories on NewsNet.

NewsNet's Online Bulletin.   Subject: NewsNet updates and hints on how to use the system. Producer: NewsNet, Inc. Also listed under Telecommunications and under Electronics and Computers categories on NewsNet.

Online Database Report.   Subject: covers on-line data base industry. Producer: Link Resources Corp. Also listed under Telecommunications and under Electronics and Computers categories on NewsNet.

Public Broadcasting Report.   Producer: Television Digest, Inc. Also listed under Government and Regulatory and under Entertainment and Leisure categories on NewsNet.

RadioNews.   Subject: The radio industry. Producer: Phillips Publishing, Inc. Also listed under Telecommunications and under Management categories on NewsNet.

Television Digest.   Producer: Television Digest, Inc. Also listed under Electronics and Computers and under Telecommunications categories on NewsNet.

The Photoletter.   Subject: Photography. Producer: Photosearch International. Also listed under Education and under General Business categories on NewsNet.

The Seybold Report on Publishing Systems.   Producer: Seybold Publications, Inc. Also listed under Electronics and Computers and under Telecommunications categories on NewsNet.

Travelwriter Marketletter.   Producer: Robert Scott Milne. Also listed under Public Relations and under Entertainment and Leisure categories on NewsNet.

Viewdata/Videotex Report.   Subject: All aspects of the videotex industry, with emphasis on graphics-oriented systems. Producer: Link Resources Corp. Also listed under Telecommunications and under Electronics and Computers categories on NewsNet.

Wiley Book News.   Producer: John Wiley & Sons. Also listed under General Business and under Research and Development categories on NewsNet.

Worldwide Videotex Update.   Producer: Worldwide Videotex. Also listed under Telecommunications and under Electronics and Computers categories on NewsNet.

REAL ESTATE

Crittenden Bulletin.   Producer: Crittenden Financing, Inc. Also listed under Building and Construction and under Finance and Accounting categories on NewsNet.

Crittenden Report.   Producer: Crittenden Financing, Inc. Also listed under Building and Construction and under Finance and Accounting categories on NewsNet.

Real Estate Investing Letter.   Producer: HBJ Newsletter Bureau. Also listed under Investment and under Taxation categories on NewsNet.

Research and Development

Federal Research Report. Subject: Covers Federal research and development. Contains announcements of deadlines, contracts, and contact addresses. Producer: Business Publishers, Inc. Also listed under Education and under Social Sciences categories on NewsNet.

Hi Tech Patents: Data Communications. Producer: Communications Publishing Group. Also listed under Telecommunications and under Electronics and Computers categories on NewsNet.

Hi Tech Patents: Fiber Optics Technology. Producer: Communications Publishing Group. Also listed under Telecommunications and under Electronics and Computers categories on NewsNet.

Hi Tech Patents: Laser Technology. Producer: Communications Publishing Group. Also listed under Telecommunications and under Electronics and Computers categories on NewsNet.

Hi Tech Patents: Telephony. Producer: Communications Publishing Group. Also under Telecommunications and under Electronics and Computer categories on NewsNet.

Research Monitor News. Producer: National Information Service. Also listed under Energy and under Government and Regulatory categories on NewsNet.

Retailing

Fraud and Theft Newsletter. Producer: LPS Marketing, Inc. Also listed under General Business and under Advertising and Marketing categories on NewsNet.

Social Services

Behavior Today. Subject: Research developments in fields of behavior and mental health. Producer: Atcom, Inc. Also listed under General Business and under Advertising and Marketing categories on NewsNet.

ChurchNews International. Subject: Social and religious news from press offices of churches and religious agencies. Covers a range of issues from peace to women's rights. Producer: Resources for Communication. Also listed under Politics and under International categories on NewsNet.

Marriage and Divorce Today. Producer: Atcom, Inc. Also listed under General Business and under Advertising and Marketing categories on NewsNet.

RFC News Service. Producer: Resources for Communication. Also listed under Corporate Communications and under Public Relations categories on NewsNet.

Sexuality Today. Producer: Atcom, Inc. Also listed under General Business and under Advertising and Marketing categories on NewsNet.

United Methodist Information. Producer: United Methodist Communications. Also listed under Public Relations and under Publishing and Broadcasting categories on NewsNet.

Taxation

CCH State Tax Review. Producer: Commerce Clearing House. Also listed under Government and Regulatory and under law categories on NewsNet.

CCH Tax Day: A Digest of Federal Taxes. Producer: Commerce Clearing

House. Also listed under Finance and Accounting and under Law categories on NewsNet.

Charitable Giving.   Producer: Walter S. Bristow III, P.C. Also listed under Investment and under Law categories on NewsNet.

Corporate Acquisitions & Dispositions.   Subject: Tax aspects of corporate reorganizations, liquidations, incorporations, and the like. Producer: Mark A. Stephens, Ltd. Also listed under Law and under Finance and Accounting categories on NewsNet.

Employee Retirement Plans.   Subject: Federal regulations, court decisions, and legislation affecting employee benefits. Producer: Mark A. Stephens, Ltd. Also listed under Law and under Finance and Accounting categories on NewsNet.

IRS Practices and Procedures.   Producer: Mark A. Stephens, Ltd. Also listed under Law and under Finance and Accounting categories on NewsNet.

The Small Business Tax Review.   Producer: Tax Analysts. Also listed under Finance and Accounting and under Law categories on NewsNet.

Tax Notes Bulletin Service.   Producer: Tax Analysts. Also listed under Finance and Accounting and under Law categories on NewsNet.

Tax Notes Today.   Producer: Tax Analysts. Also listed under Finance and Accounting and under Law categories on NewsNet.

Telecommunications

CableNews.   Subject: Cable television industry. Producer: Phillips Publishing Co. Also listed under Government and Regulatory and under Entertainment and Leisure categories on NewsNet.

Cellular Radio News.   Subject: Technology and marketing of cellular radio for mobile telephone service. Producer: FutureComm Publications. Also listed under Government and Regulatory and under Research and Development categories on NewsNet.

Communications Daily.   Subject: Communications and information industry. Producer: Television Digest, Inc. Also listed under Electronics and Computers and under Publishing and Broadcasting categories on NewsNet.

Data Channels.   Subject: Data communications industry. Producer: Phillips Publishing, Inc.

DataCable News.   Subject: Interactive cable television industry and related technologies. Producer: TeleStrategies Publishing. Also listed under Electronics and Computers and under Publishing and Broadcasting categories on NewsNet.

DBS News.   Subject: Satellite broadcasting industry. Producer: Phillips Publishing, Inc. Also listed under Aerospace and under International categories on NewsNet.

Fiber Optics and Communications Newsletter.   Subject: Industry news, including personnel changes and developments in relevant technology and policy. Producer: Information Gatekeepers. Also listed under Electronics and Computers and under Aerospace categories on NewsNet.

Fiber Optics and Communications Weekly Newsletter.   Subject: Industry news. Producer: Information Gatekeepers. Also listed under Electronics and Computers and under Aerospace categories on NewsNet.

Fiber/Laser News.   Subject: Marketing, trends, regulatory action, and other news of interest to the optical fiber industry. Producer: Phillips Publishing, Inc.

Also listed under Research and Development and under International categories on NewsNet.

Home Computer News.   Producer: Phillips Publishing, Inc. Also listed under Electronics and Computers and under Management categories on NewsNet.

LAN.   Producer: Information Gatekeepers. Also listed under Electronics and Computers and under Office categories on NewsNet.

On-Line Computer Telephone Directory.   Producer: J.A. Cambron Co., Inc. Also listed under Electronics and Computers and under Corporate Communications categories on NewsNet.

Satellite News.   Producer: Phillips Publishing, Inc. Also listed under Aerospace and under International categories on NewsNet.

Satellite News Bulletin Service.   Bulletin Service. Producer: Phillips Publishing, Inc. Also listed under Aerospace and under International categories on NewsNet.

SMR News.   Producer: FutureComm Publications, Inc. Also listed under Research and Development and under Government and Regulatory categories on NewsNet.

Telecommunications Counselor.   Producer: Voice & Data Resources, Inc. Also listed under Management and under Electronics and Computers categories on NewsNet.

Telephone Angles.   Producer: Telephone Angles. Also listed under Office and under General Business categories on NewsNet.

Telephone Bypass News.   Producer: TeleStrategies Publishing, Inc. Also listed under Electronics and Computers and under General Business categories on NewsNet.

Telephone News.   Producer: Phillips Publishing, Inc. Also listed under Government and Regulatory and under General Business categories on NewsNet.

Telepoints.   Producer: Telecomputer Research. Also listed under Management and under Electronics and Computers categories on NewsNet.

VideoNews.   Producer: Phillips Publishing, Inc. Also listed under Management and under Entertainment and Leisure categories on NewsNet.

Viewtext.   Producer: Information Gatekeepers. Also listed under Electronics and Computers and under Office categories on NewsNet.

New data bases are continually being added. Contact NewsNet for a current list.

THE SOURCE

The Basics

Hours: On-line 6:00 A.M. to 4:00 A.M. Eastern Time, seven days a week.

Dual structure: Can move around the system with commands or can use the menus.

Baud rate: 300/1200 baud. (Additional charge at 1200 baud.)

Initial charge: $100.

Monthly minimum: $10. ($1 of this is for "account maintenance" and is added to the bill no matter what. The other $9 is chargeable against connect time.)

Training not available and not necessary.

Reference manual: Subscription to THE SOURCE includes a User's Manual, an Introductory Guide, and a Command Guide. The manual is about an inch thick, which makes it fairly intimidating. It is easy enough to use, however, and makes an excellent reference manual. Unfortunately, it is not very useful as an introduction to the system. The trick to using it is to realize that you do not have to read it from beginning to end before signing on to THE SOURCE. Instead, treat it as a reference guide, dipping into it for specific information about specific areas on the system as necessary. *Sign On,* the Introductory Guide, is a thin pamphlet that will tell you most of what you need to know before you start. *The Command Guide* is another thin pamphlet. It does for THE SOURCE what a telephone book does for the phone system. As with the *User's Manual,* the Guide is a well-designed tool for using THE SOURCE but not for learning about it. Additional manuals are available for specific areas of THE SOURCE—primarily for using the programming languages, the text editor, and INFOX, a data-base management program.

Updates: *Update,* a monthly "User's Manual Supplement," is sent to all subscribers. This "Supplement" announces changes to the system. It usually also highlights one section of THE SOURCE, typically discussing what's on that section and giving some tips on how to use it.

On-line updates are also available under "What's New" on the entry menu.

Available through:

SOURCENET (THE SOURCE's own network. Check with THE SOURCE for current availability in your area).
Telenet
Tymnet
Uninet
Datapac (in Canada)

There is no extra charge for any of these telecommunications networks. WATS Lines are also available for $15 per hour in areas where none of the standard services is available.

For further information, contact:
Source Telecomputing Corp.
1616 Anderson Road
McLean, VA 22102
Phone: (800) 336-3366
         (703) 734-7500 (in Virginia)

Price Structure

Prices on THE SOURCE vary by time of day, baud rate, and service used, with all Source Plus services billed at a single higher rate than the standard Source services.

At 300 baud, the charges for standard services are: $20.75 per hour on weekdays from 7:00 A.M. to 6:00 P.M. $7.75 per hour on evenings, weekends, and holidays.

At 1200 baud, the charges for standard services are: $25.75 per hour on weekdays from 7:00 A.M. to 6:00 P.M. $10.75 per hour on evenings, weekends, and holidays.

At 300 baud, the charges for Source Plus services are: $29.75 per hour on weekdays from 7:00 A.M. to 6:00 P.M. $14.75 per hour on evenings, weekends, and holidays.

At 1200 baud, the charges for the Source Plus services are: $34.75 per hour on weekdays from 7:00 A.M. to 6:00 P.M. $19.75 per hour on evenings, weekends, and holidays.

Description

THE SOURCE, like CompuServe, is one of the larger general-interest utilities. It is also probably the best known, to the point where *InfoWorld* has called it "the granddaddy of the nation's information utilities." As with CompuServe, size is measured both in terms of the number of subscribers (currently in the tens of thousands) and in terms of the number of individual data bases available on the system (currently over 800).

Any general description of THE SOURCE and CompuServe is bound to emphasize their similarities rather than their differences. As with CompuServe, services on THE SOURCE include games (even some of the same games), wire news (but UPI this time instead of AP), on-line shopping (computerized classifieds again, and another gateway to COMP*U*STORE), business and financial news, on-line conferences, and even programming.

As with CompuServe also, there's enough on THE SOURCE so that you'll almost certainly find something there to interest you.

And unfortunately, as with CompuServe, if there is any single most important failing in the system, it is simply that when you first get on it, you are likely to feel overwhelmed.

The categories on THE SOURCE are not quite as arbitrary as those on CompuServe. Plans are currently under way to change the main menu (more on that shortly), but as of this writing, there are eight categories. They are:

News and Reference Resources
Business/Financial Markets
Catalog Shopping
Home and Leisure
Education and Career
Mail and Communications
Creating and Computing
Source Plus

The only category here that is clearly arbitrary is Source Plus, which contains all data bases that are charged at premium rates.

This turns out not to be a problem when you're looking for a data base though. For the most part, you can reach any given data base from any category in which you can reasonably expect to find that data base. Post, for example, is a bulletin board where you can post the computerized version of classified ads among other things. Because this is a bulletin-board service, you can reach it through the "Mail and Communications" choice on the main menu. But because Post is a kind of on-line shopping service as well, you can also reach it through "Catalog Shopping." You will find some cross-referencing of this kind on CompuServe also, but it is simply not as thorough as it is on THE SOURCE.

This cross-referencing of data bases simplifies life enormously when it comes to finding your way around the system. In fact, it is one of the nicer features of THE SOURCE. Unfortunately, THE SOURCE doesn't bother to tell you about it, and until you figure it out, you're likely to feel lost.

The problem here is not with THE SOURCE itself but with a lack of foresight in helping newcomers learn how to use the system. It would be relatively easy for THE SOURCE to do much the same thing that Delphi does—namely, provide an introduction that touched on the most important points and helped newcomers feel comfortable with the system. Instead, you're left pretty much on your own. Or worse. The menu selection entitled "Using THE SOURCE" buries you in information that you don't need when you're first starting. It would be much more helpful if the information were at least divided into tips for beginning, intermediate, and advanced users. (Another menu choice does give tips, but here again, there's a bit too much information for a new user.)

As of this writing, THE SOURCE is in the process of developing a new set of menus. The new version of the main menu will reduce the number of choices to six. The point is to make the system seem less overwhelming. Unless current plans are changed, the categories will be:

News and Sports
Business and Financial Information
Travel Services
Games
Communications
Consumer Services

The data bases within these new categories will still be reachable through any reasonable route. Post, for example, will be available through Communications, but also through Consumer Services under an Online Market or Shop-at-Home menu choice.

Finally, THE SOURCE, like CompuServe, has a dual structure. You can find your way around the system through the menus, but if you know where you want to go, you can get there directly by giving the name of the program or data base you want. THE SOURCE also has a kind of hybrid method for getting around the system. If you know the menu route, or at least part of it, you can skip the intervening menus by giving a single menu-route command. MENU 231, for example, is read by the system as "Item 2 on this menu, followed by Item 3 on the next menu, followed by Item 1 on the third menu."

Services Available

As you might expect, any general-interest utility with over 800 data bases will have services that fall into just about any category you can think of, plus a few that don't fall neatly into any single category.

Communications Services

Communications services on THE SOURCE include Electronic Mail, Online Conferences, and Bulletin Boards.

Electronic Mail is the single most popular service on the system. It is generally considered more difficult to learn than Electronic Mail on CompuServe, but it is also more flexible—meaning that you can do more with it. In addition to simply sending a message to another SOURCE user, for example, you can send a "carbon copy" (the recipient is listed on all other copies) or a "blind copy" (the recipient is not listed on other copies). Other features include "delayed delivery" (the recipient will not be able to read the mail until some specified date) and "reply requested" (you will automatically be notified when the letter has been scanned or read). You can even create "distribution lists" (Read: mailing lists) so that you only have to send a letter once for it to show up in any number of mailboxes. (This is useful for inter-office memos and the like.)

THE SOURCE does not have any Special Interest Groups as such, but it does have a service called Participate, which is essentially a series of individual bulletin boards, or conferences if you prefer. Each of these "conferences" works like an extended public discussion carried on through a newspaper's Letters-to-the-Editor page. These conferences, though, can be organized around just about anything: a political discussion, a hobby, a professional interest, and so on. Many of them amount to User's Groups, organized around particular computer systems, for example.

You can also start your own conference on Participate, but be aware that whoever starts the conference has to pay the storage charges for all messages posted under that conference. This isn't necessarily as open-ended as it sounds, and it can be useful. You can make a conference private simply by listing the people who are permitted to use it. This means you can set up a conference on THE SOURCE for a business, a club, or a research group and have what amounts to a private bulletin board. Participate is also suitable for real-time conferences, with everyone on-line. When you're through, you have a complete record of the conference available as "minutes." If you don't want to leave the conference in THE SOURCE's computers, you can download a copy to your own system, then delete the record from THE SOURCE, in which case there will be no storage charges.

A private conference is private to the extent that non-participants cannot get into it—either to read messages or to enter any. Don't forget, though, that the information is going out over phone lines, which can be tapped.

In addition to Participate there is also Chat and Post, two related services.

Chat lets you talk to another user but without saving the information.

Post is strictly a bulletin-board service; it is not suitable for on-line conversations. As of this writing Post includes more than 80 bulletin boards organized around such subjects as aircraft, art, politics, pets, soap operas, and VisiCalc. (New bulletin boards are being added continually as interest warrants.) You are free to read any bulletin board that interests you, to enter comments, to have your comments answered, and even to post want ads or for-sale ads, as appropriate. The most popular bulletin boards are organized around particular hardware or software. These amount to User Group bulletin boards, where users trade information on how to get the most out of their systems.

You can also send Western Union Mailgrams through THE SOURCE, with next (business) day delivery anywhere in the U.S. if sent before 4:00 P.M. Eastern Time. Check with THE SOURCE for current prices.

Transaction Services

THE SOURCE has several interesting transaction-based services. I've already mentioned Post, where you can post computerized classified ads. Catalog shopping includes lists of records, tapes, video tapes, and books—with tapes and video tapes available at a discount. A more specialized catalog lists classic radio programs available on tape (Jack Benny, and Fibber McGee and Molly, among others).

More interesting, perhaps, is the Barter network, where you can exchange goods and services with other SOURCE users. Three-cornered deals—where A gives to B, B gives to C, and C gives to A—are not uncommon, I'm told.

THE SOURCE also acts as a gateway to COMP*U*STORE, with its 50,000 items available at 10 to 40 percent discount.

Information Services

THE SOURCE provides information on a wide range of topics. These include financial and business news, general news, airline schedules, a home medical guide, movie reviews, restaurant guides, and even a guide to wine.

Specific data bases include:

UPI newswire, which you can search by key words to find the stories you're interested in.
Management Contents, which lists abstracts of 27 leading business journals.
Media General, which provides analysis of stock performance for more than 3100 stocks from the New York Stock Exchange, the American Stock Exchange, and Over-the-Counter stocks.

One newer service that is specific to THE SOURCE is Business Update, or BIZDATE. This electronic business "magazine" is updated 80 times each business day between 8:30 A.M. and 7:00 P.M. It covers stock prices, market indicators, commodities indexes, currency rates, and general business, financial, and economic news. Most of the information in BIZDATE is also available elsewhere on THE SOURCE from UPI, Media General, Commodity News Service, and other data bases. The point of

BIZDATE is that it makes all the information available in one place in a single "easy-to-read" format. In effect, BIZDATE is an electronic business and financial oriented newsclipping service.

Other Services

Other services on THE SOURCE include games of various kinds (adventure games, board games, word games, and more).

You'll also find Employ, a service that lists employers on the one hand and resumés on the other. These are divided into 40 categories that you can search by various keys, including geographical location and salary.

Another interesting service is PUBLIC, which consists of publications produced and maintained by users on THE SOURCE. In the print industry this is known as vanity publishing. With the electronic equivalent, though, this capability seems to have more in common with the idea of setting up your own independent newspaper. At any rate, I'm told that this is one of the most popular services on the system.

Finally, there is a section of THE SOURCE called "Creating and Computing," which gives you programming capabilities and some limited text-editing features. You have to know what you're doing before you can use these features though. Some information is available on-line, but you are better off ordering the appropriate manuals before you try this section.

DATA BASES ON THE SOURCE

(A Partial List)

Data Base List

THE SOURCE's *Command Guide* provides an excellent, cross-indexed list of the system's 800 data bases. Rather than trying to duplicate the *Command Guide,* I've limited this section primarily to listing categories of data bases along with a few examples in each category. As with the data base list for CompuServe, the major exceptions to this are for newspapers, magazines, newswires, and the like, where I have listed the names of all current data bases. Where appropriate, I've also included a short explanation of the data base and the name of the producer. As with the CompuServe list, I have not included communications services such as electronic mail, on-line conferences, or Mailgram message service. I have listed only those categories that are built around a data base of some sort.

Post: Bulletin Boards/Special Interest Groups

As I've pointed out elsewhere, bulletin boards on THE SOURCE are each organized around a particular subject and provide at least some of the features of an on-line Special Interest Group. At the moment, Post contains between 80 and 90 bulletin boards. Here are some examples, grouped by category:

Computers: Apple, Atari, Basic, CP/M, Commodore, DEC, Hayes, Heath, IBM, Novation, Osborne, Pascal, TI-99/4A, Hardware Sale, Hardware Wanted, Hardware Rent, Software Sale, Software Wanted, VisiCalc.

Professional or Hobbiest Interests: Aircraft, Antiques, Art, Aviation, Engineering, Games, Ham Radio, Music, Photography, Sports.

Other: Apartments, Automobiles, Fairs and Festivals, Overseas, Property/ Houses, Satellite TV, Soap Operas.

EMPLOYMENT SERVICE

The Employment Service on THE SOURCE is a listing of jobs and resumés. These are broken into about 40 categories, including Accounting, Advertising, Computers, Consulting, Education, Finance, Law, Mathematics, Real Estate, Sales, Travel, and Transportation. As a prospective employer, you can enter a job description or read resumés. As a prospective employee, you can enter a resumé or read job descriptions.

ON-LINE SHOPPING—TRANSACTION SERVICES

Computerized Classifieds: Any of the bulletin boards on Post can be used for classifieds.

Barter: For trading and bartering.

Catalog Shopping Includes: COMP*U*STORE (also available on CompuServe, Dow Jones). Books (for ordering in-print books available in the U.S.). MusicSource (for audio and video tapes). Radiosource (for classic radio programs).

Travel Services: You can make airline and hotel reservations through THE SOURCE. Also, by filling out a questionnaire, you can become a member of THE SOURCE Travel Club (no dues). This entitles you to special tours and group discounts on tours throughout the world. And, of course, you can reserve a spot on any available tour. (A current list of tours is available on-line.)

NEWSLETTERS

U.S. News Washington Letter: Subject: Political and economic news. Producer: U.S. News & World Report, Inc.

COLUMNS (NEWS FEATURES)

THE SOURCE carries about 75 feature columns distributed by United Media Features Syndicate. These are broken down into eight categories: "Viewpoints," "The Arts," "The Locker Room," "Around the House," "Confidentially…," "Leisure," "Science and Health," and "Lifestyles." You can find the column you want by choosing from menus or by searching for the author, date, key word, or title of the column. (The columns are kept for 30 days.)

UNITED PRESS INTERNATIONAL NEWS WIRE

This includes financial news, business news, national and international general news, sports, and weather. THE SOURCE UPI data base holds stories for one week before taking them off the system.

Note: The UPI wire is also available on NewsNet, NEXIS, and DIALOG but in different forms than on THE SOURCE. NEXIS and DIALOG do not take stories off the system, which makes their UPI files suitable for researching background or "historical" information. ("Historical" in this context means one week old.)

Neither system carries the current day's stories though. The NewsNet version of UPI is searchable only by NewsFlash, the system's electronic newsclipping service. On THE SOURCE the news is on-line essentially immediately (with a three or four-minute delay) and is fully searchable.

FINANCIAL AND BUSINESS DATA BASES

Business Update: Subject: Covers stocks, financial markets, and general business, financial, and economic news. Includes Dow Jones Indexes, New York Stock Exchange Indexes, latest status and gold trading worldwide, latest metal market activity, Standard & Poor's hourly indexes, commodities indexes, and the latest currency trading. The information in Business Update is extracted primarily from other data bases on THE SOURCE and is updated 80 times each day. Producer: THE SOURCE.

Management Contents: Subject: Index to and abstracts of 27 leading business journals. Producer: Management Contents, Inc. This is a subset of Management Contents as available on BRS, BRS/AFTER DARK, and DIALOG.

Commodity News Service: Newswire. Updated continuously. Subject: Contains news, prices, and information on the commodities market. Producer: Knight-Ridder Newspapers, Inc. Also available on CompuServe.

Unistox: Subject: Covers trading activity on stocks, bonds, money markets, and mutual funds. Producer: UPI.

GAMES

THE SOURCE's Entertainment section includes about 75 games of all kinds.

EDUCATION

THE SOURCE's Education section consists of about a dozen drills, including a pictorial counting drill for non-readers, an alphabet-teaching program for young children, a program designed to teach the order and spelling of the days of the week, and a program designed to teach typing.

GENERAL INFORMATION

Movie Reviews: Available from several sources, primarily Cineman Movie Reviews. Producer: Cineman Syndicate. Also available on Dow Jones.

Television Reviews.

New York City Entertainment Guide.

Travel Services and Information: Airline schedules, restaurant guides, and hotel guides. (See also On-line Shopping.)

PUBLIC

Because Public is a user publishing area, the subjects covered are as varied as the creators' interests. This section includes newsletters, advice columns, games, and more. The range is broad enough to cover just about every other category on THE SOURCE.

This is only a partial list of data bases on THE SOURCE. For a complete current list, contact Source Telecomputing Corporation.

OTHER UTILITIES

In addition to the major general-interest systems that we've covered so far, there are also several hundred other on-line utilities that are either too small or too narrowly focused to warrant covering in detail. This section covers about 50 of these utilities.

All the systems included here are available in the United States. With one exception, they are available to members of the general public—meaning anyone who is willing to pay for the service. The one exception is MINET, which is restricted to members of the medical profession.

Some systems that meet these two criteria were ruled out because, as a matter of policy, they do not provide information on themselves for publication.

These 50 systems are located in North America, mostly in the United States. They are grouped here in six categories. The categories are:

General Interest
Law
Science and Medicine
Employment—Job Listings
Industry-Specific
Business, Economic, Financial, Investment, Advertising and Marketing.)

One comment: A few of these systems have simple price structures. In those cases, I have included the prices along with the rest of the information for that system. For most systems, though, the pricing is anything but simple. In those cases you'll find information about start-up fees and minimum monthly fees or annual subscription fees as appropriate. These will generally give you a good indication of the cost of using the system, but be aware that there are other costs involved as well.

GENERAL INTEREST

First, here are five systems that are of reasonably general interest even though they are more restricted than the systems we have looked at in detail:

ORBIT Search Service
PLATO
ITT Dialcom
Info Globe
VU/TEXT

ORBIT Search Service

SDC Information Services
2500 Colorado Ave.
Santa Monica, CA 90406
Phone:(800) 421-7229
        (800) 352-6689 (in California)

ORBIT has much in common with BRS and DIALOG. Each is a large bibliographic information-retrieval system consisting primarily of data bases that contain indexes and abstracts. There is even some overlap of data bases.

ORBIT tends to concentrate more on scientific and technological areas than BRS or DIALOG. SDC says that the system is targeted largely to researchers in these fields. Even so, it contains information that will be useful to others as well.

SDC feels that one of the strongest points of the system is the consistency of file structure from one data base to the next. Of particular note is the CROSSFILE searching capability. This includes some unique features that speed the chore of searching more than a single data base. One of the more interesting features is that ORBIT will let you suspend a search in one data base to run a search on a second data base. You can then go back to the first data base, pick up the search where you left off and still be able to read the information you found in the second search. This can be useful in certain data bases when you are in the middle of a search and need to dig some information out of a related "reference" data base before you can go on.

ORBIT has roughly 80 data bases—slightly more than BRS but many fewer than DIALOG. ORBIT groups these into 13 categories. These are:

Business
Chemistry
Electronics
Engineering
Energy
Environment
Government and Legislation
Industry-Specific
Life Sciences
Multidisciplinary
Patents
Social Sciences
Science and Technology

Training

The start-up fee on ORBIT varies, depending on the training option. The choices are:

$125—Self-Instructional Workbook Program. This includes a workbook with exercises, a system reference manual, and five data base manuals of your choice. The fee also includes $300 of on-line time on selected files for practice. This must be used within three months after getting the password.

$200—Training Workshop Package. This includes the same manuals as used in the self-instructional program plus training for two people at a regularly scheduled, one-day, basic-skills seminar. The seminar includes on-line practice time under an instructor's supervision. The package also includes $150 of on-line time for practice on selected files. This must be used in a six-month period from the day of the workshop.

Custom Workshop Package: One-day seminars custom-designed to client needs. Prices begin at $450 and vary with travel expenses, the number of manuals needed, and the number of people being trained. The package includes a total of $400 connect time for training purposes. As with the other training options, this practice time is limited to selected data bases and is for use over a six-month period from the day of the workshop.

Price

Data bases range in cost from $35 to $160 per hour plus an $8 telecommunication cost on Telenet or Tymnet. About half the data bases are $80 per hour or less. About 70 percent are $90 per hour or less.

There is a minimum billing of $10 for any month in which the service is used.

For further information, contact SDC Information Services.

PLATO

Control Data Corporation
Box O
Minneapolis, MN 55440
Phone: (800) 328-1109
 (612) 853-7518 (in Minnesota)

Available to universities and corporations on a subscription basis. The cost of the package varies, depending on needs. Subscription includes dedicated terminals when necessary.

Available to individuals with the purchase of PLATO Access Disk ($50). This includes a manual and password. As of this writing, the Plato Access Disk is available only for the IBM PC. Plans are to offer similar programs for other machines. Check with PLATO for current availability.

For individuals there is a $10 annual fee. All other charges are strictly for on-line time at $5 per hour.

PLATO is primarily concerned with computerized education and training. It offers on-line courses in over 1000 subjects. The PLATO catalog divides these into 27 categories.

Categories include: Agriculture, Astronomy, Aviation, Biology, Botany, Business, Chemistry, Computer Science, Demography, Economics, Education, Engineering,

Games, Languages, Mathematics, Medicine, Music, Nursing, Personal Development, Physics, PLATO topics, Psychology, Securities Industry, Statistics, Utilities, Veterinary Medicine, and Vocational Training.

Individual courses vary from such general-interest topics as Planning for Retirement to such specialized courses as Heat and Thermodynamics. Some other courses are: Aviation Ground School, Multi-national Corporations, Computer Concepts, Management by Objective, and The Metric System. For the complete list of courses, contact PLATO.

The system also has communication services, including electronic mail, bulletin boards, and on-line conferences.

ITT Dialcom, Inc.

Corporate Headquarters
1109 Spring St., Suite 410
Silver Spring, MD 20910
Phone: (301) 588-1572

ITT Dialcom carries a great deal of "general" information, but it is marketed as a business-oriented system. Data bases include UPI Wires (including UNISTOX), Los Angeles Times/Washington Post Syndicate, Federal Rulings on Business, and the OAG (Official Airline Guide), and other travel services. Dialcom also offers a gateway to DIALOG and BRS.

A $100 monthly minimum fee is chargeable against use.

Info Globe

The Globe and Mail
444 Front Street West
Toronto, Ontario
Canada M5V 2S9
Phone: (416) 585-5250

On-line edition of the Canadian newspaper, *The Globe and Mail*. Also carries Marketscan, a data base of stock-market information. *The Globe and Mail* is $150 per hour in prime hours. Marketscan is $60 per hour in prime time.

VU/TEXT Information Services, Inc.

(A Wholly Owned Subsidiary of Knight-Ridder's Business Information Division.)
P.O. Box 8558
Philadelphia, PA 19101
Phone: (215) 854-8297 (in Pennsylvania)
     (800) 258-8080

VU/TEXT carries the full text of newspapers and other general information sources. Data bases on the system include Media Wire, *The Washington Post, The Philadelphia Enquirer,* the *Philadelphia Daily News,* the *Lexington Herald-Leader,* the Academic American Encyclopedia Database, the *Wall Street Transcript,* and the Pennsylvania Legislative Database (consisting of the Pennsylvania Bill Inquiry data base and Pennsylvania Legislator Statistics).

All newspapers and similar daily materials are on a one-day delay. Once on the system, the information stays. Start dates range from January 1980 for the *Philadelphia Daily News* to April 1983 for *The Washington Post.* All data bases are fully searchable by key words using any combination of AND, OR, and NOT.

Charge is for connect time only. Costs vary with data base, but most are in the $60- to $80-per-hour range. There is no additional charge for 1200 baud. Contracts are available with reduced charges for guaranteed minimum usage.

LAW

Two systems of interest primarily to lawyers:

AUTO-CITE

Lawyers Co-operative Publishing Co.
50 Broad St.
Rochester, NY 14694
Phone: (800) 462-6807
        (800) 828-6373 (in New York)

Legal data base for checking current status of case citations. Data base includes references to *American Law Reports.*

Start-up fee of $150 includes manual, training, and 30 days of unlimited use. Monthly minimum is $36 (equivalent to 30 cites per month).

AUTO-CITE is also available through LEXIS.

WESTLAW

West Publishing Co.
50 West Kellogg Blvd.
St. Paul, MN 55165
Phone: (612) 228-2433

Data bases on legal cases, statutes, and regulations. Also includes on-line versions of *Shepards Citations, Black's Law Dictionary,* and the *Forensic Services Dictionary.* One of WESTLAW's newer data bases is Insta-Cite, a system designed to check the history and current status of case citations. Insta-Cite will retrieve both the prior and subsequent history of citations searched. (AUTO-CITE, a competing service, retrieves only the subsequent history.)

Unlike LEXIS, WESTLAW can communicate with just about any ASCII-based system. WESTLAW works at 1200 baud only.

Subscription fee of $100 per month is *not* chargeable against on-line time.

SCIENCE AND MEDICINE

Here are seven utilities with data bases on various aspects of science and medicine. They are further divided into three sub-categories: chemistry, medicine, general.

Chemistry

Cas Online

Chemical Abstracts Service
P.O. Box 3012
Columbus, OH 43210
Phone: (614) 421-3600
   (800) 848-6533

CAS ONLINE has a Chemical Structure data base and the CAS Abstracts data base. (Much the same information is available on DIALOG as a bibliographic data base—without the abstracts.)

Start-up fee is $50.

NIH/EPA Chemical Information System

User Support
Computer Sciences Corp.
P.O. Box 2227
Falls Church, VA 22042
Phone: (703) 237-1333
   (800) 368-3432

Twenty-three data bases dealing with all aspects of chemicals, including Regulation, Toxicity, Environmental Effects, Spectroscopy, and Modeling. The system contains raw data in numerical and textual format. It also includes references to other sources of raw data.

Start-up fee is $300 (waived for non-profit, publicly supported libraries). No minimum usage fee.

Pergamon International Information Corporation

1340 Old Chain Bridge Road
McLean, VA 22101
Phone: (703) 442-0900
(800) 336-7575

Twenty data bases on Patents, Chemistry, Business, and Materials Technology (includes rubber, metals, plastics, and textiles).

There is a $10 minimum charge for any month during which the system is used.

Medicine

BRS/Colleague Medical

BRS
1200 Route 7
Latham, NY 12110
Phone: (800) 833-4707
(800) 553-5566 (in New York)

BRS/COLLEAGUE Medical is a service of BRS tailored to the needs of practicing physicians, medical researchers, and medical libraries. This system offers the medically related data bases of BRS at $22 to $25 per hour, depending on the subscription option chosen. Data bases include *The New England Journal of Medicine* and the Critical Care data base.

Start-up fee is $50. The $50-per-month subscription fee includes two hours of on-line time each month. Individual or group annual rates are also available.

Subscribers to BRS/COLLEAGUE Medical can also use non-medical BRS data bases at normal BRS rates.

National Library of Medicine

MEDLARS Management Section
8600 Rockville Pike
Bethesda, MD 20209
Phone: (301) 496-6193

Roughly 15 data bases on all aspects of medicine and medical research, including the history of medicine. Chiefly of interest to practicing physicians and medical researchers.

A $15 monthly minimum is chargeable against on-line time.

The MINET Medical Information Network

GTE Telenet Communications Corp.
8229 Boone Blvd.
Vienna, VA 22180
Phone: (800) 838-3638

Seven medically related data bases. Six of these are provided by the AMA. The system includes information on Drugs, Disease, Socio-Economic Literature, Procedural Terminology, an Index to and Abstracts of Medical Journals, and a series of Continuing Medical Education Modules. A seventh data base, PHYCOM, is an industry-sponsored pharmaceutical data base comparable to *Physicians Desk Reference*.

Start-up fee is $100. The monthly minimum of $45 is chargeable against on-line time.

MINET is available only to members of the medical profession.

General

ISI Search Network

Institute for Scientific Information
3501 Market St.
University City Science Center
Philadelphia, PA 19104
Phone: (215) 386-0100
        (800) 523-1850

Four data bases covering a range of hard sciences including Biomedicine, Computers, Mathematics, Statistics, and Geology. There is also a Multi-disciplinary Index to both conference proceedings and multi-author books dealing with the hard sciences.

EMPLOYMENT—JOB LISTINGS

CLEO

The Copley Press, Inc.
Los Angeles, CA

CLEO is an acronym for Computer Listings of Employment Opportunities, which pretty well describes the service. The system works in much the same way as a newspaper's want ads. If you're an employer, you place an ad and pay for it. If you're looking for a job, you can read the ads for no charge. As of this writing, the system is confined primarily to jobs in California and mostly to positions in technical and financial industries.

To place an ad, call **(213) 618-0200.**

To browse through the ads (at 300 baud only), call **(213) 618-8800.**

If you're having trouble in signing on to the system, call **(213) 618-1525** for assistance.

Connexions

55 Wheeler St.
Cambridge, MA 02138
Phone: (800) 562-3282
   (617) 497-4144

Connexions is a data base of job listings. The system focuses on those people who are most likely to have access to terminals. This means that most listings deal with engineering, data processing, and the computer sciences. Another strong area is sales and management positions in high-technology companies. As the number of people with access to computers grows, so will the areas covered on the system. Connexions will not "post" your resumé for employers to read, but it will let you store your resumé and send it in response to any job listings that interest you.

Cost is $15 for two hours of connect time.

Industry-Specific

Here are nine industry-specific utilities for a variety of industries. They are arranged alphabetically by utility name. The first line in each entry identifies the industry. The second line is the name of the utility.

Agricultural Industry

AgriData Network (formerly AgriStar)

AgriData Resources, Inc.
205 W. Highland Ave.
Milwaukee, WI 53203
Phone: (414) 278-7676
   (800) 558-9044

Agricultural economics and agricultural financial information, including agricultural market news, commodity reports, and financial-market and stock-market information. Also includes information on agricultural technology.

Subscription fee is $399 for the first year, $39 per month thereafter. Connect charges are additional.

Aviation Industry

Aircraft Technical Publishers

101 S. Hill Drive
Brisbane, CA 94005
Phone: (415) 468-1705
(800) 227-4610

General Aviation aircraft maintenance.

Start-up fee is $250 or $350, depending on choice of manual (paper or microfiche). Yearly updates are $50 or $100, again depending on choice between microfiche and paper.

Telecommunications Industry

Arthur D. Little, Inc.

25 Acorn Park
Cambridge, MA 02140
Phone: (617) 864-5770

On-line data base covers the telecommunications industry. Other services are available as well.

Annual subscription fee for on-line data base access is $15,000.

Construction—Architectural and Engineering

Berkeley Solar Group

3140 Grove St.
Berkeley, CA 94703
Phone: (415) 843-7600

This system contains historical (*not* current) data on weather, with hourly readings for more than 250 locations. Of interest to architects, engineers, and others working in building energy analysis.

Start-up fee is $25. Monthly minimum usage is $25.

Music Industry

Billboard Information Network

Billboard Publications, Inc.
1515 Broadway
New York, NY 10036
Phone: (212) 764-7424

Billboard Music Charts of best-selling records.

Start-up fee is $200 for record companies, $25 for individuals.

Horse Racing and Breeding

Bloodstock Research Information Services, Inc.

801 Corporate Drive
P.O. Box 4097
Lexington, KY 40544
Phone: (606) 223-4444

Information on thoroughbred horses: pedigrees, race records, stakes results, and depreciation schedules.

$50 minimum monthly usage.

Construction Industry—Architectural and Engineering

Bowne Information Systems

435 Hudson St.
New York, NY 10014
Phone: (212) 807-7280

Construction specifications for architectural and engineering use.

Basic annual fee is $100. Additional fee varies with data base, from a low of $100 per year to a high of $550 per year plus a minimum of $300 per month. (One data base is $1100 for the first year only, or $975 for CSI members.)

Energy Industry

Oil Price Information Service

Division of United Communications Group
8701 Georgia Ave., Suite (800)
Silver Spring, MD 20910
Phone: (301) 589-8875

Information for the energy/petroleum industry.

Yearly subscription fee varies with data base. The lowest charge is roughly $400 per year per data base. This is *not* chargeable against connect time.

Energy Industry

World Energy Industry Information Services

Division of Business Information Display, Inc.
4202 Sorrento Valley Blvd.
San Diego, CA 92121
Phone: (619) 452-7675

Data bases on world energy industry. Information is available by country for about 100 countries. It is available by commodity for nuclear energy, gas, coal, and the like. System automatically converts different units of measure into like units, thereby simplifying comparisons among countries.

Annual subscription fee is $750. This includes the *World Energy Industry Quarterly*, which is essentially the printed equivalent of the on-line data base.

Business, Economic, Financial, Investment, Advertising and Marketing

Here, finally, are 24 systems that deal exclusively with various aspects of business, economics, financial, investment, and advertising and marketing information. Some of these systems have more than 100 data bases. Others have only one or two. Some deal with most or all of the subject areas included in this category. Others deal with only one. This section also includes systems with industry-specific data bases on more than one industry. Because of the nature of the information, many of the systems in this category are relatively expensive.

The listing is arranged alphabetically by utility name. The first line in each entry indicates the kind of information on the system; the second line is the utility name.

Financial

ADP Financial Information Services, Inc.

East Park Drive
Mount Laurel, NJ 08054
Phone: (609) 235-7300

Stock, Bond, and Commodity Market Information. Also has gateways to related data bases from selected sources, including Dow Jones, Standard & Poor's, Monchik-Weber, and Commodity News Service.

Minimum monthly fee is "in the neighborhood of $1000." This includes leasing of terminal equipment. The system should soon be available on personal computers as well. Check with ADP for current information and price.

Financial

ADP Network Services Division of Automatic Data Processing, Inc.

175 Jackson Plaza
Ann Arbor, MI 48106
Phone: (313) 769-6800

Roughly 35 data bases covering financial, banking, securities, and economics (including both historical information and projections).

$100 monthly minimum, chargeable against connect time. Some data bases have subscription fees as well as connect-time charges.

This utility is only now becoming available on microcomputers. Check with ADP for current list of compatible systems.

Financial

Bridge Data Company

10050 Manchester Rd.
St. Louis, MO 63122
Phone: (314) 821-5660
        (800) 325-3986

Financial information.

Complex fee structure. Contact Bridge Data Company for information.

Business

CBD OnLine

(A subsidiary of United Communications Group)
8701 Georgia Ave., Suite 800
Silver Spring, MD 20910
Phone: (301) 589-8875

On-line version of *Commerce Business Daily,* a publication of the U.S. Dept. of Commerce. This covers all government procurements and awards.

CBD OnLine has a $10 monthly minimum, chargeable against connect time. (Also available on DIALOG.)

Business—Management, Construction Industry, Agriculture

CYBERNET Services

Control Data Corp.
P.O. Box O
Minneapolis, MN 55440
Phone: (612) 853-8100

Data bases dealing with construction industry, agriculture, and management.

Economic and Financial

Chase Econometrics/Interactive Data Corp. (CEIDC)

486 Totten Pond Road
Waltham, MA 02154
Phone: (617) 890-1234

With roughly 120 economic and financial data bases, this is one of the largest systems specializing in economic information.

Monthly charge is $150, *not* chargeable against usage.

Economic, Financial, Business

CitiShare

Box 1127
New York, NY 10043
Phone: (212) 572-9600

Financial, economic, and business data bases.

Minimum fee of $250 per month, chargeable against on-line time.

Financial—Commodities and Stocks

Commodity Systems, Inc.

200 W. Palmetto Park Rd., Suite 200
Boca Raton, FL 33432
Phone: (305) 392-8663
         (800) 327-0175

Information on commodities, stocks, commodities options, and stock options.

Start-up fee is $60. Minimum charges vary with data base but start at $32 per month, with 10 percent discount for evening use.

Business and Financial

Computer Directions Advisors, Inc.

11501 Georgia Ave.
Silver Spring, MD 20902
Phone: (301) 942-1700

Business and financial data bases covering ownership of companies and performance of funds.

Start-up fee is $100. Cost per year varies with data bases used. Some data bases are on a strictly pay-for-use basis. Others require an annual subscription fee. The most expensive is $2500 per year.

Business and Financial

Control Data Corporation/Business Information Services

500 W. Putnam Ave.
P.O. Box 7100
Greenwich, CT 06836
Phone: (203) 622-2000

Roughly 50 data bases covering marketing, demographics, business, and financial subjects.

Minimum $200-per-month fee, chargeable against on-line time.

Economic and Financial

Data Resources, Inc.

Corporate Headquarters
29 Hartwell Ave.
Lexington, MA 02173
Phone: (617) 863-5100

National and international economic, financial and demographic information. Also includes industry-specific data bases. An interesting feature of this system is VisiLink, a communications package that lets you buy a "data Kit" —a small, predefined data base in VisiCalc format. Once you download the data kit to your own system, you can play with it off-line, using VisiCalc.

Start-up fee is $100. $12 monthly fee is *not* chargeable against connect time.

Call the above number for the closest regional office.

Economic and Financial

General Electric Information Services Co.

401 N. Washington St.
Rockville, MD 20850
Phone: (301) 340-4000

Roughly 45 data bases in a wide range of categories, including Economic, Financial, Marketing, and Demographic. Industry-specific categories include Petroleum, Agricultural, Pharmaceutical, and Health Industry.

Start-up fee is $100. Minimum fee is $40 per month per data base "catalog." (Each "catalog" typically contains several data bases.)

Business and Financial

I.P. Sharp Associates

Box 418, Exchange Tower
2 First Canadian Place
Toronto, Ontario
Canada M5X 1E3
Phone: (416) 364-5361

Roughly 100 data bases on a variety of business and financial subjects. Categories are: Aviation, Economics, Energy, Financial, Insurance, Banking, and Securities.

Business and Financial

INFONET Network

Computer Sciences Corp.
2100 East Grand Ave.
El Segundo, CA 90245
Phone: (213) 615-0311

Covers foreign exchange rates, financial markets, costs for offshore oil and gas exploration.

Contact INFONET for prices.

Financial

M.J.K. Data Retrieval Service

M.J.K. Associates
122 Saratoga Ave., #11
Santa Clara, CA 95050
Phone: (408) 247-5102

Commodities futures (historical and current information).

Start-up fee is $25. A $15 monthly minimum is chargeable against use.

Marketing and Advertising

Management Science Associates, Inc.

5100 Centre Ave.
Pittsburgh, PA 15232
Phone: (412) 683-9533

MSA data bases are most useful to large advertisers and advertising firms. The system has roughly 10 data bases on product movement at factory, warehouse, retail, and consumer levels. Another half-dozen media data bases contain demographics and usage statistics of magazine readers and television viewers.

Subscription fees vary with the data base. The least expensive is roughly $2500 per year. Usage fees are additional.

MSA has branch offices in Washington, New York, and Chicago. The phone numbers are:

Washington (301) 997-3660
New York (212) 398-9100
Chicago (312) 693-0343

The New York and Chicago offices use the name "Market Science Associates."

Financial

National Computer Network of Chicago, Inc.

1929 N. Harlem Ave.
Chicago, IL 60635
Phone: (312) 622-6666

Information on commodities, stocks, options, bonds, and indexes. In addition to using the system to find information, users can also manipulate the information while on-line.

Subscription fee varies with the data base. The most expensive is $500 per month. This fee is not chargeable against on-line time.

Financial

Nite-Line

National Computer Network of Chicago, Inc.
1929 N. Harlem Ave.
Chicago, IL 60635
Phone: (312) 622-6666

Nite-Line provides raw financial data for home-computer use. This is a less-powerful and less-expensive version of NCN's full service. Subscribers to Nite-Line can search and download the same information as subscribers to the regular service, but there is no capability for analyzing the information by manipulating it while on-line. Although Nite-Line gets its name from having started as an after-hours service, it is no longer limited to evening hours.

Start-up fee is $15. There is no minimum usage.

General Business and Economics

On-Line Research, Inc.

200 Railroad Ave.
Greenwich, CT 06830
Phone: (203) 661-1395

Four data bases covering economic, demographic, agricultural, general business, tax, and financial information.

The agricultural data base has an annual minimum fee of $1000. The other data bases have no annual minimum charge.

Financial

STSC, Inc.

2115 East Jefferson St.
Rockville, MD 20852
Phone: (301) 984-5000

Data bases include national and international financial information, industry-specific financial information for the airlines and oil industries, and demographic information.

A $150 monthly minimum is chargeable against on-line time.

Financial

Securities Data Company, Inc.

62 William St., 7th Floor
New York, NY 10005
Phone: (212) 668-0940

Several financial data bases dealing with corporate securities, municipal debt issues, mergers and acquisitions.

Subscription fees (not chargeable against use) vary with data base but run between $10 per month and $50 per month per data base.

Advertising and Marketing

Telmar Media Systems, Inc.

90 Park Ave.
New York, NY 10016
Phone: (212) 949-4640

Roughly 30 data bases with various aspects of advertising and marketing information, including demographics, consumer product usage, and media audience data. Major users are advertising agencies, advertisers, publishers, and broadcasters. Data covers North America, Europe, South Africa, and the Far East.

Subscription fee varies with data base and amount of use.

Financial

Time Sharing Resources, Inc.

777 Northern Blvd.
Great Neck, NY 11021
Phone: (516) 487-0101

Two financial data bases. No start-up fee. No monthly minimum.

Investment Information—Business and Corporate Information

Wall Street Transcript

120 Wall St.
New York, NY 10005
Phone: (212) 747-9500

Full text of *Wall Street Transcript*. This is a weekly publication containing in-depth round-table discussions on the business and economic outlook for two industries each week. The *Transcript* covers the investment potential for the industries discussed and for specific companies within those industries, giving the opinions, analyses, and forecasts of professionals in the business and investment world. It also contains verbatim transcripts of interviews with executives of publicly traded companies. Approximately 500,000 words per week.

On-line fees vary from $180 per hour to $290 per hour.

Economics and Energy Industry

Wharton Econometric Forecasting Associates

3624 Science Center
Philadelphia, PA 19104
Phone: (215) 386-9000

Roughly 25 data bases covering energy, domestic economics, and international economics. About half of these have been taken over from CISInetwork.

Data bases are available only to those who are already subscribers to the printed *Wharton Econometric Forecasts*. Annual subscription to the data bases themselves is $3000.

Index to Services Available on On-Line Systems

How to Use This Index

This is not an index to on-line data bases. There are any number of such indexes available already, some of which you will find recommended in the Appendix to this book.

Data base indexes are necessarily organized around the subject categories that the data bases fall into. These indexes can be useful but they tend to go out of date quickly as data bases go on- and off-line or move from one system to another. Also, because these indexes are organized specifically around *information*-based services, they tend to be of limited usefulness when trying to track down other kinds of services.

This index is organized primarily around *kinds* of services. This includes information-based services, of course, but it also includes transaction-based services and communications-based services.

To use the index, start by looking up the kind of service you're interested in. Some possibilities are: Bibliographic Data Bases, Newspapers, Bulletin Boards, and Directories. Each category contains a list of on-line systems that deal in that kind of service. In many cases you will also find notes indicating differences among the utilities. Under Wire Services, for example, you will find comments telling you which systems carry current information and which carry historical information. Under Bibliographic Data Bases you will find a list of subject categories for each system. At the end of the index you will find a list of specific data bases that are available on more than one system.

Keep in mind that although specific data bases are mentioned in many cases, this is primarily an index to the information utilities themselves, not to the data bases. Even when *specific* data bases or services change, the *kinds* of data bases and services on each system are likely to remain the same—all of which should keep this index useful and current for a relatively long time.

Some items here were only in the planning stage when this list was compiled. See the entries for each system for further information. In each case you can check with the utility for current availability.

Also, be aware that although this index refers to some of the utilities covered under "Others," it is still primarily an index to those systems covered in some detail. For a more complete list of systems, use this along with the list of utilities in the "Others" section. These are already broken down by category.

BIBLIOGRAPHIC DATA BASES

Data bases in this category include indexes to magazines, journals, newspapers, books and scientific papers. Many of these are well-known works available at most libraries; *Books in Print* falls into this category, for example. Typically, where there is both a print version and an on-line version of a bibliographic data base, the on-line version is "full text" in the sense that it contains the same information as does the print version. Since the print version itself is a bibliographic data base, though, the on-line version is listed that way.

Many of the data bases in this category also contain abstracts of the items indexed.

BRS.   BRS consists primarily of bibliographic data bases. The BRS manual lists them in the following categories:

Sciences & Engineering   health and medicine, dentistry, computers, mathematics, agriculture, biology, chemistry

Business & Finance   data on specific industries, management, industrial standards, patents, economics

Education   education for the handicapped, exceptional child education, vocational education, computer applications

Social Sciences & Humanities   alcoholism, drug abuse, marriage and family, psychology, mental health, religion, architectural history, sociology, all social sciences

Energy & Environment   energy, environment, pollution, conservation

Reference   general and multi-disciplinary directories, including *Books in Print* and *Monthly Catalog of Government Printing Office*

BRS/AFTER DARK.   As with BRS, BRS/AFTER DARK consists primarily of bibliographic data bases. The BRS/AFTER DARK manual lists them in the following categories:

Sciences & Engineering   health and medicine, dentistry, computers, mathematics, agriculture, biology, chemistry

Business & Finance   general business and financial information, patents

Education & Educational Practices   includes exceptional child education

Social Sciences & Humanities   marriage and family, psychology, mental health, religion

Energy & Environment

Reference   includes *Books in Print*

DIALOG.   As with BRS, DIALOG consists primarily of bibliographic data bases. Because there are roughly three times as many data bases as in BRS, DIALOG has organized them into a greater number of categories. Notice, though, that many of the subjects that have their own categories on DIALOG are also present on BRS as part of some other category. "Patents," for example, is listed under "Business & Finance" on BRS. The DIALOG categories are:

Chemistry

Agriculture & Nutrition

Medicine & Biosciences

Energy & Environment

Science & Technology   physics, engineering, geology, computer science, microcomputers

Materials Science   metals, textiles, paints, and other materials

Patents

Business/Economics   includes industry-specific information

Law & Government

Current Affairs   magazines, newspapers

Social Sciences/Humanities   political science, psychology, child abuse, language, history, philosophy, music, all social sciences

Education

Foundations & Grants   DIALOG lists these as bibliographic but most are directories to foundations and available grants

Reference

KNOWLEDGE INDEX.   KNOWLEDGE INDEX also consists primarily of bibliographic data bases. The KNOWLEDGE INDEX manual lists them in the following categories:

Agriculture

Books

Business Information

Computers & Electronics

Corporate News

Education

Engineering

Government Publications

Magazines

Medicine

News

Psychology

MEAD: NEXIS.   NEXIS is known for its full text data bases but it also carries INFOBANK, which has a section called "The Abstracts" and another called "Advertising Marketing Intelligence." These are both bibliographic data bases. (The Abstracts covers general news.)

THE SOURCE.   Contains one business-oriented bibliographic data base: Management Contents.

OTHERS

See ORBIT Search Service; Science & Medicine category in Others.

BULLETIN BOARDS/SPECIAL-INTEREST GROUPS   See also On-Line Shopping for Bulletin Boards that function as Computerized Classifieds.

COMPUSERVE.   CompuServe's Special Interest Groups, or Forums, are one of the strong points of this system. The SIGs are built around bulletin boards but include other capabilities as well.

DELPHI

DIALOG

KNOWLEDGE INDEX

THE SOURCE

BUSINESS & FINANCIAL INFORMATION

Includes information on stock and commodity markets. See also: Bibliographic Data Bases; Numeric & Statistical Data Bases.

Note: For a list of business and financial data available from more than one utility, see the list for Bibliographic Data Bases.

COMPUSERVE: Market information, background information on a variety of companies.

DOW JONES: Market information, background information on a variety of companies. Also transcripts from the PBS series, WALL $TREET WEEK ONLINE.

THE SOURCE: Market information, background information on a variety of companies. Business Update, a data base with general business and financial information, updated throughout the day.

OTHERS: See Industry-Specific Category. Business, Economic, Financial, Investment, and Advertising and Market category in "Others."

CB SIMULATION

COMPUSERVE
DELPHI

COLLEGE ENTRANCE & COLLEGE FINANCIAL INFORMATION

COMPUSERVE

COMMUNICATION SERVICES

See Electronic Mail; On-Line Conferences; CB Simulation; Bulletin Boards

COMPUTERIZED CLASSIFIEDS

See On-Line Shopping

CURRENT AWARENESS SERVICE

See Electronic Newsclipping

DIRECTORIES

See also Employment Service

BRS

DIALOG. DIALOG is strong in this area. It has business directories such as the ELECTRONIC YELLOW PAGES (for various classifications of business) and more general directories such as job-placement directories, American Men and

Women of Science (also on BRS), and Marquis Who's Who. (See also DIALOG's Foundations & Grants category under BIBLIOGRAPHIC data bases.)
DOW JONES

EDUCATIONAL DRILLS

THE SOURCE
OTHERS: See PLATO in General Interest category in "Others."

ELECTRONIC BANKING

COMPUSERVE
DELPHI

ELECTRONIC MAIL

BRS: A somewhat limited (I'm tempted to say "primitive") system.
BRS/AFTER DARK
COMPUSERVE
DELPHI: Delphi will also transfer messages to other systems. See Delphi section for details.
KNOWLEDGE INDEX
THE SOURCE: Electronic mail on THE SOURCE is one of the system's strong points.

ELECTRONIC NEWSCLIPPING

BRS: Available on all data bases. Information is searched as it is put on-line. Matches are printed and sent by mail.
DIALOG: Essentially identical to BRS newsclipping service.
NEWSNET: Available on all data bases. As with BRS or DIALOG, information is searched as it is put on-line, but unlike BRS or DIALOG, the information is not printed and sent by mail. You have a choice of two methods of delivery. The system will either notify you of any hits the next time you sign on or it will call you up and print the information on your printer. See NewsNet section for details.

EMPLOYMENT SERVICE/RESUMÉ SERVICE

COMPUSERVE   Supplies a gateway to Connexions.
DIALOG   listed on DIALOG under Directories.
THE SOURCE
OTHERS: See Employment—Job Listings category in Others (includes CLEO and Connexions).

GAMES

COMPUSERVE
DELPHI
THE SOURCE

GENERAL INFORMATION

See also: College Entrance & College Financial Information; Government Publications; Movie Reviews; Television Reviews; Weather

THE SOURCE: General news features (columns) on a variety of subjects.

GOVERNMENT PUBLICATIONS

COMPUSERVE: Full text of an assortment of government publications.

MEAD: NEXIS: Full text of Federal Reserve Bulletin, Code of Federal Regulations, Federal Register.

INFORMATION RESEARCH SERVICES

COMPUSERVE
DELPHI
THE SOURCE

JOURNALS/MAGAZINES: FULL TEXT DATA BASES

BRS: Chemistry, medicine, business. Contains full text of the *Harvard Business Review*, all 18 journals of the American Chemical Society, the *Kirk Othmer Encyclopedia of Medical Science*, the *New England Journal of Medicine*, and other medical journals.

BRS/AFTER DARK: *Harvard Business Review.*

COMPUSERVE: *Better Homes and Gardens, Popular Science, Computers and Electronics.*

DIALOG: *Harvard Business Review.*

DOW JONES: Dow Jones News section covers *The Wall Street Journal* and *Barron's* as well as the Dow Jones News Service.

MEAD—NEXIS: Full text of about 30 magazines. These range from general interest (*Newsweek*) to specialized (*Byte, Chemical Week.*)

LAW & LEGAL DATA BASES

See also: Government Publications; Bibliographic Data Bases

MEAD—LEXIS

OTHERS: See AUTO-CITE; WESTLAW in Law category in Others

MAGAZINES: FULL TEXT DATA BASES

See Journals/Magazines.

MOVIE REVIEWS

COMPUSERVE
DOW JONES
THE SOURCE

NEWSLETTERS

See also: Business & Financial Information.

COMPUSERVE: Newsletters cover money market, investments, microcomputers.

MEAD—NEXIS: Full text of about 40 newsletters in a wide variety of fields, from politics, to finance, to industry.

NEWSNET: With nearly 200 newsletters on-line or in the planning stage, NewsNet is the obvious system to go to for newsletters. There is some overlap between newsletters on NewsNet and on Nexis.

THE SOURCE: Carries one newsletter: *U.S. News Washington Letter.*

NEWSPAPERS: FULL TEXT

See also: Journals and Magazines.

COMPUSERVE

DOW JONES: Carries Wall Street Journal Highlights On-Line.

MEAD—NEXIS: Full text of about a dozen newspapers (on a delayed basis). These range from general-interest newspapers (*The New York Times* and *The Washington Post*) to specialized industry-specific newspapers (*ComputerWorld, Legal Times*). NEXIS also carries Today, an on-line, abridged version of *The New York Times.*

OTHERS: See VU/TEXT and Info Globe in General-Interest category in Others.

NUMERIC & STATISTICAL DATA BASES

The data bases in this category are "full text" in the sense of containing all relevant information rather than referring you elsewhere. The information, though, is primarily statistical or numeric rather than textual.

BRS: Does not have any data bases that are strictly or even primarily numeric, but it does have several Business and Financial data bases that contain statistical or numeric information along with textual information.

COMPUSERVE: Contains financial and business data bases with current and historical market quotes, annual reports, and other numeric information.

DIALOG: Contains a sub-category of Business and Economic Numeric data bases.

DOW JONES: Contains several business and financial oriented numeric data bases, including current historical market quotes.

OTHERS: See Business, Economic, Financial, Investment, and Marketing and Advertising category in Others.

ON-LINE CONFERENCES

COMPUSERVE
DELPHI
DIALOG
KNOWLEDGE INDEX
THE SOURCE

ON-LINE SHOPPING

BRS/AFTER DARK: Swap Shop (computerized classifieds), catalog shopping for computer software, downloading of software directly from the system.

COMPUSERVE: Computerized classifieds, gateway to COMP*U*STORE.

DELPHI: Bazaar (computerized classifieds, with option for auction), Catalog (a Delphi-specific computerized catalog), gateway to COMP*U*STORE.

DOW JONES: Gateway to COMP*U*STORE

THE SOURCE: Computerized classifieds, gateway to COMP*U*STORE and other catalog shopping for books, records, tapes.

PROGRAMMING

This is a time-sharing function. It lets you write programs in a language stored on the host computer.

COMPUSERVE
THE SOURCE

REFERENCE WORKS

BRS: *Academic American Encyclopedia.*

BRS/AFTER DARK: *Academic American Encyclopedia.*

COMPUSERVE: *World Book Encyclopedia.*

DELPHI: Kussmaul Encyclopedia (cross-indexed with back files of wire news stories).

DIALOG: *Academic American Encyclopedia*, UPI back files.

DOW JONES: *Academic American Encyclopedia.*

MEAD—NEXIS: *Encyclopaedia Britannica, Forensic Services Directory*, Associated Press Political Service.

RESEARCH SERVICES

See Information Research.

RESUMÉ SERVICE

See Employment Service.

SELECTIVE DISSEMINATION OF INFORMATION

See Electronic Newsclipping.

SELF-PUBLISHING

DELPHI
THE SOURCE

SHOP-AT-HOME SERVICES

See On-Line Shopping.

SPECIAL INTEREST GROUPS

See Bulletin Boards.

STATISTICAL DATA BASES

See Numeric Data Bases.

TV REVIEWS

THE SOURCE

TRANSACTION SERVICES

See On-Line Shopping; Electronic Banking; Information Research

TRAVEL INFORMATION/RESERVATIONS

COMPUSERVE
DELPHI
THE SOURCE: In addition to airline schedules, hotel availability, and other information you would expect to find in this category, THE SOURCE also contains restaurant and entertainment guides.

UTILITY PROGRAMS

This category contains simple programs for calculating such things as amortization of a loan or net worth.

COMPUSERVE
DELPHI

WEATHER

COMPUSERVE: CompuServe is probably strongest on weather service, with a range of weather data bases suitable for different purposes. Among the choices are: Aviation Weather, Marine Weather, and Global Weather.
DOW JONES
THE SOURCE
OTHERS: See Industry-Specific category in Others.

WIRE SERVICES

COMPUSERVE: AP wires, Commodity News Service.
DELPHI: AP wires.
DIALOG: UPI wires, but not current. DIALOG carries UPI with a 48-hour delay, and holds the stories "forever." (The back file starts in March 1983.) This is in contrast to other systems such as THE SOURCE, which carry the current day's stories but do not keep the stories for long.
DOW JONES: The news, sports, and weather reports on Dow Jones are extracted from UPI wires.
MEAD—NEXIS: Currently carries about ten wire services on a 12- to 48-hour delay. (The delay varies from wire service to wire service.) As with DIALOG, NEXIS holds the stories "forever." Current wire services are: AP, Jiji Press Ticker Sevice, Kyodo English Language News Service, PR Newswire, Reuters North European News Service, Reuters General News Report, UPI World, National, Business, Sports, and States wires, Xinhua (New China) News Agency wire.
NEWSNET: UPI, PR Newswire, and some more-specialized bulletin services. (UPI on NewsNet is available only through the system's NewsFlash, or electronic newsclipping function. It is not searchable otherwise, and there is no back file.)
THE SOURCE: UPI. Carries current UPI stories and holds them for one week.

LIST OF DATA BASES AVAILABLE ON MORE THAN ONE SYSTEM
(Does not include data bases on systems in others)

BIBLIOGRAPHIC DATA BASES

Agriculture

AGRICOLA (Available on BRS, BRS/AFTER DARK, DIALOG, KNOWLEDGE INDEX.)

Biological Sciences

BIOSIS PREVIEWS (Available on BRS, BRS/AFTER DARK, DIALOG, KNOWLEDGE INDEX.)

BUSINESS/FINANCIAL

See also NEWSLETTER List for business/financial newsletters on more than one system.

ABI/INFORM (Available on BRS, BRS/AFTER DARK, DIALOG, KNOWLEDGE INDEX.)

COMMODITY NEWS SERVICE (Newswire. Available on CompuServe, THE SOURCE.)

DISCLOSURE II (Directory Available on DIALOG, Dow Jones.)

DUN'S MARKET IDENTIFIERS (Directory. Available on DIALOG, Dow Jones.)

HARFAX INDUSTRY DATA SOURCES (Available on BRS, DIALOG, NEXIS.)

MANAGEMENT CONTENTS (Available on BRS, BRS/AFTER DARK, DIALOG. A subset of this data base is also available on THE SOURCE.)

PATDATA (Available on BRS, BRS/AFTER DARK.)

PREDICASTS See PTS.

PTS ANNUAL REPORTS ABSTRACTS (Available on DIALOG. Also available on BRS as Predicasts Annual Report.)

PTS F&S INDEXES (Available on DIALOG. Also available on BRS as Predicasts F&S Indexes.)

PTS INTERNATIONAL FORECASTS (Available on DIALOG. Also available on BRS as Predicasts Forecasts.)

PTS INTERNATIONAL TIME SERIES (Available on DIALOG. Also available on BRS as Predicasts Historical Time Series.)

PTS PROMT (Available on DIALOG. Also available on BRS as Predicasts Promt.)

PTS U.S. FORECASTS (Available on DIALOG. Also available on BRS as Predicasts Forecasts.)

PTS U.S. TIME SERIES (Available on DIALOG. Aso available on BRS as Predicasts Historical Time Series.)

STANDARD & POOR'S NEWS (Available on DIALOG, KNOWLEDGE INDEX.)

TRADE AND INDUSTRY INDEX (Available on DIALOG, KNOWLEDGE INDEX.)

CHEMISTRY

CHEMICAL ABSTRACTS (Available on BRS, BRS/AFTER DARK.)

COMPUTERS

DISC (Available on BRS, BRS/AFTER DARK.)

INTERNATIONAL SOFTWARE DATABASE (Available on DIALOG, KNOWLEDGE INDEX.)

CURRENT AFFAIRS

NATIONAL NEWSPAPER INDEX (Available on DIALOG, KNOWLEDGE INDEX.)

NEWSEARCH (Available on DIALOG, KNOWLEDGE INDEX.)

EDUCATION

BILINGUAL EDUCATION BIBLIOGRAPHIC ABSTRACTS (Available on BRS, BRS/AFTER DARK.)

ERIC (Available on BRS, BRS/AFTER DARK, DIALOGUE, KNOWLEDGE INDEX.)

EXCEPTIONAL CHILD EDUCATION RESOURCES (Available on BRS, BRS/AFTER DARK, DIALOG.)
SCHOOL PRACTICES INFORMATION FILE (Available on BRS, BRS/AFTER DARK.)

Energy/Environment

ENERGY DATABASE (Available on BRS, BRS/AFTER DARK.)
ENERGYLINE (Available on BRS, DIALOG.)
ENVIROLINE (Available on BRS, DIALOG.)
POLLUTION ABSTRACTS (Available on BRS, DIALOG.)

Engineering

COMPENDEX (Available on BRS, DIALOG, KNOWLEDGE INDEX.)

Law & Government

LEGAL RESOURCE INDEX (Available on DIALOG, KNOWLEDGE INDEX.)

Mathematics

MATHEMATICAL REVIEWS ONLINE (Available on BRS, BRS/AFTER DARK.)

Medicine

HEALTH PLANNING AND ADMINISTRATION (Available on BRS, BRS/AFTER DARK, DIALOG.)
INTERNATIONAL PHARMACEUTICAL ABSTRACTS (Available on BRS, DIALOG, KNOWLEDGE INDEX.)
MEDLARS ON LINE AND BACKFILES (Available on BRS, BRS/AFTER DARK.)
MEDLINE (Available on DIALOG, KNOWLEDGE INDEX.)
PRE-MED (Available on BRS, BRS/AFTER DARK.)

Reference

AMERICAN MEN AND WOMEN OF SCIENCE (Available on BRS, DIALOG.)
BOOKS IN PRINT (Available on BRS, BRS/AFTER DARK, DIALOG, KNOWLEDGE INDEX.)
GPO MONTHLY CATALOG (Available on BRS, DIALOG.)
GPO PUBLICATIONS REFERENCE FILE (Available on DIALOG, KNOWLEDGE INDEX.)
MAGAZINE INDEX (Available on DIALOG, KNOWLEDGE INDEX.)
ULRICH'S INTERNATIONAL (Available on BRS, DIALOG.)

Religion

RELIGION INDEX (Available on BRS, BRS/AFTER DARK.)

Science (Multi-disciplinary)

NTIS (Available on BRS, BRS/AFTER DARK, DIALOG, KNOWLEDGE INDEX.)
INSPEC (Available on BRS, DIALOG, KNOWLEDGE INDEX.)

Social Science/Humanities

MLA BIBLIOGRAPHY (Available on BRS, DIALOG.)

FAMILY RESOURCES (Available on BRS, BRS/AFTER DARK.)

NATIONAL INFORMATION SOURCES ON THE HANDICAPPED (Available on BRS, BRS/AFTER DARK.)

PRE-PSYC (Available on BRS, BRS/AFTER DARK.)

PSYCINFO (Available on BRS, BRS/AFTER DARK, DIALOG, KNOWLEDGE INDEX.)

PUBLIC AFFAIRS INFORMATION SERVICE (Available on BRS, BRS/AFTER DARK, DIALOG.)

SOCIAL SCIENCE CITATION INDEX AND BACKFILE (Available on BRS, BRS/AFTER DARK, DIALOG.)

SOCIOLOGICAL ABSTRACTS (Available on BRS, DIALOG.)

NON-BIBLIOGRAPHIC DATA BASES

Magazines/Journals

HARVARD BUSINESS REVIEW ONLINE (Available on BRS, BRS/AFTER DARK, DIALOG.)

Newsletters

Update/The American States (Available on NEXIS, NewsNet.)

Newspapers

The Washington Post (Available on NEXIS, CompuServe.)

Reference

ACADEMIC AMERICAN ENCYCLOPEDIA DATABASE (Available on BRS, BRS/AFTER DARK, Dow Jones.)

Wire Services

The ASSOCIATED PRESS World, National, and Business wires. (Available on NEXIS on a delayed basis. Current stories are available on CompuServe.)

PR NEWSWIRE (Available on NEXIS, NewsNet.)

UNITED PRESS INTERNATIONAL News Wires (Available in different forms on Dow Jones, DIALOG, NewsNet, and THE SOURCE. As noted elsewhere, DIALOG and NEXIS have a delayed version of UPI, which makes their files suitable for researching "historical" information. UPI is available on NewsNet only through that system's NewsFlash service, making NewsNet's UPI wire ideal for a "newsclipping" service on any subject that interests you. THE SOURCE, finally, carries UPI current stories. These are fully searchable but are held on the system for only one week).

FREE SERVICES
THE PUBLIC ACCESS BULLETIN BOARDS

The charges for the utilities cataloged in Chapter 8 vary, but in each case there *is* a charge: You have to pay someone for the use of the system.

There are hundreds of other systems that you can get on for free, or at least for the price of the phone call. We touched on them briefly in Chapter 1. These small systems, the Computerized Bulletin Boards, or CBBSs, are also known as Public Access Message Systems, or P.A.M.S. Whatever you call them, they are worth knowing about and they are worth taking the time to look at.

It's hard to say anything definitive about bulletin boards. For one thing, there are too many to keep track of them effectively. More important, trying to describe what to expect from a bulletin board is like trying to describe what to expect from a telephone call; it all depends on who's on the other end of the line.

Some systems are run by businesses. The most common of these are run by computer stores and center around the equipment that these stores sell. As you might expect, many of the messages on these systems amount to advertisements for the stores. Even so, these bulletin boards are still a good place to get information about the computers covered. You can post questions and you can find tips about how to get the most out of your system.

Computer retail stores are not the only businesses with bulletin boards. Novation, the modem manufacturer, runs a bulletin board with information on its own modems and on modems in general. You can't post public messages on this board, but you can send messages to Novation or ask questions through the bulletin board's Electronic Mail option.

More interesting, perhaps, are bulletin boards run by businesses that have nothing to do with computers. These are few and far between, but they include at least one brokerage house where you can get closing prices on more than 2000 stocks. Bulletin boards like this may turn out to be aberrations, but they may also be early signs of a field that is beginning to move out of its hobbiest stage and onto a more mature level.

Many systems are strictly hobbiest in nature. They are run by groups, clubs, or even individuals. They can function as a club's private message service or as its meeting hall. In some cases the bulletin board itself is the hobby for whoever is running it.

Most systems are (theoretically, at least) organized around something— usually a hobby or a specific computer, but sometimes a professional interest. Typical subjects are astronomy, ham radio, games, computer graphics, the IBM PC, S-100 bus systems, and various versions of the TRS-80, Apple, and Atari computers. Less common are bulletin boards organized around medicine, real estate, or education. Still, such systems do exist, and here again, they may be a sign that the field is beginning to move out of its hobbiest stage.

Most bulletin boards have a range of services available. These may include a library of articles to read, a library of free, public-domain software available for downloading, or a library of software for sale and also available for downloading. Services almost always include access to the bulletin board itself—a place where you actually read or post messages. Typically, you can designate a message as private so that the only one who can read it is the addressee.

Many systems will let anyone call in and use any service available. Some systems, however, allow only limited access until you become a "registered user." (How you do this varies from system to system.) This is a security measure. It's aimed at keeping out those few people who make a hobby of trying to make other people's systems crash.

Each bulletin board, finally, has its own personality. This is determined in large part by the System Operator, or Sysop—the person or persons who run the system.

At one extreme, I have seen systems that take a crisp, business-like approach to what they're doing, even if what they are doing is discussing games. At the other extreme, I have seen systems that take a *National Lampoon* style, fun-and-games approach. (If the sign-on message reads something like "Fee, Fie, Fo, Fum, I smell the blood of a Computer Bum," you're probably on a "fun-and-games" system: a good place for trading jokes, or making bad puns.) And, of course, there are systems at any given level between these extremes.

Using a less pleasant measurement of system personality, I've seen systems with obnoxious racist "jokes" on them, systems where the Sysop makes an effort to delete such items when they show up, and systems where the Sysop has instituted a security system to prevent that sort of thing. (Usually this means that public messages must be read and okayed by the Sysop before the system will display them.)

All the above amounts to an overview, a mosaic of impressions distilled from a random sampling of perhaps 50 bulletin boards. There are, however, hundreds of bulletin boards available, with more popping up (and many disappearing) every day. The only way to find out what's out there now, and what might interest you, is to get into the fray yourself. There are only a few things you have to know before you start. They deal with the mechanics of calling a bulletin board, the mechanics of using a bulletin board, and the not-so-incidental question of where to get the phone numbers to call.

For the most part, the mechanics of calling a bulletin board are the same as with any other utility. You call up, let the modems establish communication, sign on to the system, and go about your business. There are a couple of things to watch out for, though.

To begin with, although some bulletin boards are active 24 hours a day (barring unforeseen problems), many systems are available only during certain hours. If you have a number that isn't answering, try calling at different hours of the day before you give up on it. Also be aware that some bulletin boards need to be warned that they're about to get a call. On these systems you have to call, ring once, hang up, then call back.

Parameters and communications protocols are pretty much the same as with any other utility. Virtually all bulletin-board systems will talk to a 103-compatible modem. Some, but not all, will talk to a 212-compatible modem. Very few will talk to a Racal Vadic 3400-compatible modem. The safest approach is to stick with 300-baud, 103-compatibility unless you know that a particular bulletin board uses something else.

Parameters are not usually a problem. Most of the time you can leave them at your software's default setting and not worry about them. In fact, any one of five sets of parameters will usually work. They are:

  7 data bits, even parity, 2 stop bits
  7 data bits, odd parity, 2 stop bits
  8 data bits, no parity, 1 stop bit
  8 data bits, even parity, 1 stop bit
  8 data bits, odd parity, 1 stop bit

Occasionally you will have trouble communicating with a system using one of these settings. If that happens, try changing to one of the other four and keep trying until you find one that works. If you still can't talk to the system, ask other users about it by leaving messages on other bulletin boards.

The mechanics of using a bulletin board vary from system to system, depending on the software it uses. Fortunately there are few software packages available for bulletin-board operators, which means that once you learn a given set of commands, you'll be able to use them on several systems. Even when jumping from one kind of bulletin-board system to another, you will find that being familiar with one set of commands makes it easier to learn another set.

The basic point is: Don't worry about mistakes. Expect to make false starts, and be willing to make them. In the meantime, while you're learning how to use the system, use the help screens. Browse around the bulletin board and see if there's anything there to interest you.

Be aware that most bulletin boards are limited to being used by one person at a time. This means you may have to call a bulletin board several times before you get a ring instead of a busy signal. You'll also find that many systems will put you on a clock, typically allowing you 25 or 30 minutes, after which they will politely but firmly ask you to sign off.

Finally, there is the problem of getting the phone numbers to call. Once you get started, you'll find that it's easy. Virtually all bulletin boards contain a list of numbers for other systems, and most new bulletin boards make a point of announcing themselves by posting messages on other systems. You can also post a message asking if anyone knows about bulletin boards that cover your particular interest.

Getting started isn't much of a problem either. If you are a subscriber to THE SOURCE, CompuServe, or Delphi, you can get a list of bulletin boards just by asking for it.

You'll find it on THE SOURCE at PUBLIC 112; on CompuServe at MAUG XA4; and on Delphi in Infomania, under Member's Choice, listed as P.A.M.S.

Each of these is the same list. It is compiled and maintained by Bill Blue (with a lot of help from his friends, as he says on the heading to the list). If you are not a subscriber to any of these services, you can get the same list by calling the **People's Message System in Santee, California,** on-line 24 hours a day.

The phone number is (619) 561-7277.

The system will ask for your name, city, state, and phone number. When you've finished this sign-on routine, type "?" for a list of commands, then "O" for "Other systems current summary." You'll want to either print the list as it comes or capture the information and save it to disk. The list currently includes roughly 800 phone numbers and takes about 20 minutes to send at 300 baud.

This same list is also available on many other, if not most bulletin boards. If California is a long-distance call for you, you can cut down on your phone bill by getting only part of the list from Santee, then picking a local number to call for the rest of the list. Check the data on the list you download, though. On a single day on two different bulletin boards I found one list that was less than a month old and another that was more than a year old.

Another good place to start is *The On-Line Computer Telephone Directory,* published by Jim Cambron.

The OLCTD currently costs $9.95 for a one-year subscription or $15.95 for a two-year subscription. The address is:

OLCTD

P.O. Box 10005

Kansas City, MO 64111-9990

Published four times a year, the OLCTD contains reviews of bulletin boards, news about new equipment, and articles that delve into the quasi-technical side of telecommunications (the mysteries of RS-232 ports, for example). Most important, it contains an updated list of bulletin-board services.

Jim Cambron says that he and Bill Blue exchange information freely, which means that there is quite a bit of overlap between this list and the P.A.M.S. list. There is a difference though.

As of this writing, the P.A.M.S. list contains roughly 800 phone numbers as opposed to roughly 600 for the OLCTD list. (This may have changed, probably upward, by the time you read this.) The difference is largely because the P.A.M.S. list tends to be inclusive, which means that it's slower about weeding out deadwood. In practical terms, this means that you will find more disconnected phone numbers, or numbers that do not answer, on the P.A.M.S. list. On the other hand, the OLCTD may occasionally eliminate numbers that are still active but didn't happen to be working when the OLCTD tried to confirm them.

The OLCTD should be available over NewsNet by the time you read this.

That's all there is to bulletin boards. From this point, it's like swimming: You have to jump in the water to find out what it's like. Just remember to relax, to enjoy yourself, and to be careful about running up long-distance bills. (And if you haven't signed up with Sprint or MCI yet, this would be a good time to check them out too.)

10

ON THE NEAR HORIZON

Each of the systems we've looked at so far has one thing in common. No matter what they call themselves, no matter what services they offer, no matter who their target audience is, they are all ASCII-based. They are in the business of transmitting text only, and transmitting it using ASCII coding.

There is another kind of information utility—one that is qualitatively different even when it's delivering the same kind of information. It is different because it deals not just with words in a row but with colors and graphics as well.

I am talking, of course, about Prestel and Prestel-like systems. I've ignored these for the most part because as of this writing there are no such systems generally available in this country. Still, there are rumblings. Correction: There are more than rumblings. There have been market tests, there have been "unofficial" rumors, and—more to the point—there have been announcements.

Things are starting to happen.

One local Prestel-like utility is already available in Dallas, Texas. As of this writing, its terminals are located only in shopping malls, retail stores, and the like, but the utility will soon be available for business and home use.

At least two more systems should be coming on-line in Florida at about the time this book is published.

Software that will let you use your computer as a graphics terminal is rapidly becoming available for more and more computers.

AT&T, meanwhile, is introducing its first computer-related consumer product: a graphics-oriented terminal with no computer capabilities.

Some of the other companies involved in these activities include CBS, Sony, and Viewdata Corporation, a subsidiary of the Knight-Ridder newspaper publishing group.

Add this up and it doesn't take much in the way of fortune-telling ability to see that we're going to hear a lot more about graphics-based information utilities in the near future. Given the inherent flexibility of any computer-based system, though, and given the tendency of words to shift meaning in this industry depending on who's using them, it's a good bet that much of what we're about to hear is going to be more bewildering than informative.

Consider this chapter a basic survival guide to help make sense out of what promises to be a confusing situation.

PRESTEL-LIKE SYSTEMS

Throughout this book I have been using the term "Prestel-like system" rather loosely to refer to any information utility that is capable of transmitting graphics and colors as well as text. While there is nothing wrong with using the term this way, it does leave room for confusion once you start looking at such systems a little more closely.

To begin with, Prestel is a specific system; it uses a specific set of communications protocols and it has specific capabilities and limitations. Other systems, with different protocols, may be Prestel-like in the sense that they deal with colors and graphics, but they may also have a different set of capabilities and limitations. More than that, because they each use their own protocols, you need different equipment (or at least different software) to talk to them.

Theoretically, you can set up a graphics and color-oriented information utility using any set of protocols that you like. Some in-house systems, for example, use the RCA Videotex Data Terminal and its protocols. TEXNET, a "special edition" of THE SOURCE, uses protocols appropriate for the Texas Instruments TI-99/4A. You can just as easily set up a system aimed at the Atari, the Apple, or the TRS-80 Color Computer.

As a practical matter, it doesn't make much sense to use different protocols for different systems. For the information utility, this approach would limit the number of potential customers. For the information user, it would mean having to get different terminals for different systems, or at least having to get and learn how to use any number of terminal programs to make your computer act like any number of terminals.

The two protocols that count right now—the two that you're likely to be hearing about—are Prestel and NAPLPS (North American Presentation Level Protocol Standard). NAPLPS is also known (incorrectly) as PLP protocol. It is backed by AT&T.

In practical terms (meaning what shows up on your screen), the major difference between these two protocols is that NAPLPS can transmit much more detailed (high-resolution) graphics while Prestel can transmit its information more quickly.

We'll come back to these differences shortly, but it might help first to take a look at Prestel and what it can do.

PRESTEL

Prestel (the utility *and* the protocol) is an onging concern in England. An abortive attempt was made to introduce Prestel (the utility) to the U.S. in 1982. This was dropped in early 1983, mostly because the system is aimed at British needs and is not quite appropriate for the U.S. market. (You can get a listing of British television programs, for example. This is useful if you're in London, certainly, but not if you're in Ohio.) You can still get Prestel from the U.S., but only by calling England directly and paying the long-distance phone charge. (There are some subscribers who do precisely this.)

As far as function and use are concerned, Prestel doesn't differ in any important way from CompuServe, THE SOURCE, Delphi, or Dow Jones. You call the utility by phone, you log on, and the system presents you with menu choices.

Like CompuServe or THE SOURCE, Prestel has a dual structure: You can use the menus to find your way around or, if you know the page number you want, you can key it in and go there directly.

Also, services on Prestel are no different in scope from those on various ASCII-based systems. They include information services, transaction services, and communications services. You can get travel information or stock-market reports; you can order wine or make hotel reservations; you can send electronic mail or read a bulletin board.

One important aside here: There are three kinds of Prestel terminals. The "Standard Prestel Terminal" consists of a screen and a numeric keypad. This lets you pick numbers from a menu or designate page numbers but otherwise limits what you can do. You cannot, for example, send electronic mail very easily with a numeric keypad. This kind of terminal is sufficient, though, for the "standard" Prestel service. It also has the advantage of being inexpensive.

The second kind of terminal is a Prestel or Videotex adaptor that is used along with a television set. The adaptor has a standard typewriter QWERTY keyboard. This means that in addition to being able to pick numbers from menus, you can use it for sending electronic mail or for posting messages on bulletin boards.

The third kind of terminal is a computer equipped with appropriate software (usually using a color television for a screen). These terminals represent a relatively recent addition to Prestel. They have opened the door to services that were not previously available on the system, including downloading of games and other programs to use on your computer. These additional services have been combined into a separate section of Prestel called Micronet 800.

The point here is that if you are using the third kind of terminal, there is effectively no difference between what you can do on Prestel and what you can do on an ASCII-based system such as THE SOURCE or CompuServe. There is also little or no difference in the information that travels between you and the utility. Most of it is in the form of text. When simple graphics show up on Prestel, they tend to be more decorative than informative.

The difference between Prestel and ASCII-based systems is mostly a matter of *how* the information shows up on your screen. Both kinds of systems may give you menus and information in the form of words in a row, but Prestel adds some basic graphic design to the words. Prestel's pages are similar to the text-oriented graphics you've seen on network news shows in reporting the results of a poll or an election. Background colors vary, headings may use large letters, some words or lines may be emphasized by putting them in a different color from the rest, and so on.

The effect, quite simply, is that the screen is more attractive with Prestel—more interesting to look at.

The cost is that it takes longer to get the same information out of the system.

Twelve hundred baud on an ASCII-based system works out to about 1200 words a minute if there are no interruptions. This is faster than most people can read even by skimming.

Three hundred baud on an ASCII-based system works out to about 300 words a minute. This is slow enough so that most people can comfortably keep up but fast enough that even fast readers won't feel they're being slowed down too much.

It's hard to make a direct speed comparison with Prestel because the utility isn't sending so-many-characters-per-second. Instead, the information it's sending deals with what colors go where on the screen. At any given baud rate, the length of time it takes to form a page on Prestel remains reasonably constant but the number of words per page can vary tremendously, from one or two words up to a maximum of about 200 words.

At 1200 baud, Prestel takes about five seconds to form a page. This generally translates to fewer words per second than you'll get from an ASCII-based utility *at 300 baud.* This is slow, but not slow enough to be annoying. And the slowness is made up for, in part at least, by a more interesting screen.

At 300 baud, Prestel takes about 20 seconds to form a page. In my experience, sitting in front of a computer screen or television set for 20 seconds is a long time when you're waiting for a response. Having to wait for 20 seconds between each page is simply not tolerable—no matter how pretty the page looks when it's finally finished.

All of which brings us back to the comparison between Prestel and NAPLPS.

NAPLPS has the capacity for high-resolution graphics. The problem here is that the more detailed the graphics get, the slower the system gets. In order to draw high-resolution graphics on your screen, an NAPLPS utility has to send more details over the phone lines. More details mean more information (in a technical sense). At any given baud rate, more information per page means more time needed to transmit each page. With NAPLPS protocol, the time can vary from two or three seconds per page on up. The time involved in sending a screenful of detailed graphics could actually be measured in minutes.

Prestel supporters claim that the extra time in using NAPLPS is enough to make NAPLPS annoyingly slow and that the increase in visual detail won't be worth the extra wait. NAPLPS supporters disagree. And, of course, NAPLPS has the economic muscle of AT&T behind it.

Which of these protocols will become *the standard* is not yet clear. The real test will come in the marketplace, when people who are using these systems start voting with their dollars.

Some Graphics-Oriented Utilities

With Prestel and NAPLPS scarcely in their infancy in this country, it's a bit premature to compile a list of "major" graphics-oriented utilities. Here instead is a starter list: three systems that have been announced and that should be coming on-line at about the same time this book is published.

You will notice that each of these utilities is essentially local. This is a marketing strategy, not based on any technical requirements. It means that the system can be modeled in part on a local newspaper. In addition to carrying information in general (an on-line encyclopedia, a wire service, stock-market reports), they can also carry information that is only of local interest (local weather, restaurant guides, ads from small retail stores).

This "local newspaper" model is more than just an analogy. Newspapers around the country are at least partners in the development of many utilities that are still in the planning stage.

Viewtron, one of the three systems listed here, is itself a subsidiary of the Knight-Ridder newspaper publishing group. As of this writing, Viewtron has signed joint-venture agreements with companies that represent *The Boston Globe; The Kansas City Star; The Fort Worth Star-Telegram; The*

Baltimore Sun; The Plain Dealer in Cleveland; *The Rocky Mountain News* in Denver; the *Memphis Press-Scimitar;* the *Star-Ledger* in Newark, New Jersey; *The States-Item* in New Orleans; the *Pittsburgh Press; The Oregonian* in Portland, Oregon; and *The Seattle Times* in Seattle, Washington.

Unless something disastrous happens to the first Viewtron system in Florida, you can expect to see at least some of these additional local Viewtron systems relatively soon.

Here, then, is the list:

InSource, in Dallas, Texas, was developed by **HVC Corporation.** It uses Prestel protocols.

InSource went on-line in April 1983. It started as a teledirectory service with terminals located in shopping malls, hotel lobbies, and retail establishments in Dallas. Services included travel information, local real-estate information, and a consumer directory. This last service amounted to an on-line Yellow Pages with information about local restaurants, stores and services.

As of this writing, InSource is "gearing up for individual users." Among other things, this means adding newswires, electronic banking, travel services, on-line shopping, games and entertainment sections, and the ability to download software for use on home or business computers. InSource will also offer a gateway to several ASCII-based systems, including BRS and NewsNet. Other gateway possibilities are currently "being discussed."

InSource should be available in Dallas by the time you read this. HVC is also planning to expand InSource to other Texas cities in the near future and has long-term plans (extending to 1996) for expansion into many more cities throughout the U.S.

For further information, contact InSource.
InSource Corp.
Heritage Square
4852 LBJ Freeway, Suite 110
Dallas, TX 75234
Phone: (214) 960-2050

TeleQuest, located in Ft. Lauderdale, Florida, should also be on-line by the time you read this. The system will use Prestel protocols to begin with, but it will also be able to communicate with ASCII and NAPLPS terminals. Current thinking is that the system will take advantage of NAPLPS graphics capabilities as new services are added. (This is not a serious problem if you are using a computer for a terminal. You simply switch to a communications program that uses NAPLPS protocols.) Initially the system will be geared toward the immediate Ft. Lauderdale area, although expansion into other markets is planned for the near future.

TeleQuest will be structured as a series of specialized data bases. Each of these will deal with a specific interest, and each will need a separate subscription. This is similar in concept to a publishing house that turns out a series of specialized magazines. Initial offerings will be aimed primarily at fields of professional interest, although consumer-oriented services are also planned for the near future.

As of this writing, the specific data bases have not been announced. For current information, call or write TeleQuest.

TeleQuest
3015 No. Ocean Blvd., Suite 116 A
Ft. Lauderdale, FL 33308
Phone: (305) 566-7400

Viewtron, from Knight-Ridder's Viewdata Corporation of America, is the third and last utility on this list. It is also the one you are likely to be hearing the most about simply because AT&T has a finger in the pie. In 1980 and 1981, Viewtron ran a joint marketing test of its service with AT&T in southern Florida.

The commercial version of the service, which should be on-line by the time this book is published, will be available in Florida in a three-county area that includes Miami, Ft. Lauderdale, and West Palm Beach.

Viewtron will use NAPLPS protocols. As of this writing, plans are for the system to be marketed along with the AT&T Sceptre terminal, which means that if you want to use Viewtron, you have to buy the Sceptre terminal. According to Viewtron, this is strictly a marketing decision; there is no technical reason why you couldn't use another NAPLPS terminal. It shouldn't be long before the marketing strategy changes, at which point you'll be able to use the system without having to buy the AT&T terminal. The introduction of the Sceptre, incidentally, was timed to coincide with the commercial introduction of Viewtron. AT&T has announced that the list price will be $900 but that it will sell the terminal to the first Viewtron customers for $600.

The Viewtron system will take advantage of the superior graphics capabilities of NAPLPS in those instances "where the graphics add information." This includes graphs, maps, or pictures on advertising pages. The system is designed so that most pages will take three to five seconds to form, with an occasional page taking as long as ten seconds. The idea is that by using higher-resolution graphics primarily for adding information rather than for decorative purposes, the extra time required for the detailed pages will be worth the wait.

Services on Viewtron will include electronic banking, on-line shopping, news, stock prices, airline schedules, electronic mail, bulletin boards, and announcements of community events. Specific information services will include the *Academic American Encyclopedia, Marquis Who's Who,* and the Official Airline Guide.

Finally, in addition to the joint-venture agreements with the 12 local newspapers around the country, Viewtron has announced its intention to start operations in various additional Knight-Ridder markets, including:

Charlotte, North Carolina
Detroit, Michigan
Philadelphia, Pennsylvania
San Jose, California
St. Paul, Minnesota

All told, plans are to establish Viewtron systems in some 30 to 35 areas over the first ten years of operation.

For current information, contact Viewtron.
Viewdata Corp.
1111 Lincoln Road
Miami Beach, FL 33139
Phone: (305) 674-1444

In addition to these three systems, there are others still in the planning stages. Expect them to start springing up like mushrooms throughout the country.

TURNING YOUR COMPUTER INTO A PRESTEL OR NAPLPS TERMINAL

As graphics-oriented utilities become available, you can expect to see more software that will allow computers to be used as graphics terminals. Here's a list of some of the communications software that exists now for various computers.

Apple II

Appletel—Prestel protocols, 300 baud only.

Available from: Not currently available in the U.S.

Appletel 2.0 is somewhat limited in that it works only with the Hayes Micromodem at 300 baud. Also, before you can get the pages in color, you have to buy a special color card. A minimal system requires 48K and one disk drive. Two drives are recommended.

Commodore 64

Avcor, a division of Southam Communications Publishing Co., sells a program to turn the Commodore 64 into an NAPLPS terminal. For further information, contact:
Avcor
Toronto, Ontario

IBM PC

A combination hardware/software package is available from:
Wolfdata, Inc.
187 Billerica Rd.
Chelmsford, MA 01824
Phone: (617) 250-1500

The software part of the combination is available in two separate programs, one for Prestel protocols and one for NAPLPS protocols. This software can be used with the standard IBM color board, but it is then limited to using four colors.

The hardware part of the combination is a replacement for the IBM color board. This will give you all the functions of the IBM board with other programs. It will also give you 16 colors instead of four when using the IBM as a terminal.

The Wolfdata hardware and software will work with any 212-compatible, 1200-baud modem.

S-100 Bus Computers

Metrotel manufactures an S-100 board that will turn most CP/M S-100 bus computers into Prestel-compatible terminals. The board will work with any 212-compatible, 1200-baud modem. Metrotel is a British-based company. As of this writing, it has no offices in the U.S.

Finally, Prestel-compatible software, or hardware-software combinations, also exist for Commodore 64 and for TRS-80 Models I, III, and 4. As of this writing, these are not yet available in this country. For current information ask the utility you're interested in signing up with.

THE VIDEOTEX(T) DEFINITION DEBATE REVISITED: JUST WHAT IS VIDEOTEX(T)?

In Chapter 1 we covered about half a dozen different definitions of videotex. By now you're in a better position to appreciate the argument, and the confusion, behind them.

On the one hand, there is Dow Jones, THE SOURCE, CompuServe, and Delphi—each one an ASCII-based system and each one claiming to be a videotex service. (Delphi, in fact, is a trademark of General *Videotex* Corporation.)

On the other hand, there are people like Fred Madeira, former Operations Manager at Torch Computers.

Madeira is adamant about ASCII-based systems not qualifying as videotex. He even goes so far as to draw a distinction between videotex and videotext. Videotext, according to Madeira, is a generic term that applies to both ASCII-based and Prestel-like systems. Videotex should be reserved for Prestel and similar utilities.

Madeira is not alone in his objections by any means. Others make the distinction by talking about videotex systems and videotex-like systems. When *Viewdata/Videotex Report,* an industry newsletter, covered the Videotex 83 conference, it thought it worthwhile to report that Dow Jones and THE SOURCE gave demonstrations "without anyone questioning whether those services were 'really' videotex."

As this last comment indicates, Madeira's position seems to be gradually losing ground. Odds are that over the next few years the broader definition of videotex will win out so that it will eventually be defined as "any interactive information utility where the information is presented primarily as a series of menu choices." Madeira's distinction is still a useful one though. The term that seems to be emerging to cover graphics-oriented systems is "viewdata." At least, I have yet to see anyone apply this term to an ASCII-based utility.

Complicating matters further is that the distinction between ASCII-based systems on the one hand and viewdata systems on the other is beginning to blur.

I've mentioned TEXNET elsewhere. This is a "special edition" of THE SOURCE that takes advantage of the color, graphic, and sound capabilities of the TI-99/4A. A more interesting development is SOURCELINK, a communications program from THE SOURCE for the IBM PC. (As of this writing, an Apple version is under development.) SOURCELINK contains graphics capabilities similar to Prestel's. At the moment, these graphics are used only on the "introductory" pages to various sections of THE SOURCE, but it's a good bet that THE SOURCE has other uses in mind.

The distinction between viewdata and ASCII-based systems is being erased from the other direction as well. As I've already noted in the "starter list" above, InSource in Dallas, Texas, plans to offer a gateway to various ASCII-based systems.

Modem technology, meanwhile, continues to improve. Communications specialists are talking about developing modem protocols that will transmit reliably at 2400 baud or better over standard voice-grade phone lines. With speeds like this, the waiting time for detailed graphics becomes minimal and the speed advantages of ASCII-based systems becomes irrelevant for most purposes.

The general direction in which utilities are moving—the blurring of distinctions between ASCII-based and graphics-based systems—seems clear enough. How long it will take to erase these distinctions is not so clear.

I, for one, am not making any predictions.

APPENDIX
STAYING CURRENT

If you've learned anything at all from this book, it should be that the world of on-line information is in a state of change.

Hardly a month goes by without a new utility coming on-line or an old utility revamping its structure in some significant way.

Hardly a day goes by without new data bases being put on-line, or without older data bases either being offered where they were not previously available, or being removed from systems where they were previously available.

All this makes it difficult, at best, to keep up with exactly which data bases are available where at any given moment.

Once you get on-line, you'll find that this isn't as much of a problem as it might seem. Depending on your needs and interests, you'll probably find that a few data bases on one or more utilities will pretty much meet your needs. The regular updates from the utilities will keep you posted on any changes you need to know about.

On the other hand, the utilities you subscribe to will not go out of their way to let you know what's happening on other systems, which means that keeping posted on new developments elsewhere can be a problem. Here, then, are some sources for keeping up with on-line systems in general. Be forewarned that many of them are aimed at librarians and other professional researchers, which means the prices are a bit steep for individuals. Some, however, are reasonably inexpensive, and one is even free.

Database Update is probably of interest to the broadest range of on-line users, although it might be a bit expensive for many individuals. This is a monthly newsletter that covers just about anything related to on-line systems—with special emphasis on announcements of new data bases and changes in the availability or structure of old data bases. Reports on the data bases themselves typically include a thumbnail description of the data base and a name, address, and phone number to contact for further information.

One nice touch is a section called "Media Scan." This lists current magazine articles that cover everything from software or hardware reviews to general introductions to on-line utilities. Each month's newsletter also contains a "Special Report" section that focuses on some given aspect of on-line systems.

The newsletter's layout, finally, makes it a useful reference tool as well a worthwhile monthly newsletter. Headlines are not only informative, they are printed in large type and in a different color from the surrounding text. This makes it easy to find information when looking through back issues. Also, the newsletter comes with pre-punched holes suitable for a three-ring looseleaf binder.

The current cost of *Database Update* is $97 per year. This includes a free copy of *Guide to Online Databases*, compiled by Robert Davidson III, editor of *Database Update*.

For current subscription information, contact:

Database Update
10076 Boca Entrada Blvd.
Boca Raton, FL 33433
Phone: (800) 345-8112
        (800) 662-2444 (in Pennsylvania)

Online and **Database** are two magazines from ONLINE, Inc. *Online* is a bi-monthly. *Database* is a quarterly. Each is aimed primarily at librarians and other professional researchers. Both contain articles on search strategies and the content of various data bases. Jeffrey Pemberton, President and Publisher of ONLINE, Inc., feels that "about half the articles in *Online* would be of interest to the casual data base searcher. Probably about seventy-five percent in *Database Magazine."*

The subscription price for individuals is $39 per year for *Online* and $28 per year for *Database*. If you want to take a look at either magazine, your best bet is to look for it in university libraries or corporate business libraries.

For further information, contact:

ONLINE, Inc.
11 Tannery Lane
Weston, CT 06883
Phone: (203) 227-8466

Directories

There are several data base directories available. Like any directory, these start going out of date before they've been printed, but they can still be useful. Some are updated frequently enough to keep them reasonably current.

The **Directory of Online Databases** from Cuadra Associates is one of the better-known directories. This is published four times a year, with two completely new editions each year alternating with two supplements. The number of data bases covered is currently well over 1700 and growing with each issue. The data bases are listed alphabetically. Each listing includes basic information about the subject covered, the producer, price, availability on-line, and content of the data base. Indexes in the *Directory* include listings by subject, by producer, and by on-line system.

The Cuadra *Directory* is aimed primarily at librarians and other research specialists, and is priced accordingly. (As of this writing, it is $75 per year for a one-year subscription within the U.S., $85 per year in Canada and Mexico, and $92 per year elsewhere. Single issues are available at $45 each.)

For current subscription information, contact:

Cuadra Associates, Inc.
2001 Wilshire Blvd., Suite 305
Santa Monica, CA 90403
Phone: (213) 829-9972

Online Business Information Sources is a special edition of Cuadra's *Directory of Online Databases,* available only through NewsNet. As the title implies, this is a business-oriented version of the Cuadra *Directory.* As such, it contains about half as many data bases as the standard directory. Among other things, it includes descriptions of all NewsNet newsletters as of the directory's publication date.

This guide is available free to NewsNet subscribers.

The On-Line Computer Telephone Directory is devoted to small bulletin-board systems. (See Chapter 9 for a closer look at the OLCTD.)

The OLCTD is published quarterly. The current price is $9.95 for one year, $15.95 for two years.

For current subscription information, contact:

OLCTD
P.O. Box 10005
Kansas City, MO 64111

Finally, there are future editions of this book. Plans are to revise it as often and as completely as necessary to keep it both current and useful. For up-to-date information, get on-line and look it up in *Books-In-Print*.

INDEX